THE FISHBOURNE
car ferry

Wight connection

John Faulkner

Colourpoint

6 5 4 3 2 1

© John Faulkner
  2004

Designed by Colourpoint Books, Newtownards
Printed by The Universities Press (Belfast) Ltd

ISBN 1 904242 30 8

Colourpoint Books
Colourpoint House
Jubilee Business Park
21 Jubilee Road
Newtownards
County Down
Northern Ireland
BT23 4YH
Tel: 028 9182 0505
Fax: 028 9182 1900
E-mail: info@colourpoint.co.uk
Web-site: www.colourpoint.co.uk

John Faulkner was born in Reading in 1953 and has lived on the Isle of Wight since the age of four. He was educated at Sandown Grammar School before taking up a technical apprenticeship with the British Hovercraft Corporation and qualifying with an HNC in Mechanical Engineering. Much of his early career was taken up with hydrodynamic testing in the company's test tanks. Today his principal employment is certification testing of flight-critical aircraft structures. His interests include photography and cycling. A cycle ride from Land's End to John O'Groats in 1998, mostly on A and B roads, convinced him that the roads of the Isle of Wight are not as quiet as is often claimed. Perhaps surprisingly, given the subject of this book, he is a proponent of sustainable transport and he hasn't taken his own car on a ferry for many years!

Photo credits:

Front cover: A mere forty years elapsed between the minuscule *Fishbourne* departing from the Portsmouth to Fishbourne ferry and the giant *St. Clare* arriving. During that period the fleet capacity grew from 48 to 754!

Fishbourne – George Osbon, courtesy World Ship Society
St. Clare – John Faulkner

Rear cover: A modern day view of Wootton Creek with Fishbourne on the left, Woodside to the right and Wootton in the distance. Despite possessing the Isle of Wight's busiest ferry terminal the estuary remains a quite backwater compared with the River Medina and the western Yar.

John Faulkner

Frontispiece: The pioneer ferry *Fishbourne*, an ungainly platform for cars perhaps, she was state-of-the-art in her day. All man-made machinery evolves gradually, with the occasional giant leap. *Fishbourne's* introduction may not have been a defining moment in history but she represented a big step forward in the design of coastal and estuarine ferries. Many ferries around our shores can trace their lineage back to this radical concept. She is seen here during her final condition, with rebuilt, electrically operated prow ramps, approaching Portsmouth in 1961.

George Osbon, courtesy World Ship Society

Contents

Acknowledgements

Research into the life and fate of the early Fishbourne ferries for a society magazine article, eventually evolved into the compilation of a book about the entire history of the Portsmouth to Fishbourne service and gave me the pleasure of meeting many interesting people. Many other sources of information must be accessed before compiling a book of this type. A bibliography of documentation and previous publications used for reference is appended at the end of the book. A problem was conflicting information. One can expect people's memories to fade with time but when existing publications or official documentation were at variance it sometimes proved to be a real head-ache deciding which was correct and which was not. If I have remained unsure I have qualified statements with non-affirmative inflections.

During the course of research, it quickly became apparent that official documentation and records for the early days were more thoroughly archived than for recent times; today there seems to be no place for old records – even traffic figures. Privatisation and changes of ownership bring new brooms that sweep clean in order to present a fresh image – all the more important to provide an up-to-date record. But no amount of official documentation can tell the whole story. So much of the history of the Fishbourne ferry service existed only in the minds or private archives of former company servants. I am indebted to many people whose own work or whose assistance has gone towards the compilation of this book. There were those who sacrificed their own time to provide me with information. No less important are those who checked or amended the content, made confirmatory comments and those who have simply provided leads that have opened up new avenues to follow. All are due credit.

Ray Butcher, who served as mate on the first generation ferries and later became the Gunwharf Terminal Supervisor (following in his father's footsteps), has been the principal supporter of the project. Without his input and his vast selection of photographs this book would not have been worth producing. His colleague Ray Perry was able to give me valuable insights into the technical aspects of the earlier ferries. Tony Rogan, Sealink's Chief Naval Architect from 1969 until his retirement in 1994, and his right hand man Eddy Robson, enthusiastically offered information on the design concepts of the later tonnage. There could have been no better person than Tony to write a foreword to the book, but sadly he passed away before its completion.

My thanks to Wightlink's current management team, Mike Aiken (Wightlink Group Chief Executive), Captain Bill Frampton (Marine Director) and in particular Janet Saville (Marketing Director) who had to endure sustained requests for information. I would also like to offer my thanks to the following current members of Wightlink staff; Tim Bayley, Kerry Jackson, Paul Dolling, Rachel Dunn, Roger Keyzor, John Monk, Chris Tilley, Alasdair Watt and Simone Wort. Of former company servants I would like to thank Jim Ashby, Roger Bartrum, Brian Bowers, Ted Coote, Maelor Jones, Andy Lavies and Roger Rees.

Credit is also due to the following; Tim Cooper, whose knowledge of any railway related matter appears to be second to none. Alan Brown, author of two excellent books, who gave me access to his own information and gave me many tips and leads for my own production. John Mason and Steve Taylor of EC Goldsworthy and Co. (the UK Voith agents). Michael O'Sullivan of the Shannon ferry who led me to Mr C Dekker of G Doeksen & Zonen, the Dutch purchasers of two of the pioneer ferries. Thanks to Rob Kamps for interpreting a Dutch oil company circular. My thanks are also due to Andrew Cooke, Tom Lacey, the late Cliff Matthews, Hilton Matthews, Bert Moody, Richard Seville, Les Windeler and my father, Eric Faulkner who all provided valuable information based on their own observations, whilst Richard Maycock and Cynthia Sherwood placed some of their own researches at my disposal. My appreciation is also extended to Frank Basford, Robin McInnes and Dave Moore of the Isle of Wight Council. Thanks also to Keith Allen, Grahame Bowler and Hubert Smythe for providing leads.

I must also extend my thanks to Kathleen Harrison, the former head librarian at Cowes, Caroline Woodford of Warsash Nautical College, Richard Smout of the IW County Records Office, Andrew Morris of the Isle of Wight Council, Hal Matthews of Isle of Wight Tourism and Paddy Jardine of the Isle of Wight Steam Railway, who either provided information or saved my time by leading me to exactly what I was looking for.

I am also heavily indebted to those who have trusted me with their photographs. Selecting photos was always going to be the most difficult part of this project – there were too many to choose from. There were still more that I would have liked to have included, but some of those seem to have vanished without trace, whilst others no doubt will turn up but not without a prohibitively long delay. Photographers or collectors of photographs have been acknowledged beneath their photos, those not credited being by the author.

To all the above and anybody else whose name I may have inadvertently omitted, my warmest thanks.

Introduction

15 March 1926 saw the opening of a new six mile car ferry service between Portsmouth and the Isle of Wight. The Island terminal was situated at the mouth of Wootton Creek, in the tiny village of Fishbourne. Remote from the main Ryde to Newport road, the community comprised little more than a cluster of houses and an inn surrounding a pleasant circular green with a large oak tree at its centre. Today, Fishbourne is the principal gateway to the Isle of Wight; the village, however, is still bereft of a shop and has no other public transport links.

The ferry service, which became popularly known as the Fishbourne car ferry by Island residents, remained a secondary route for the first thirty-five years of its life, but since the early 'sixties it has grown at a phenomenal rate. As more and more people became car owners so they abandoned the traditional passenger ferries, instead taking their cars with them across the Solent. In the twenty-nine years between 1961 and 1990 the vehicular capacity of the Fishbourne ferry fleet grew by 1000% whilst the capacity of the nearby Portsmouth to Ryde passenger ferry decreased by a corresponding proportion. All of the car ferry routes to the Island have prospered but none more so than the Fishbourne car ferry. This is largely due to the convenience of its location and heavy investment in new tonnage at a time when it was really needed.

The Fishbourne ferry's history can be split into three distinct phases. The first began when the Southern Railway transferred the Island terminal of a primitive towboat service from a tidally restrictive berth next to Ryde Pier. Over the next four years they transformed the service by introducing three small, slow, but revolutionary ferries. These ships lasted for over thirty years, the longest period in recent history (and probably ever) that a cross Solent service has operated with a completely unchanged fleet. The second phase, between 1961 and 1983, was a period when the operating company constantly struggled to accommodate the inexorable increase in traffic. A pair of new ferries soon proved to be decidedly undersized and two considerably larger ships were added to the fleet. When the later pair where still quite new their capacity was increased further by the installation of mezzanine decks but still the company was hard pressed to cope with the traffic. The operating company took the bull by the horns and over a period of seven years introduced a fleet of four so-called 'super ferries'j during the third and current phase of the life of the route. When capacity problems once again became an issue an even larger, fifth ferry was added to the fleet in 2001 confirming the route as the principal gateway to the Isle of Wight. Today, the operator is faced with the same dilemma as at the end of the first and second phases, ie the service is full to capacity at peak periods. Further radical changes will probably take place in the near future.

This book looks back at the history of the Fishbourne car ferry and speculates on what may lie ahead. It examines traffic trends over the years and takes an objective look at fares – always the most hotly debated topic on cross-Solent ferries, but one that is rarely discussed in books of this type. This book is intended to be of general interest and should provide something for local historians and shipping enthusiasts alike. Also placed on record are some of the more interesting technical features of the ships (a frequently ignored subject) as well as recollections of the men who operated them.

Chapter 1: Historical background

Although vehicular ferries have only been running between Portsmouth and Fishbourne since 1926, the preceding service for wheeled vehicles and livestock had been operating between Portsmouth and Ryde since time immemorial, using 'towboats'. The practice of using these towed barges probably began during the sailing ship era and crossings would have been dependent on the weather. They may also have been somewhat tide dependent due to the vast presence of Ryde sands, which extended from the shoreline out as far as a mile at low water. A jetty was built on the site of the present pier (c1796) primarily to facilitate the transportation of livestock to market on the mainland, but it too was only usable at high water. The Ryde Pier Company purchased the jetty after Parliament passed an Act authorising construction of the new pier in 1812.

With the advent of steam a more reliable service for transporting livestock and carriages could be provided, however the first steamship service was abortive. PS *Britannia* commenced service in the spring of 1817 but lasted only a month because she had been designed for use on the Thames Estuary and could not cope with the rough conditions sometimes experienced in the Solent, especially when berthing at the pier. Success came eight years later when, in 1825, PS *Union* commenced regular service between Portsmouth and Ryde. Livestock and carriages were accommodated as required in two small boats towed along behind. In 1831 the Southampton company followed suit when they introduced a similar towboat service to Cowes and five years later towboats also commenced running between Lymington and Yarmouth.

The Portsmouth towboat service was advertised as "for the conveyance of carriages, horses and cattle, which will be enabled to walk to and from the beach when shipped and landed". The towboats were small shallow draught open barges with a bottom hinged stern access door kept watertight by packing it with sacking and pulling up tight with a block and tackle. At first they operated literally off beaches. Once loaded, they were poled out into the channel where they were taken in tow by the regular passenger steamer. At the end of the passage they were released and poled towards the shore. Livestock and carriages got off wherever the vessels grounded. Planks were usually used to allow wheeled vehicles easier access. Later, proper slipways were brought into use. At Portsmouth the public slipway at the end of Broad Street, Portsmouth Point, formed the mainland terminal and was usable at all states of the tide. At Ryde the George Street slipway, just to the east of the Pier, was initially used. This was only usable for two hours or so either side of high water. At other states of the tide livestock, carriages and wagons were faced with a long journey over Ryde sands. In 1864 the Tramway Pier was built alongside the Promenade Pier at Ryde, and this incorporated a slipway on its eastern side close to the Pier Head. This was accessible at all states of the tide and allowed a much more flexible operation.

The towboat service was operated initially by the Portsmouth and Ryde Steam Packet Company. On 1 January 1852 they amalgamated with a rival concern called the Portsea, Portsmouth, Gosport and Isle of Wight New Steam Packet Company (which had been formed in 1849) to create a new company called the Port of Portsmouth and Ryde United Steam Packet Company Limited. In 1856 another new company called the Isle of Wight Ferry Company was authorised to build a second pier (the Victoria Pier), two basins and a slipway to the east of the existing pier and slipway at Ryde. The company intended to run a chain ferry from the Victoria Pier to Stokes Bay Pier at Alverstoke (Gosport), but the Admiralty objected to the laying of chains under Spithead, so that idea was abandoned. The company built the new slipway and the two basins to specification, but a lack of resources meant that the new pier, intended to be 2,420ft long, only ever reached 970ft in length, stopping well short of the low water mark. The Isle of Wight Ferry Company was always in dire financial straits and it was purchased by the Ryde Pier Company in 1865.

The Isle of Wight Ferry Company possessed three vessels; two were conventional paddle steamers, which operated between Stokes Bay and either the Victoria Pier or Ryde Pier (depending on the height of the tide), but their third ship was far more radical. This vessel is worthy of some discussion as her design has some relevance to the topic of this book. Named *Victoria*, she was built at Wallsend-on-Tyne in 1860 and was designed specifically for the purpose of carrying vehicles. This vessel had a fold down stern door and was in effect a steam-powered towboat. Her length was 65feet, beam 13feet, depth 6feet, draught 3feet (loaded), gross tonnage 36 and her cargo capacity was 14 tons. She may well have been the first self-propelled roll-on roll-off ship in Britain and was the first vessel ever to be constructed at the Neptune Yard of Wigham, Richardson & Co, which merged with Swan Hunter in 1903. Very little is known of her service on the route so presumably she was not a success.

Another unusual vehicular carrying vessel was to have been introduced by one of the Southampton companies in 1862. In October of the previous year, the Southampton, Isle of Wight and Portsmouth Improved Steam Boat Company, launched their third iron steamer, *American*. Built by the Vulcan Iron Works at Millbrook, this paddle driven vessel had a clear through-deck, no masts and was double-ended with rudders fore and aft. Presumably, owing to the presence of rudders at each end, she was intended for pontoon berthing. Driven by an 80hp engine, her dimensions were 130'0" x 25'6" x 8'3". Her draught at launching was only 2'3" forward and 2'6" aft. Her gross tonnage was 173.27. To keep the main deck clear, it was extended along most of its length to the outer edge of the paddle-boxes on each side, and on these sponsons, long, narrow saloons were erected for passengers' accommodation. She had Muntz's patent paddles, which were a novelty in British waters at that time. Muntz were specialists in solid rolled brass and copper tubes. It would appear that, like *Victoria*, *American* was not a success, in fact it is doubtful if she ever entered service. Between 28 December 1862 and 8 February 1863 she was advertised in the local press as being about to commence service on the Southampton to Cowes passage, but thereafter the advertisements ceased. In February 1863 local newspapers reported that she had rammed the pontoon at Cowes, possibly during a trial trip. The Improved Steam Boat Company was soon taken over by the extant Southampton, Isle of Wight and South of England Royal Mail Steam Packet Company Limited, better known today as Red Funnel, who acquired the two passenger steamers but not *American*. Implausible though it sounds, *American* was converted into a screw-driven collier during the 1860s. Renamed *Allerwash*, she plied for the best part of sixty years between the northeast coal ports and St Helens (IW). She was sold to German owners in 1921 and scrapped about two years later. It may have been that *Victoria* and *American* were too far ahead of their time during the 1860s and it was not until 1927 that a satisfactory self-propelled free-running vehicular ferry was introduced.

Meanwhile at Portsmouth, with the Isle of Wight Ferry Company now defunct, the Portsmouth and Ryde United Steam Packet Company had lost its only serious competition. Eventually, however, it fell into railway ownership. The first railway reached Portsmouth in 1847 when the line from Brighton, operated by the London, Brighton and South Coast Railway (LBSCR), reached the terminus at Commercial Road, now known as Portsmouth and Southsea. The following year London and South Western Railway (LSWR) trains from the Fareham direction began using the same line. From the junction at Port Creek to the terminus a Joint Committee of the two companies operated the line. It was to be another eleven years before a direct link with London came into being when the South Western completed the line between Godalming and Havant, and not until 1876 that the railway was extended to the present terminus at Portsmouth Harbour. The following year the Joint Railway Company, as they called themselves, was authorised to build a new railway in Ryde

linking the existing railway terminus at St Johns Road, on the southern side of the town, with the Pier Head steamers. This line was completed in 1880 and although owned by the Joint Railway Company the Island railway companies always operated it. By now the Isle of Wight was a fashionable holiday resort, not least owing to Queen Victoria having her country residence at Osborne. The Joint Company had rail connections on both sides of the Solent and in order to exploit the full potential of the Island as a resort, in 1880 they took control of all the ferry companies operating out of Portsmouth. The towboat service was, of course, included in this acquisition. The Fishbourne ferries' railway lineage thus stems from this date.

The new Railway Pier at Ryde had been built alongside the Tramway Pier and in order to make way for it the Pier Head slipway was demolished. The towboat service was therefore compelled to revert to using the much less convenient George Street slipway once again, not that the Joint Company would have been overly concerned about any inconvenience on that service, their principal business was, after all, the running of railways. George Street slipway was frequently given the alternative name of 'Horse Boat Slipway' owing to the towboats being known as 'horse boats'. It could easily have received a second alternative name because the crews often called the vessels 'pig boats'.

When the Joint Railway Company took over the service, the practice of using the passenger steamers as towing vessels was gradually phased out in favour of screw driven steam tugs, which were either purchased or hired for the purpose. Occasionally, in the event of the unavailability of the usual tug, the Gosport ferry was pressed into service as a towing vessel and this practice continued right up to the termination of towboat operation. Very few details of the towboats have survived and information is somewhat conflicting regarding towboat numbers 2 and 3 so the details may not be totally accurate. Of the pre-Joint Railway Company towboats No 1 was built by Messrs Hayles in 1870 at a cost of £225 and survived into the Southern Railway era when it became No 6. It had a length of 45'0", a beam of 16'0" and a gross tonnage of 19. The gunwales were 4'0" high but the draught was only 2'0" loaded, and 1'6" unloaded. Number 2 is also recorded as being built in 1870. Number 3 was apparently built in 1864 and lasted until 1912. Records of the Joint Company towboats seem to be more certain. Number 4 (SR No 7) was built in 1904 by Dibles at a cost of £250 and measured 48'0" by 16'0". Number 5 (SR No 8) was larger (50'0" by 17'0") and was built in 1912 by the same company at a cost of £450. The larger of the towboats could accommodate six cars each.

Information regarding some of the tugs is also rather vague. The 1910-built *Ada* (the second ship to carry this name, the first being a 182'0" cargo vessel) was a regular vessel on the towboat service until she was lost in 1917 (qv). *Ada* was replaced temporarily by *Bandit* (formerly *Crampton*) until 1919

Before 1926 the Island terminal of the vehicular service from Portsmouth was at Ryde. This view shows a tug and towboat departing from Horse Boat Slipway, next to Ryde Pier. The tug is thought to be Bandit, *which was used for a while after the loss of* Ada *in 1917.*   Ray Butcher collection

The children of old Portsmouth pose with the crew of a towboat at Portsmouth Point. This slipway was the mainland terminal from the mid nineteenth century until 1961.

Ray Butcher collection

when *Adur II* was purchased second hand for £3,250. *Adur II* was perhaps the best known of the steam tugs. She measured 75'0" in length by 15'9" broad and had a draught of 6'0" forward and 7'3" aft. Powered by a 2-cylinder engine, she was built by Hepple & Co Ltd of South Shields in 1912 for Thomas L Westray of London. They already owned a vessel named *Adur*, hence the suffix. She was first sold to REV James Ltd of Southampton before being purchased by the Joint Committee. *Adur II* was sold out of the company in 1928 to the Shoreham Harbour Trustees. She lasted until August 1947 when she was lost in the Bristol Channel.

Although the first shipment of a motor vehicle went unrecorded it probably occurred during the first few years of the 20th century and, once started, the practice steadily increased. Crossings were initially advertised at fixed times of the day and therefore motorists would have been confronted with the vast expanse of Ryde sands to drive their cherished vehicles across on the occasions when they arrived at low water. Such an environment was an inconvenience to wagons, livestock and the men controlling them but as far as a motor car was concerned it was a disaster. Even with today's six year anti-corrosion warranties there would be few motorists who would be willing to take their cars onto a wet and sandy beach, so it would be hardly surprising if the early twentieth century motorist was less than enchanted at the facilities provided to ship his very expensive vehicle across to the Island. The timetable was subsequently changed, presumably simply to appease motorists, and towboats were advertised as departing from Broad Street two hours before high water and returning from George Street slip half an hour before high water. This was about the only concession that the motorist got.

The towboat service may have been state of the art when it was introduced in 1825 but nearly one hundred years later it was becoming increasingly archaic. During the crossing, water was frequently shipped, either over the bulwarks or through the stern doors. The crew, who were usually togged up in oilskins, sou'westers and thigh-boots, spent most of the crossing pumping the water out with stirrup pumps. They sometimes called on passengers to muck in – and not always in the friendliest of terms; comments such as "if you buggers don't help us pump this thing out, we'll sink" were not unknown. Things have moved on a bit since those days! Cars frequently shared the towboats with livestock, which were always carried on the hoof. It must have been a terrifying experience for livestock, particularly under adverse weather conditions, and the body has its own special way of expressing a feeling of sheer terror! Although motorcar drivers and their passengers were given the option of travelling on the conventional steamer there must have been many occasions when they were anything but thrilled when they were reunited with their beloved machines.

At the end of the passage from Portsmouth the tug and towboat used to head for the beach at full power. The tug

captain would aim for a point one side of the slipway or the other, depending on the wind or tide, and then sweep round as close to the slipway as possible. The crewmember in the leading towboat blew a whistle when he wanted the tug to release the towrope. The towboats were then poled up to the slipway and if possible they were beached side by side. Meanwhile the tug would drop anchor or moor up at the Pier Head and then the skipper (Captain Lewis latterly) would come ashore and supervise loading.

With such a haphazard operation there were bound to be some mishaps. Most, fortunately, were of a minor nature. A serious accident, however, occurred on 26 January 1917 when the tug *Ada* and towboat No 1 were swept against the eastern side of Ryde Pier by a sudden gust of wind while they were departing for Portsmouth. Both tug and towboat sank. The towboat had been carrying 22 'beasts', 53 pigs and one pony. Fourteen 'beasts' and six pigs were saved alive and £62 was obtained for the carcasses recovered from the sea and washed ashore along the coast as far as Quarr Abbey. *Ada* was salvaged, when the engines etc were removed, but received further damage making her a total wreck. The towboat was refloated and repaired.

There was little about the towboat service that was ideal, although it was probably regarded as the norm at the time. Livestock brought to the Ryde terminal by rail was off-loaded at Ryde St Johns Road Station and then herded along Monkton Street and onto the Esplanade. My father recalled an incident when a shipment of pigs was being herded along this street. Evidently one of the sows was on heat and a boar was trying to do what any self-respecting boar would attempt to do under the circumstances. All this was being witnessed by a group of seamstresses who worked on the top floor of one of the houses in Monkton Street. Apparently they spent most of their time looking out of the window and on seeing a herdsman breaking up the pigs fun one of them opened the window and yelled out "Shame". There was another time when he witnessed a pig making a bid for freedom when it was being loaded onto a towboat at George Street slipway. The large, fully-grown pig ran into the sea and swam under the pier and then suddenly appeared on the Western Esplanade beach. It was summer time and the beach was crowded with bathers. Needless to say women and children screamed with terror and scattered in all directions. For several minutes the pig quite happily grunted and sniffed about (like pigs do) on the now deserted beach, until two men, who had been faced with a long walk round the top of the railway tunnel mouth, arrived with sticks and herded the unfortunate creature back to the slipway. The sight of a large pig swimming ashore on a crowded holiday beach and the pandemonium that followed remains one of my father's more vivid childhood memories.

Perhaps the best way to envisage how nasty a passage on board a towboat could be is to read from the reminiscences of Tom Lacey of the Bembridge furniture removal company, concerning his experiences in the year following the Southern Railway take over of the route:

> I write my experience of conveying of vehicles on the Southern Railway car ferry Ryde/Portsmouth and vice versa in 1924.
>
> All traffic was loaded onto flat bottom barges 30' long x 10' wide and would hold one 10-ton lorry and one car. Sheep and pigs were driven on after loading of vehicles. My company was one of the first to carry out removals to and from the Isle of Wight by road and sea.
>
> The crossing could take anything from 4 to 5 hours. I recall a very frightening experience, we left Ryde Pier Head in thick fog, and as you may know a lot of large shipping was in and out of Southampton docks. We were half way across, the fog thickened, we could hear a siren blowing in very close proximity. The next thing that we knew was the side of a very large liner appeared, the tug Captain spotted the liner in the nick of time and chopped the tow line, it was a very dangerous moment. Our troubles were not yet over, the three barges were drifting with the tide and in the fog it took a long time for our tug to locate us, happily he did and we eventually reached Portsmouth.
>
> At Portsmouth the Tug Master would tie the barges to a buoy and a motor boat would push one barge at a time on to the slipway at Broad Street (the slipway is still there situated where the old Gosport chain ferry departed).
>
> In rough weather it was a very hazardous trip, nothing to have a foot of water aboard. There was a seaman on each of three barges pumping continuously to keep us afloat, often I would take a turn pumping (what a difference today and still people grumble if the ferry is late!!)

Of course a trip lasting between 4 and 5 hours only occurred during adverse weather conditions. In calm seas the journey usually took less than an hour, but was somewhat dependent on the power of the tug and the number of towboats. The service passed to the control of the Southern Railway in 1923.

The Southern was notable for the modernisation and economical improvements that it brought about throughout its system. Although, like their predecessors, their main function was the running of an efficient and profitable rail network, they were forward thinking and it was hardly surprising that they frowned upon their newly acquired and archaic towboat service to the Isle of Wight, and they wasted no time at all in initiating a programme of improvements to the service.

Classic view of the tug Adur II *and two towboats at Fishbourne in 1926 during the first season of the Fishbourne service.*

Ray Butcher collection

Chapter 2: The First Phase, 1926 to 1961

On 1 January 1923 the railways of Britain were grouped into four large companies. The south and south east of England fell under the auspices of the Southern Railway and included all the railways of the Isle of Wight except for the Freshwater, Yarmouth and Newport Railway (FYNR). This minor company held out for several months hoping for better terms, and they appealed to the Amalgamation Tribunal claiming that no account had been taken of the proposed Solent tunnel scheme. Had this scheme come to anything it would certainly have altered the course of history of the Isle of Wight and its ferry links. The scheme had been on the table since 1901 and was intended to provide a rail link between the Lymington branch and a point on the Freshwater line approximately midway between the terminus and Yarmouth station. Although the LSWR, who had owned the Lymington branch prior to the grouping, were outwardly supportive of the scheme they had stood to lose on their heavy investment jointly with the LBSCR on the Portsmouth to Ryde steamer service and negotiations broke down. Several attempts were made to revive the scheme but nothing ever materialised. The FYNR were unsuccessful in their appeal and the Southern Railway absorbed their line later in 1923. The Ryde Pier Company (RPC) was also excluded from the Southern Railway takeover at the beginning of 1923. Their property comprised the pedestrian pier and the tramway but not the railway pier. The RPC remained independent longer than the FYNR, but it too was absorbed during 1924. The Southern Railway take-over included the railway owned ferry services to the Isle of Wight, these being the Lymington to Yarmouth Ferry, the Portsmouth to Ryde Steamer service and the Portsmouth to Ryde towboat service. At that time the Portsmouth towboat fleet comprised the tug *Adur II* and three towboats, numbers 1, 4 and 5.

One of the first significant actions that brought about modernisation of the Portsmouth to Ryde towboat service was from a leading and influential resident of Ryde, Mr GH Harrison. On 14 March 1923 he wrote to Mr AW Langworthy, the Marine Superintendent at Portsmouth, saying that he had been asked by many Island friends, amongst them the Commander-in-Chief at Portsmouth, to write to ascertain if some better means could be devised for landing and transporting motor cars from Ryde. Mr Harrison suggested that the cars should run up and down Ryde Pier and be loaded and unloaded to and from the towboats by means of platforms or trays at the crane on the Pier Head, similar to an arrangement then in use at Southampton in dealing with cars for the Le Havre ships.

Mr Langworthy made his first report to the General Manager, Sir Herbert Walker, on 17 March 1923. On 13 May he also wrote to the Docks and Marine Manager, Mr Gilbert S Szlumper, asking for an interview to discuss the subject and a meeting was subsequently held at Southampton on Friday 18 May. By this time the suggestion had already been made that a terminal at Fishbourne in the tidal estuary of Wootton Creek, some two miles west of Ryde, would be a more suitable terminal on the Island for the towboat service. A number of other options were also investigated and the matter was considered in some detail when the Southern Railway chiefs-of-staff met to discuss inspections of the Isle of Wight section of the system on Thursday, Friday and Saturday, 30 August to 1 September 1923.

It was reported that motor car traffic to and from the Isle of Wight was very much on the increase and that the arrangements provided by the railway company for dealing with it were inefficient, with the result that a larger proportion of the cars were passing to and from the Island by means of the ships of the Southampton, Isle of Wight and South of England Royal Mail Steam Packet Company (Red Funnel) via Southampton and Cowes. Of the two railway owned routes the bulk of the traffic passed by the Portsmouth to Ryde service but the service was very inefficient owing to the fact that the slipway at Ryde could only be used an hour or two before and after high water. Moreover, silting up of the jetty there was a serious matter.

The officers reported that they had considered four alternative schemes, viz.:

1 Dredging at Ryde so as to make the existing slipway available at all states of the tide. This, however, had to be ruled out on account of the very high first and continued cost that would be involved.

2 The provision of a 5-ton crane at the end of Ryde Pier so that motor cars could be lifted out of the towboats on to the Pier at any state of the tide, proceeding thence along the Promenade Pier to the shore. The objection to this scheme was that the Ryde Pier Company (who were still independent at that time) required a toll of 2/6d (12.5p) for the passage of each car over their property and that the motors passing up and down the Pier would involve risk of injury to foot passengers. It remains to be seen whether or not this option would have been acceptable had the Southern Railway already absorbed the Ryde Pier Company.

3 Provision of a slipway at the company's Medina Wharf on the west bank of the River Medina on the outskirts of

Cowes. A slipway was planned to be provided in connection with the proposed rearrangement of this wharf but the distance from Portsmouth to Cowes rendered the proposition unsuitable, added to which the owners of motor cars objected to being forced to go as far west as Cowes.

4 Provision of accommodation near the village of Fishbourne, at the mouth of Wootton Creek.

This place was inspected by Sir Herbert Walker, Mr Szlumper and the other chief officers. A slipway already existed but could only be used at high tide and in order to make the place suitable it would be necessary to extend the slipway and to do a considerable amount of dredging at an estimated cost of £12,000, in addition to the purchase of the necessary property. The site, however, was admirably suited for the purpose and it was confidently expected that if suitable arrangements were made the motor car traffic to and from Portsmouth could be doubled.

During the years 1920, 1921 and 1922 the average receipts from the towboats working between Portsmouth and Ryde amounted to £3922 per annum, and the gross expenditure (including Interest and Depreciation on Capital outlay) of the tug and towboats came to £2691. The average yearly receipts from motor cars amounted to £1399 per annum.

It was recommended that the provision of a landing place at Fishbourne be taken in hand and the General Manager would advise the Estate Agent to make preliminary investigations as to purchase of the property.

Fishbourne (otherwise known as Fisseburne, Fishborn, Fisshehous or Fish-house, but frequently by its present name throughout the nineteenth century) was once the site of a thriving shipyard. Surprisingly large ships were built here, such as the 36-gun man-of-war *Magicienne* in 1812 and the Earl of Yarborough's *Falcon*. The Earl was the founder of the Royal Yacht Squadron and Falcon was the fastest opium runner of her day. By the 1920s the yard was long closed and Fishbourne had become a sleepy backwater. Things were about to change.

Once approval for the new terminal had been given proceedings went rather slowly until the property had been acquired. At the annual meeting the following September it was stated that the arrangements for the purchase of the necessary land were by then well advanced. The plot of land, measuring approximately two acres, was subsequently purchased from one Mr HE Dennis of the Fishbourne Farm Estate and construction work commenced on 10 March 1925, by which time dredging work had already been under way for two or three months. The Southern Railway built a terminal

As many as six cars are about to disembark from towboat No 6. Two more towboats await their turn. The towing vessel on this occasion was one of the Gosport ferries.

Ray Butcher collection

Slipway construction taking place at Fishbourne in 1925. There were very few residential properties in Fishbourne Lane at this time, the building visible being Fishbourne Farm.
Ray Butcher Collection

with a pleasantly rural air near the end of a quiet side road leading nowhere, except to a circular green and an unspoilt foreshore at the mouth of the creek. Fishbourne Lane was never to be so peaceful again.

Construction work was under the supervision of Mr RN Sinclair, the Assistant Docks Engineer and Mr LS Kingston, the resident engineer. The Docks Department built a new road branching off the lane and running in a straight course down into the sea, making the slipway at right angles to the mouth of the creek. The terminal buildings were all bungalows of timber construction. The terminal supervisor's house was reached first on the left. Next was the booking office, which had a petrol pump installed in front of it. Beyond the booking office was a lock-up garage. The right hand side was mostly laid out to gardens with livestock pens (to accommodate 15 cows, 100 pigs and 6 boars) and a private residence, known as 'The Cedar Box', nearer to the shore. The terminal was later equipped with a telephone. The phone number was Wootton Bridge 32, which gives a fair idea of how rare phones were in those days. The upper part of the terminal was just open ground with the new road passing roughly through the centre of it. During construction of the slipway a steamroller became stuck near the low water mark. As the tide came in bystanders watched with delight when the sea pored down the chimney! Beyond the shoreline the tidal channel was dredged to give a depth of 8 foot at low water ordinary spring tides. Near the slipway a large basin was also dredged to allow swinging of the towboats and an anchorage for the tug. The deep-water channel was marked by four timber built dolphins which were passed to starboard by inbound traffic.

Work continued apace and the new terminal was due to be opened on Monday 12 October 1925. The new road, however, proved to be substandard and was suffering damage. Work then started on constructing a reinforced concrete road and the opening was delayed until at least 1 January of the following year. In the event the construction took much longer but the road was certainly built to last because it is still there today lined either side by tarmac and more concrete. By March of 1926 the Fishbourne terminal was completed for a total expenditure of £19,230. The towboats made their final crossings to Ryde on Saturday 13 March 1926 and, there being no Sunday service, the Fishbourne terminal opened for traffic on the following Monday.

The opening of Fishbourne terminal

The new ferry service between Portsmouth and Fishbourne commenced operation with the 10.00 am departure from Portsmouth, Broad Street, on Monday 15 March 1926. On the following day there was a visit of inspection by officialdom. The party arrived at Portsmouth by the 11.43 am train and included Messrs GR Newcombe, Deputy Docks and Marine Manager, Southampton; CN Anderson, Assistant to Divisional Operating Superintendent; and RP Biddle, Assistant to the Marine Manager, Southampton. On arrival at the Harbour station the company boarded the passenger steamer to Ryde Pier, and en route they were able to view the Broad Street slipway. Luncheon was served at the Esplanade Hotel, Ryde, and immediately afterwards the party proceeded to Fishbourne in motorcars. A test of the new landing was made with two of the cars, which were easily and comfortably run on and off of the towboat. The party was received by Mr LS Kingston and Mr AF Webb, and everything was found in excellent working order, and, despite unfavourable weather conditions, a perfect landing was effected with motorcars and other vehicles. The party returned to Ryde in time for the 3.05 pm boat back to Portsmouth. That was the official line anyway. According to the reminiscences of a crewmember that was on board, the VIPs crossed to Fishbourne in one of the towboats. A fresh wind whipped up the sea sending sheets of spray over the party, there being no cover on board. On arrival at Fishbourne they were said to be very wet and miserable people and decided to forgo the pleasure of the return trip on this service.

The new service proved an instant success. The Southern Railway was now able to run a fixed timetable with two trips a day. The minimum crossing time was about 50 minutes but was often longer. Motorcar traffic had been increasing year by year, but now the process accelerated rapidly. In 1913, 742 cars had been shipped but then the First World War cut this back, to as few as 48 cars by 1918. After the war, traffic picked up again and by 1923 it had reached 1163 vehicles. In 1924, 1356 cars were carried and in 1925, the last full year of services to Ryde, the total had reached 1718. The move to Fishbourne was rewarded with a total of 4451 vehicles shipped during 1926. This was a considerable improvement but the service was still operated by the very primitive towboats of a type that had been running since several generations before the first motorcar had even been dreamt of, let alone graced our roads. Not surprisingly many motorists were still rather hostile towards the standard of service provided by the Southern Railway, but not all, as the following letter written in *The Motor* magazine on 25 May 1926 testifies:

> After reading the correspondence in The Motor relating to the new Fishbourne service between Portsmouth and the Isle of Wight, I should like to encroach on your valuable space and give a short account of my experiences.
>
> Last year I crossed several times by the old Portsmouth and Ryde service and have now crossed between Portsmouth and Fishbourne. This route, to my mind, is indeed a very great improvement, and the new waiting rooms and other accommodation at Fishbourne are a great convenience. The tug and barge started to time and there was no delay at all at either end.
>
> Capt Lewis and his men have always been most kind and courteous, and I for one am most obliged to them for their help. It has often done me good to see the patience shown by these men in getting obstinate sheep, pigs, cattle and horses on to the barges; also at times with drivers of cars who try to "show off" instead of at once entrusting their steering wheel to the able hands of Capt Lewis.
>
> It is well worth recording that he and his men carried on

> splendidly during the strike. To anyone crossing to the Isle of Wight I can thoroughly recommend the new Fishbourne service.

One could be forgiven for thinking that the writer, who remained anonymous, was a member of the Southern Railway staff or a company shareholder, or even Capt Lewis himself, but he claimed to have no connection with the company. Allegedly Capt Lewis could become quite hot under the collar if any motorist dared to touch the car's steering wheel while he was in charge, so it is not surprising if some drivers became rather agitated themselves. The above letter was one of many that had been written in response to one damning letter in *The Motor* and by the time it appeared in print the magazine had already carried out its own assessment of the service. The findings were published in an article titled 'The Truth about the New Isle of Wight Service' on 1 June 1926:

> We took the 2.00 pm service on Saturday, May 22nd, and returned by the 3.30 pm service on Monday, May 24th. On the outward journey the embarkation of cars began at 1.30 pm. There were 18 of them and three barges were required. Each car is reversed down the rather steep slipway with one of the sailors standing on the running-board or walking beside the car holding the steering wheel, leaving the driver only to control the brakes. Two wooden runways connect the slipway with the barge. Only one car can be manoeuvred at a time, at present. The total time taken in loading 18 cars was 40 minutes - a little over 2 minutes per car. Later on, it is intended to widen the slipway so that two barges at once can be loaded, which will reduce the time. The start was delayed until 2.30 and, owing to it being low tide, a longer detour than usual had to be taken, so the other side was not reached until after 3.30 pm. The crossing was perfectly smooth and no covers were required or used. As the cars at the other end only had to be driven straight off the barges on to the slipway there was little time lost in disembarkation, but, again, widening the slipway will save some minutes lost in getting the barges into position.
>
> On the return journey the barges were manoeuvred into position at 3 o'clock, embarkation having already begun on a barge in position earlier, and the return journey started promptly at 3.30 pm, reaching Portsmouth at 4.30 pm, the cars being all off the slipway about 10 minutes later.
>
> Short of having a large ferry boat on to which the cars can be driven direct, the accomplishment of which, in view of the rise and fall of the tide, might prove difficult, we do not see that much time could be saved, whichever route is taken to cross to the Isle of Wight. One has to bear in mind that there are no formalities, no emptying of petrol tanks and replenishing, and that the cars are handled very skilfully indeed, without scratching a wing or causing any anxiety. The slipways are washed down after every tide and sanded so that they are not slippery, and we consider the embarkation and disembarkation perfectly safe. On the

return journey a wave from a passing Union-Castle liner caused the towboats to rock slightly, but no water was shipped. At the same time this part of Spithead can be fairly rough, when bad sailors had, perhaps, better take the smoother passage from Lymington to Yarmouth, which is about half the distance. Against this is the fact that the journey from London (to Portsmouth, 70 miles) is increased to 94 miles and it costs more to take the car across.

The passengers sit in their cars going across the water and the journey is not an uninteresting one, especially if one of the big liners is passed en route.

The weekday service is from Portsmouth at 10.00 am and 2.00 pm and from Fishbourne at 11.30 am and 3.30 pm, but at holiday times additional passages are run. A Sunday service may be run in the holiday months. The cars should be in readiness half an hour before the advertised time of starting, and notice should be given in advance at present.

Despite the above misgivings about the suitability of a large ferry boat on this service a large self-propelled ship was exactly what the Southern Railway had in mind as the next stage of their modernisation of the service.

MV Fishbourne – a revolution in car ferry design

At sometime during 1925 or 1926, The Southern Railway Superintendent Mechanical Engineer, Mr EH Dashper was instructed by Gilbert Szlumper, the Docks & Marine Manager, to investigate the possibility of replacing the towboats with a purpose built self-propelled car ferry that would meet the following broad requirements:

1 Increased capacity
2 Easier and quicker loading
3 Improved facilities for passengers
4 Greater economy

Mr Dashper took the opportunity to discuss the matter with Sir Maurice Denny, chairman of the Dumbarton shipbuilding firm William Denny & Bros during one of the latter's periodic visits to the Southern Railway. Unfortunately nothing of any consequence came out of this meeting, which is not altogether surprising because there was no ship in existence that was suitable for docking at the existing terminal facilities ie slipways. Either the terminal arrangements would have to be altered or somebody was going to have to come up with a radical design of ship. There was probably some fear of ships grounding and there was certainly concern that propellers or rudders would be damaged if slipway berthing were used. The terminal arrangements proved to be a serious hurdle and little progress was made for some time. However, on 26 October 1926 things began to move when Mr Szlumper wrote to Sir

Maurice with a request for him to tender for the design, specification and delivery of a ship with the following particulars:

Length, 100' to 125'
Beam, 25'
Loaded draught, 4'
Speed, 8 knots minimum
Dead-weight, 25 tons
Maximum headroom 10'6"

Included in the letter was a rough sketch of the envisaged design. It had a conventional, sharp stem with a square deck protruding over it amidships. The stern had a shallow rake and a fold-down gangway. There was also what appeared to be a turntable situated close to the stern. Obviously this design was intended for slipway use at one end only. This would have been the Portsmouth end because the slipway there was public property and could not be altered. Clearly, at that time, Mr Szlumper favoured end-on pontoon loading at Fishbourne. The turntable suggests that the Company was keeping the option open to provide side-on pontoon loading at Portsmouth as well.

Sir Maurice, in his reply to Mr Dashper, noted that the Southern Railway's new request was for a larger ship than discussed earlier and he suggested that the company should examine the design of certain LMS vessels. Sir Maurice was possibly referring to the side-loading Tilbury to Gravesend ships. One of the ships, *Tessa*, was already in service (having been built in 1924) and a second ship, *Mimie*, was added in 1927. They were designed for the conveyance of vehicles and had clear decks fore and aft and no mast. *Tessa* measured 141'0" in length by 39'0" broad and was 368 registered tons. Both ships were screw-propelled and driven by coal burning steam compound engines. They could load 25 to 30 cars using ramps to connect with the pontoon landing stages.

Correspondence regarding terminal arrangements continued at some length but unfortunately the Southern Railway kept changing the requirements. In a letter to Sir Maurice, dated 2 November 1926, Mr Dashper repeated his worries about the possibility of damage being caused to propellers and rudders if slipways were used. In another letter written on the same day, and in an apparent tone of despair, he expressed his preference for the use of slipways if at all possible. At least Sir Maurice and his team had a goal to aim at and so they raised some queries regarding the slipways and their gradients. In a letter dated 18 November, Mr Dashper replied that the Fishbourne terminal was versatile (being that they owned the freehold there and they could provide any gradient required) but the Broad Street slipway was shallow at low water. The gradient of this slipway also levelled out somewhat near the high water mark, but he did not mention that. He also stated that he "had his eye on a slipway owned by the military" but he did not know the gradient. He did not say where it was either.

A frequently published photograph of Fishbourne *prior to launching from Denny's yard at Dumbarton in 1927. This view clearly illustrates the curious hull-form and the arrangement of propellers and rudders.*

National Maritime Museum

Then came another bombshell. In the same letter Mr Dashper once again brought up the possibility of alternative terminal arrangements with pontoons at each end, bow loading at Fishbourne and side loading at Portsmouth, and preferably using a 9 or 10 knot ferry. From the ensuing lack of correspondence it would be reasonable to assume that Sir Maurice had taken a long holiday in foreign climes in order to get over the trauma. In fact he had probably acquired all the information that he needed and he and his team settled down to design a ship that would be able to use the existing slipways without the risk of propellers and rudders being damaged.

When Sir Maurice submitted his design to the Southern Railway there was a feeling of total relief for all concerned. Denny's design and tender for construction were accepted and on 27 January 1927 the order was placed with them to build the ship. At this time detail design was incomplete yet within five months yard number 1200 was ready for the water. During construction the goal posts moved yet again though not significantly this time. Mr Dashper was worried that the 10'6" headroom was not going to be enough and 11'0" would be preferred, a modification that the builders could easily incorporate.

The new vessel was launched by Mr Dashper's wife on 21 June 1927. The ship was christened *Fishbourne*, the first of two vessels to carry this name, and she was something of a revolution in ship design. All cross-Solent car ferries plus many other coastal and estuarine vehicular ferries around our shores can trace their lineage back to this single radical concept. Her launch also brought to an end a dearth of ship construction at Denny's yard.

During the course of the post-launch speech Sir Maurice told the guests that they had just seen launched a very interesting little ship. *Fishbourne* was odd in that she was double-ended and had four times of everything, except perhaps the captain – four rudders, four screws and so on. He hoped she would make so much money for her owners that a second boat would be necessary. It was a pleasure for many reasons for his firm to build ships for the Southern Railway and one person he would like to mention was their superintendent, Mr Dashper. It was always a pleasure to be supervised by a gentleman who knew his business, from truck to keel, there is no part of any ship they built for the Southern Railway about which they could not ask advice from Mr Dashper and receive a definite and proper reply.

Diplomacy indeed!

Fishbourne certainly was odd. She even looked odd and brought a whole new dimension in ugliness to Solent shipping, a legacy that, arguably, has rubbed off on all subsequent short sea car ferry designs. Her design was totally functional with barely any attention being paid to aesthetics. She was a double-ended (bidirectional), double-twin-screwed, double-twin-ruddered roll-on, roll-off car ferry. The ship measured 131'0" in length, with a beam of 25'0", the depth being 8'0" and the loaded draught 4'6". Her gross tonnage was 136 tons, with a loaded displacement of 199 tons (approximately 10% of today's 'Saint class' ships). She had a completely clear deck and articulated hinged gangways fore and aft, which folded down onto the slipways to form loading ramps. The ramps were able to support a load of 6 tons. There was nothing particularly unusual about the basic arrangement, many chain ferries used a similar format, but what made *Fishbourne* so different was that she was a free-running, screw-driven motor ship. The choice of using internal combustion engines was a radical one; at that time 94% of new tonnage was steam driven. In fact *Fishbourne* was the very first railway owned ferry to incorporate this novel form of machinery.

The vehicular capacity of *Fishbourne* was variously quoted as anything between 15 and 20 cars. It is not easy to quantify vehicular capacity, particularly with such a small vessel, because cars come in all sorts of shapes and sizes and the average varies with the passage of time. Eighteen is probably a reasonable estimation of average late 'twenties-sized cars that she could accommodate, but 15 is considered a reliable figure

during her latter days. Nowadays vehicular capacity is measured in CEUs (Car Equivalent Units) or PCUs (Passenger Car Units). Both are the same and equate to cars measuring 4.1 metres by 1.7 metres (13'5½" by 5'7"). For the purposes of comparison with the present day tonnage, *Fishbourne* had a capacity of 16 CEUs.

The general arrangement of the ship is shown at Figure 1. Although double-ended she was obviously not symmetrical, and she had a designated bow and stern. The forward projection of the deckhouses and the stump mast were towards the bow, while the port of registration (Portsmouth) was painted beneath the ship's name at the stern only. Beneath the car deck the asymmetry was more obvious with the passenger accommodation towards the bow and the engine room nearer the stern. It can be seen that the ship was equipped with separate saloons (or waiting rooms as they were called) for ladies and gentlemen. These were rather basic and contained nothing more than slatted wooden seats and a few tables. However, they were less gloomy than many below-deck

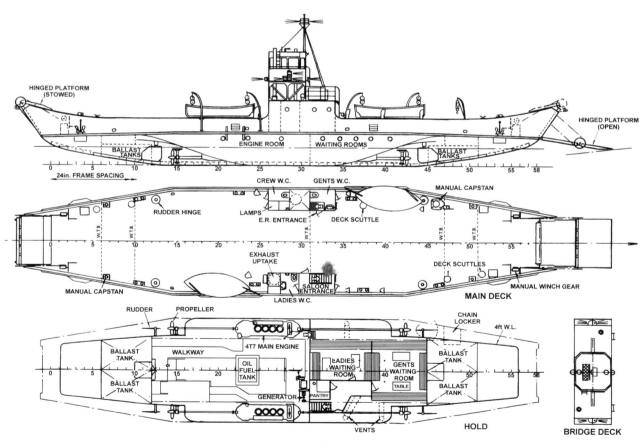

Figure 1
M.V. Fishbourne (1927) as built

saloons on later ferries because they were lit by natural light; admittedly they were not very well lit and passengers could not see out. Light found its way in via portholes in the ships sides, across a void space and through obscured glass portholes in the cabin bulkheads.

The engine room was also rather spartan. It contained little more than the two main engines and a small generator / compressor set. The main engines were 4-cylinder Gardner 4T7 heavy-oil engines. Each engine had a cubic capacity of 61.8 litres but developed only 120bhp at 340rpm. The engines were standard units apart from the employment of a clutch at both ends, from which shafts ran to the fore and aft propellers. The latter were set well away from the ends of the ship so as not to foul the slipways.

The engines were very primitive by today's standards being 2-stroke crankcase-scavenging semi-diesels – or 'hot bulb' engines. A photograph of the starboard engine taken before installation is shown below. Later and more conventional 2-stroke diesels incorporated pumps or blowers to charge scavenge (combustion) air into the cylinders; this version worked more like a standard 2-stroke petrol engine but with airless fuel injectors instead of spark plugs, flapper valves installed in the ports and no carburettors. The air intakes were the round discs seen on the crankcases. Lubrication was nothing like that found in a 2-stroke petrol engine, in which oil is mixed with fuel. On the 4T7 the lubrication oil was pumped to the main bearings, which were outside the crankcases, and a gravity system dripped oil on to the big end bearings. Oil was also thrown about by the whirling machinery. The gravity-feed oiling unit can be seen on the second cylinder from the right. Most spent oil found its way to the base of the crankcase where it was pumped out and discarded. Since the oil was used only once, the supply system had to be repeatedly replenished.

Unlike a full diesel, the compression ratio on a semi-diesel was insufficient to heat the gases to a high enough temperature to initiate spontaneous combustion, a source of red heat being required at all times. The photograph shows electric heating plugs in the top of each cylinder. These were reportedly removed before the ship entered service because there was insufficient electrical power to supply them. Instead, a conventional blow-lamp head was fixed at the top of each cylinder. These were lit using methylated spirit and the domed tops of the cylinder heads had to be glowing red before the engines would start. With a headroom of only 6'6", the atmosphere in the engine room with the heat guns operating can be left to the imagination. Above deck there was a strict no smoking regulation yet down below eight blow-lamps could be found burning away in an enclosed chamber containing petrol, paraffin and diesel fuel tanks! Once the engines had started the combustion caused heat retentive grids (the so-called hot bulbs) within the cylinder head domes to glow red, but when running on light load the injector sprays had to be manually redirected at the grids.

Each engine incorporated an air compressor, a cooling water circulating pump and a ballast pump (all positioned at the right hand end on the photograph), the latter with a capacity of 20 tons per hour for transferring water between the fore and aft peak trimming tanks. The engines were started by compressed air – already a standard means of starting marine diesels of any size – and they were reversible, although they were only run in one direction under normal circumstances. In their normal operating mode the two engines were contra-rotating and the 3'6" diameter four-bladed screws linked to each engine were of opposite pitch, thus the fore and aft propellers could not be coupled simultaneously because their thrust would oppose each other. The aft propellers provided forward thrust while those at the bow were only used for manoeuvring purposes and were otherwise allowed to idle, that is until the direction of travel was reversed, in which case they became the propulsive propellers.

The column on the left of the photograph contained the oil pump, governor and reversing gear. The hand wheel provided the reversing control and it changed the orientation of the external camshaft which drove the four injector pumps and the compressed air inlet valves. All these components are visible in the photograph.

As mentioned, the ship was also equipped with a generator/compressor set, which was designated a Gardner No 2V Electric Engine. The power plant was a hand started single cylinder engine, which ran at 550rpm and drove a 110 volt DC dynamo and the compressor. The engine was started on petrol and then ran on paraffin, which was much cheaper in those days. The engine was temperamental and could be difficult to start and difficult to stop. It could take up to an hour to get the contraption started and it had a tendency to run-on after it had been shut down. Sometimes the crew could hear it intermittently firing away after they had left the ship at the end of a day's duty. The engineers affectionately named this unit as 'One Lung'. One engineer, Frank Leach, was a dab-hand at starting 'One Lung' and he took great delight in rubbing his colleagues noses in it when he came along and started it straight away after they had been struggling for ages. The dynamo had an output of 2.5kW, which was sufficient only to supply some of the ship's lighting, the remainder being oil lamps. There was certainly not enough power to drive the four warping capstans or the prow-ramps, which were all manually operated. The services of four men (half the crew) were required to raise and lower the latter.

The hull-form on *Fishbourne* was unconventional to say the least. It was symmetrical fore and aft and was punt shaped, with a shorter and broader punt shaped section amidships (Figure 17, page 154, top left). The broad section generated its own bow wave and can have done little for the hydrodynamic efficiency of the hull. The design of the second ship would suggest that this was a problem worth tackling, as will be discussed later.

Although *Fishbourne* was a tremendous technological advance, it can be seen that in many ways she was still rather primitive. She was very much a prototype vessel and expenditure was kept to a minimum in case the experiment was unsuccessful. Nevertheless 'Denny's List' reported that the final price of the ship (£13,254) was "more than anticipated because the finish was more elaborate than had been expected". The mind boggles at just what had been expected because the vessel exhibited little more than the bare essentials. Primitive she may have been but after the spartan conditions of the towboats she was like a luxury liner. Her revolutionary features were sufficient to generate a considerable amount of favourable comment in maritime technical publications of the day and *Fishbourne* was to become the most successful ferry (in terms of longevity) that the route has yet seen.

Fishbourne had been launched in a near complete condition and after successful trials in the Gareloch, in which she achieved a speed of over 8 knots, she began her long voyage to the Solent. After arrival at the Southern Railway Marine Maintenance Depot at Southampton on 11 July the railway company's own engineers cobbled together some additional walkways over the largely open bilges in the engine room. She made a trial run from Southampton to Fishbourne on 13 July and entered service from Portsmouth five days later. Her entry into service is sometimes given as 23 July in official documentation, but 18 July appears to be more reliable. She was timetabled to make four crossings per day (reducing to two in winter) and on her first trip she carried 10 cars, 1 motorcycle combination and a six-wheeled lorry. The normal crossing time was 55 minutes, more or less the same as the towboats.

Her entry into service was a rather low-key affair, perhaps due to anticipated teething problems. Whether this was the case or not, she had her fair share of gestation problems, as would be expected with such an unconventional design. Immediately following her entry into service Mr Dashper wrote to Sir Maurice expressing his views on the ship's performance. The steering was described as "wild" and two men were required on the wheel for most of the time. He added that the engines had been used to "save the situation" on a number of occasions, from which it can be inferred that the variable thrust capability from having independent engines and four propellers had been used to a greater extent than desired for manoeuvring purposes. He raised the possibility of having two wheels fitted. Mr Dashper went on to say that several vehicles had experienced 'grounding' and that he was of the opinion that the choice of manually operated ramps and capstans "had not been a good idea". He was certainly correct about the latter but as regards to the inadequacies of the steering it would appear that the problem was purely down to lack of crew experience, because *Fishbourne* eventually proved to be very light to steer.

However, another problem with the steering soon became apparent. The crew frequently experienced problems when switching from one set of rudders to the other in order to change the direction of travel. It is not clear exactly how the system worked but only one set of rudder control cables was locked to the ship's wheel at one time while the other set was locked straight ahead. It appears that swapping from one set to the other could only be achieved satisfactorily if the ship was

This curious contraption is one of the main engines for the pioneer ferry Fishbourne, *photographed before installation. The cubic capacity of this semi-diesel engine was over three times greater than the engines installed in the new* St. Clare, *but the power output was only one eighth.*

Paul Gardner Engineering

A very busy and most interesting view of Fishbourne *disembarking vehicles at the Broad Street slipway at Portsmouth Point in the summer of 1927. The tram lines are evident to the bottom right, as is the electrified wire, terminating at the pole in front of the ferry. The ticket office was in the building on the extreme right. The Gosport chain ferry slipway is out of view to the left.* Fishbourne *has yet to receive the ramp counterbalancing towers.*

Ray Butcher collection

lying in completely dead water otherwise hydrodynamic forces would cause the rudders to move thus making it very difficult to locate the fixed rudders in the straight ahead position. There was no problem locating the working rudders because the wheel could be rotated to bring the locking mechanism into alignment, an option not available with the idle rudders.

Fishbourne was taken out of service while the problem was investigated and the towboats, which were retained for the shipment of livestock, had to deal with all traffic once again.

Surprisingly no solution was found for what would appear, on the face of it, to be a fairly minor technical hitch. The problem would undoubtedly have been investigated further had the crews not found that they could operate the ship satisfactorily by running bow first on every crossing, which they proceeded to do for the rest of her life. The bow rudders were subsequently removed, at which point *Fishbourne* ceased to have a bidirectional capability. Under the new arrangement the ship operated in a similar manner to today's 'Saint class' vessels, with Portsmouth bound vehicles facing backwards during the crossing. However, unlike the current ships, *Fishbourne* was small enough to swing straight off the berth at the Island terminal and sail out of Wootton Creek bow first.

At the Portsmouth terminal the new mode of operation was actually a little easier than before because the vessel no longer had to turn through 180 degrees in order to berth at the slipway. There were never any mooring dolphins at the original Portsmouth terminal and for a while there were none at Fishbourne either. The procedure for berthing at Portsmouth was for a member of the crew to drop a bow line to a waiting boat and while this was being tethered to a buoy situated in the entrance to the Camber Docks, stern lines were secured to an old anchor embedded in the beach. This procedure may seem very primitive by current standards, but similar practices are used around the world today for berthing considerably larger ferries.

Although *Fishbourne* was now operating successfully as a unidirectional ship her troubles were not yet over. The manual system for raising and lowering the ramps was causing some serious problems and on 5 September 1927, Mr Dashper wrote to Sir Maurice complaining that they had experienced two winch-gear shaft failures and that a third had been bent. The ramps were heavy structures and in order to offset the enormous winch loads Denny's designed a counter-balancing system comprising falling weights housed in tower-like structures. The new equipment was delivered to Southampton on 17 October and *Fishbourne* was taken out of service once again while the gear was installed, an operation which took about ten days. The towers were positioned two at each end of the ship either side of the ramps and the weights were linked to the winches by means of pulleys and wire ropes. When the ramps were lifted the weights fell, and vice versa. Some considerable effort was still required to start the ramps moving but the load gradually reduced until the weights took over.

This system worked well and lasted for almost 20 years. Another problem to beset *Fishbourne* on more than one occasion was steering gear cable failure.

The Southern Railway (and Denny's) were gaining a lot of experience with the new ship and by November 1927 the owners had drawn up a list of suggested improvements for a possible 'Fishbourne 2'. One of the suggestions was that the main engine exhaust uptakes should be split into two sections to facilitate cleaning. The silencers were cooled with salt-water sprays and in time the system became choked with salt and carbon deposits. The company's concerns were well founded. On 22 February 1928 passengers on board *Fishbourne* noticed water issuing from the starboard exhaust pipe as the ship was entering Portsmouth Harbour. There followed a loud bang and the engine stopped. Both the forward cylinder bed plate and the cylinder column had failed, the problem being traced to a choked silencer causing salt water to run back into the cylinders. The Southern Railway informed Denny's of this latest mishap and pointed out that the ship was going to be away for repairs for a fortnight and there was no spare vessel except towboats. They were not happy. *Fishbourne* returned to service on 10 March and thereafter appeared to have a relatively trouble-free life. Any future problems that did occur would have been less embarrassing to the company, anyway, because by the time *Fishbourne* had returned to service a second ship was already on the stocks.

MV Wootton, improving the breed

At a meeting of the Southern Railway board held in September 1927 it was reported that in view of the growth in traffic, and the fact that the tug and towboats would be incapable of dealing with the traffic in the event of breakdown of *Fishbourne*, it was agreed that sanction should be sought for the construction of a second motor ferry vessel. With the experience they had gained with *Fishbourne* they were able to specify a much-improved ship. The principal requirements for the new vessel were as follows:

1. Ramps to be longer to reduce grounding of vehicles
2. Ramps to be able to carry a load of 8 tons rather than six
3. Ramps and capstans to be power operated
4. Deck space to be maximised by raising lifeboats clear of the deck and positioning the life jackets elsewhere, possibly on a larger bridge
5. Accommodation to be provided for captain and crew
6. Increased electrical power

There were many more requirements, over fifty in total, and most were incorporated in the final design. An official Request for Quotation (RFQ) was placed with Denny & Bros. on 3 December 1927 and the order was confirmed on 9

January 1928. Construction was again rapid and ship number 1216 became *Wootton* when the vessel was launched on 6 June 1928. She was 4 feet longer and 1 foot broader than *Fishbourne* and also heavier, having a gross tonnage of 149 and a loaded displacement of 212 tons (see Figure 2 below). From a cursory glance she appeared very similar to *Fishbourne* but in fact she was quite different in that she was designed and built as a true unidirectional vessel and to the extent that it would have been difficult to convert her to bidirectional operation had this been required. The single-ended nature of *Wootton* was betrayed by the arrangement of the bridge deck and the location of the two lifeboats. The wheelhouse protruded forward from the bridge and there were only two windows in its rear whereas the forward side, which had angled corners, was fully windowed. The two lifeboats were stowed aft of the bridge deck thus giving the captain an unrestricted view ahead. The principal single-ended feature, and one which was not mentioned on the company's list of suggested improvements, was the hull-form. The stern section

was similar to both bow and stern sections on *Fishbourne*. *Wootton*, however, had a faired bow (compare the views at Figure 17, page 154). There were still recessed areas to accommodate the bow propellers but they were gently faired and as a whole the hull presented a much cleaner under water shape that did not generate, to such a large extent, the secondary bow wave which was always a feature of *Fishbourne*. The cleaner hull enabled this larger vessel to travel at approximately the same speed as her older consort without any additional power requirement and during trials she was reported to have achieved 8.7 knots. This said, she was generally considered to be a little slower than *Fishbourne*. Bow rudders were never fitted to *Wootton* and bow propellers need not have been either, since astern thrust could have been applied by reversing the engines. This, however, would have resulted in a small loss of manoeuvrability because the main propellers would have been less efficient thrusting against the structure ahead of them, and maximum manoeuvrability was an all-important requirement of these ships. In any case it was

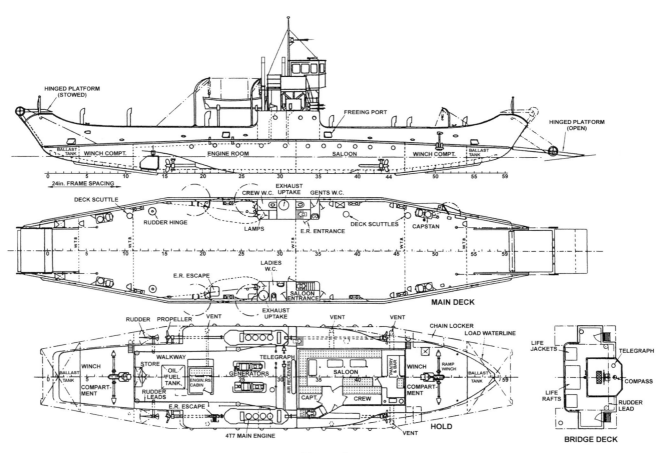

Figure 2
M.V. Wootton (1928)

considered unwise to reverse the engines because normal wear patterns could be prejudiced and engine bearing life reduced.

The main engines were identical to those fitted in *Fishbourne*. The Southern Railway (always looking for ways to save a bob or two) had, once again, wanted to omit the electric starting plugs, as had been done with *Fishbourne*, as an economy measure. This would have been a retrograde move and Norris Henty, the engine builders, agreed to carry out modifications (at no additional cost) which enabled the plugs to operate satisfactorily. The heat guns were retained as a back up but were rarely needed. The auxiliary engines on *Wootton* were quite different. She was fitted with a pair of 12.5kW generator sets, representing a 1000% increase in electrical power capability over 'One Lung' in *Fishbourne*. The English Electric generators were each driven by a hand started 4-cylinder 24bhp 4-stroke petrol/paraffin Gardner engine. In addition to driving the generator, one of these engines also drove a small air compressor whilst the other drove a bilge pump. The electrical output was sufficient to power the ramp winch system, the four capstans and all the ship's lighting as well as providing a heating system for the comfort of passengers and crew.

The vehicular loading ramps extended to 19'7", 2'6" more than those fitted to *Fishbourne*. They were more substantially built and were operated using chains (rather than wire ropes) from electric winches, which raised or lowered the ramps in less than a minute. The winch gear was housed beneath the car deck. The ramps could support a load of 8 tons. A system of chains and steel rods was also used to link the rudders to the ship's wheel in place of the failure-prone wire ropes used on *Fishbourne*. The lifeboats were mounted on davits giving them an 8 foot clearance above the deck, which kept them out of harm's way and allowed cars to park beneath them. As originally suggested the life jacket boxes were mounted on the bridge deck abaft the wheelhouse. The bridge deck itself was not only larger; it was also 11 inches higher, giving maximum headroom of 12'0". Whereas *Fishbourne* had canvas dodgers on the bridge deck, on *Wootton* timber panelling was used instead, apart from a section with open railings amidships aft. The useable deck area of *Wootton* was approximately 10% greater than that of *Fishbourne* enabling her to accommodate perhaps two extra cars. Her latter day capacity has been reliably quoted as 16. In terms of CEUs the capacity was also 16, exactly the same as the smaller *Fishbourne*. There would have been more vacant deck space but it would not have been possible to accommodate more than sixteen 4.1 metre long cars. Of course a typical load of cars would not have been all the same size and with judicious placement of large and small vehicles one or two more could have been carried.

The standard of facilities provided for both passengers and crew on *Wootton* was vastly superior to that on *Fishbourne*. The separate saloons for ladies and gentlemen were replaced by a single saloon for both sexes and the seating therein was upholstered with horsehair and velvet. Measuring 21'7" by 9'2" it incorporated a snack counter and bar at the forward end. Similarly upholstered cabins were also provided for captain, crew and engineer. There were many other improvements of a less significant nature. One feature is worth mentioning because it is another example of the Southern Railway's penny-pinching. The navigation lights fitted on *Wootton* were the stern facing lights that had been removed from *Fishbourne* after she became a single-ender.

Wootton was an improved version of *Fishbourne* in every respect except one; she tended to roll more in heavy weather due to her more massive bridge and the higher location of the lifeboats. Like her half sister she was no beauty. A particularly ugly feature was the starboard side 'funnel', or to give it a more realistic name, 'exhaust uptake', which emerged from the deckhouse abaft the bridge giving it a very long and slender appearance. Arguably her most pleasing feature was a particularly nicely finished teak-built wheelhouse. *Wootton* cost 31% more to build than *Fishbourne* but at £17,300 it sounds like a bargain today. In fact she was not very cheap at all; taking inflation into account £17,300 equates to over £½ million at 2004 prices.

The new ship arrived at Southampton at the end of her long delivery voyage on 20 June 1928. On 25 June she transferred to Portsmouth and took up service on the following day. The Southern Railway obviously had more confidence in their new ship than was the case eleven months earlier when *Fishbourne* entered service because this time they embarked on an intensive publicity campaign. Posters appeared at railway stations and elsewhere all over the country extolling the virtues of their drive-on drive-off ferries, showing pictures of embarkation on the mainland and disembarkation on the Island. One of the Broad Street staff was thereby immortalised in the embarkation picture, having been caught by the official photographer as he endeavoured to retrieve an 'offending object' (a kettle) from the side of the slipway as the picture was being taken.

The weekday timetable was increased to six sailings per day for the 1928 summer season. Each vessel performed three round trips between 9.30 am and 6.00 pm with one of them beginning and ending its daily roster at Fishbourne, where it remained berthed overnight. Traffic was increasing year by year. The year 1927 saw 7002 cars shipped, together with 340 motorcycles, 708 lorries and 459 combinations. As far as car traffic was concerned this was an increase of 2551 over the previous year, and with the towboats still holding the fort for much of time, including during periods when *Fishbourne* had broken down. 1928 saw a further 3270 increase in motor car traffic to 10,272 vehicles, but thereafter the annual increase began to slow. In 1929 the total was 12,799 and in 1930, 14,250. With two ships in service the Southern Railway had sufficient capacity to handle all this traffic plus a lot more. Of course the Southern Railway were not to know that traffic was

Hilsea *heading out for sea trials from Dumbarton in June 1930. Both* Hilsea *and* Wootton *were introduced with teak coloured bridge curtain plates and teak grained wheelhouses. Various combinations of white and teak were later used.*

Jim Ashby collection

not going to increase at such a rapid pace, but in view of the more than adequate capacity that they then had, it is perhaps a little surprising that towards the end of 1928 they were once again taking steps to obtain an extra vessel. The tone of certain correspondence, and also the original specification, suggests that perhaps they 'wanted' rather than 'required' an additional ship. Whatever the case a third ship was built.

MV Hilsea, a sister to Wootton

The first official action to acquire a third ferry came on 12 October 1928 when Mr Langworthy met Mr Biddle, the then Assistant Docks and Marine Manager, at Southampton and mentioned that traffic had reached such proportions that they ought to have an additional car ferry. He confirmed this in a report to Mr Biddle on 15 November, but it was more than a year later, on 27 November 1929, before the Docks and Marine Committee recommended and approved construction of the ship. An initial letter had, by this time, already been sent to Denny's informing them that they would be likely to require a new ship with the following specification:

1 Vessel to be 20 to 25 feet shorter than *Wootton*
2 As *Wootton*'s main electric light engine is not economical on light loads in summer, an additional small engine for lighting and the pantry is required
3 Mechanical ventilation system to be incorporated

Item 1 seems a bizarre request. Perhaps the specification of a smaller vessel was some sort of a sop, designed to encourage Board Room blessing in case they deemed another ship of the size of *Wootton* to be an expensive and unnecessary luxury. A smaller vessel would hardly have been

a sensible economic concession, as the Board must have realised. Not only would there have been additional design costs but also the ship would have had less revenue earning potential. Common sense prevailed and a vessel almost identical to *Wootton* was eventually built. Named *Hilsea* she was launched on 12 June 1930. During her trials in the Gareloch she achieved a speed of 8.74 knots. This was roughly the same trial speed as her sister but *Hilsea* was always considered to be the faster boat. Immediately after her trials she set sail for the Solent and entered revenue-earning service on 21 June 1930, a mere nine days after her launch.

Although *Hilsea* was fitted with the specified fan assisted ventilation system she did not receive a small auxiliary generator. The two auxiliary units fitted, however, were of a slightly lower output to those in *Wootton*, each being 12kW. They were driven by a pair of Gardner 2L2 high-speed 4-stroke diesel engines, making *Hilsea* the first all diesel ship. The twin-cylinder engines developed 19bhp at 1000rpm. Although hand started, these engines were state of the art in their day, technologically vastly superior to the main engines installed in the same ship and not dissimilar to the auxiliary engines fitted today in *St. Cecilia* and *St. Faith*.

In order to combat the poor generator efficiency on *Wootton* an additional smaller unit was subsequently installed in this ship. It was powered by a single cylinder engine of a more advanced type than that fitted to *Fishbourne* and gave an electrical output of 3kW. Meanwhile *Fishbourne* had already been fitted with an additional auxiliary unit, approval having been granted in March 1928. The power plant was a 3-cylinder petrol/paraffin Gardner engine of a similar type to the 4-cylinder units fitted in *Wootton*. The electrical output is not known but was probably about 9kW.

The main engines fitted in *Hilsea* were identical to those

Fishbourne *berthed at Fishbourne in 1934 with a shipment of military personnel and more horses than you could shake a stick at. Externally* Fishbourne *is in her original condition except for the installation of the ramp counterbalancing towers and removal of the navigation lights for stern-first operation.*   Ray Butcher collection

Wootton *crossing Spithead during the Fleet Review of 1937. A paintbrush has been used to make the best of a curious looking vessel, but she was never going to compete with the sleek lines in the near background!*
                                                                                          National Maritime Museum

A view of the Fishbourne terminal in the late 1930s. The photo was taken by Henry Willford of Havenstreet and shows his entourage about to depart for a holiday in Scotland. They would have been fairly typical of the Fishbourne Ferry's clientele in the early days, being towards the wealthier end of the market. The terminal was equipped with a petrol pump, which is partly obscured by the booking office sign. The old terminal buildings were not replaced until 1972.

Hilton Matthews collection

A fully loaded Fishbourne *approaching Fishbourne in 1938, by which time her lifeboats had been raised well clear of the deck. A member of shore staff has gone out in a boat to secure a stern line. The oak tree is extant whilst, in 1998, decking was laid on top of the old dolphins to form a jetty for the Royal Victoria Yacht Club. The jetty on the right was demolished in 1960.*

Eric Faulkner

An idyllic view of the Fishbourne terminal in the early days taken from the main gate. The concrete road (simply lanes 7 and 8 in today's terminal) ran in a straight line down into Wootton Creek, where Hilsea *can be seen at the slipway.*

fitted in the other two ships, but the clutches were of a higher rating. More advanced Gardner engines of the required power output were by then available but to have fitted such units would have meant an additional stock of spares would also have been required, so it was decided, probably wisely, to keep all three ships the same in this respect. *Hilsea* was fitted with improved engine silencers because the supposedly better systems fitted to *Wootton* were found to be flimsy and already in need of replacement.

Although almost identical to *Wootton*, *Hilsea* could accommodate one more car than her twin sister could. There is no positive explanation of why this should be so, but it is probably down to a different arrangement of bollards or other obstacles on the car deck.

From a casual glance *Hilsea* and *Wootton* appeared to be identical. There were, in fact, numerous minor differences between them of which only a few are worth mentioning. *Hilsea* had slightly shorter 'funnels' and the one on the starboard side was a good deal plumper up as far as bridge deck level. The prow end deck lights were in a different position and the forward white navigation light was stepped lower down the mast. The most obvious difference was that two of the ventilator cowls, associated with the powered ventilation system, had mushroom shaped tops in place of the traditional open mouthed Fyfe vents.

By now the tow boats were long since redundant although the dates of their last passages appear to have gone unrecorded. In October 1928 the tug *Adur II* was sold to Shoreham Harbour Trustees for £850. A small replacement

vessel registered *Alice* was acquired for tendering purposes. Towboat number SR8 (presumably the last) was recorded as being sold for £40 to one Frank Barnet on 15 October 1930. One of the towboats was converted into a houseboat and resided at the Kench on Hayling Island until it was destroyed by fire in June 1981.

Routine service

Whether or not there really was a need for a third vessel at that time is a matter for conjecture, but in the long term it turned out to be a wise investment. As traffic levels increased all that the Southern Railway needed to do was increase the frequency of service. Surprisingly this only extended to a three-ship timetable on summer Saturdays, though all three ships frequently did operate together at other times during summer. Most of the time the service was infrequent and hence the vessels spent a lot of time out of traffic. Out of service car ferries were usually tied up just to the south of the coal hulk, which lay parallel to the Portsmouth Harbour Station passenger ferry berth. The 'hulks' were static vessels that were used for coaling the paddle steamers as well as providing a convenient mooring for out of service ships. One of these vessels, a former naval coal barge designated C11, built 1902, was on station from 1932, until close to the end of paddle steamer operations in the 'sixties.

The car ferries were of such shallow draught that the Swashway did not present much of an obstacle to their passages. The Swashway is the name given to part of a large triangular shoal extending between Gilkicker Point, Portsmouth Harbour entrance and out beyond Spit Sand Fort. The Bar Channel, scoured by the tidal race from Portsmouth Harbour, runs close to the Southsea shoreline and to the north and east of Spit Sand Fort. There are two passages across the Swashway. The deeper one, known as the Swashway Channel, is approximately aligned with St Jude's Church Spire and Southsea War Memorial. The other, today known as the small boat channel, runs close to the Haslar shoreline. The two channels are separated by the Hamilton Bank, which comes very close to drying out at equinoctial low spring tides. At most states of tide the ferries were able to use the inner route but at low water they had to take the slightly longer passage via the main Swashway channel. Unlike today's ships they were never compelled to take the much longer deep water passage around Spit Sand Fort at low water spring tides.

Mindful of the improvements to the Fishbourne service the Southampton company took steps to increase their own vehicular carrying capability. For some years they had been pontoon loading cars on to the foredecks of their passenger steamers, and this they continued to do, but in the 1927/1928 winter the 42-year-old paddle steamer *Her Majesty* was converted into a car carrier. The deck saloons were removed to allow her to carry cars ahead and astern of the funnel, in which guise she could carry approximately 18 cars. To maximise vehicular capacity cars were sometimes manoeuvred around the decks using skids placed beneath the wheels. *Her Majesty* lasted until 1940 when she was sunk during an air raid on Southampton. Usually her services had been required only during peak summer weekends and bank holidays, whilst at other times the normal passenger steamers could handle the traffic.

After the war, the Southampton company (Red Funnel) introduced another unusual car carrying vessel. In 1947 they purchased a redundant tank landing craft (LCT). The new acquisition was converted into a vehicular ferry with vehicular access via a small fold-down, single-piece ramp at the bow. Limited, but well appointed passenger accommodation was provided aft. She was named *Norris Castle* and remained in service until 1962. The ship could accommodate 30 cars, a substantial increase over the Fishbourne ferries, but she was slow, the passage time being $1^{1}/_{4}$ to $1^{1}/_{2}$ hours.

As a means of wooing motorists to their service, the Southampton company tried to extol the virtues of the superior facilities they provided for car drivers and their passengers. In 1931 they even went to the extent of making their own publicity film, complete with sound track. Much was yet to be learnt about the making of publicity films. "A lot of people use the Southampton company vessels because they can have a meal on board" the commentator confidently stated "and what better experience than having a meal on board a ship when you're hungry". He added "Oh, and by-the-way you will find no fancy fares on the Southampton company steamers". There's no doubt about it; they just don't make commentaries like that

anymore! With its longer route the Southampton company was in a thankless situation. The convenience of the Fishbourne ferry gave it an edge that it has rarely lost.

The Fishbourne car ferry now settled down into a settled routine that barely changed for the next thirty years, but an atmosphere of peace and tranquillity did not always accompany the service. There was soon disquiet over the terminal arrangements at Portsmouth. The terminal there was far from ideal, and comprised nothing more than a residential street that ran into the sea at Old Portsmouth Point. To make matters worse the Gosport chain ferry shared the same site using a separate slipway, which was aligned with the Gosport shore. As early as 1929 complaints were registered about the volume of traffic queuing up in Broad Street for the two ferry services. Residents were not happy either that livestock was sometimes able to wander around willy-nilly in the street. This was, after all, an urban area and about as remote from a farmyard as you could get. It must have been something of a culture shock having cattle leaving their calling cards on one's doorstep, although it must have been going on for some time, though perhaps not to the same extent. In addition to the above, fishermen and other mariners grumbled that ferries berthed at Broad Street partially blocked the entrance to the Camber Docks and that the space remaining was too shallow to allow passage at low water. Representations were made that the Portsmouth terminal should be relocated in the area of the Camber Docks known as 'Dirty Corner', an unofficial but appropriate name for the area bounded by Broad Street, East Street and the Camber. Local mariners had an even less kindly name for it, which was included in a short rhyme to describe the inward passage from the English Channel:

First the Nab and then the Warner,
Blockhouse, Point and Shit-House Corner.

Portsmouth City Council went as far as approving a scheme to construct a new slipway, car parking areas and cattle pens, and they had already purchased a number of properties in East Street and Broad Street that were to be demolished as part of the scheme, which would cost a total of £8,600. An amendment was later tabled that the Southern Railway should contribute towards the costs, but this was lost. In October 1931 the Council Committee reported that they were aware of the opinion that the urgent necessity for carrying out the scheme no longer arose, owing to careful management of the boat traffic, better co-ordination between the Harbour Master and the Company's Marine Superintendent and the introduction of an additional vessel on the service Why such a scheme was not considered during 1926 when the Southern Railway were worrying about the inadequacies of the Broad Street slip is not known, but it was more than likely down to the age old reason; cost. They did not appear willing to even contribute towards the costs in 1929 let alone pay it all, as would likely have been the case in 1926 before the Council had become involved. Over the years the congestion problems in Broad Street worsened again as traffic levels built up and the company did eventually move their terminal to Dirty Corner, but not until 1961.

Residents at the other end of the passage had been voicing their own gripes. The minutes of the Docks and Marine Committee, dated 27 April 1932, reported the following:

Referring to minute of 3 October 1928, approving an arrangement with Mr AT Page for the construction of a sea wall on the eastern side of Wootton Creek to protect his property, the Docks Manager reported that a complaint had been received from Mr ES Bates, who owns certain land on the western side of the Company's property, that owing to the dredging operations carried out by the Company, damage has been done to his land by erosion.

Although it is not admitted that this damage has been caused entirely by the Company's operations, it is recommended

For many years livestock was carried on the hoof, as seen in this post-war view at Broad Street. The gentleman on the left was Bert Butcher, who initially crewed on the tow-boat service and later became the Portsmouth Terminal Supervisor. His son, Ray, followed in his footsteps.

The News, Portsmouth

Circus animals were normally carried on the hoof on special sailings before or after the day's regular services. Here, an elephant walks ashore at Fishbourne in the early morning summer sunshine, circa 1960. On the left is Ernie Young, a familiar figure at Fishbourne in the old days.

Cliff Matthews

that certain protective works to Mr Bates` frontage should be carried out by the Company at a cost of, approximately, £250 on condition that he will contribute a sum of £85 towards the expense and that this Company is not under any obligation to maintain such protective works thereafter.

How little things change! In 1996/7 the Isle of Wight Council was in dispute with the present operators, Wightlink, over erosion of the shoreline allegedly being caused by the ferry operations. Although absolved of responsibility Wightlink contributed £20,000 towards the cost of protective works.

At Fishbourne in 1930 there was even a complaint from a member of staff, and from no less than the terminal supervisor himself, who was then designated the Wharfinger. He complained that his garden had not been fenced in except by means of temporary posts and wires that he had erected himself, and that when cattle were being unloaded they frequently broke through this fence and got into his flower beds. He agreed to erect a more substantial fence himself provided the company supplied suitable concrete posts and some wire, which they duly did.

For many years the terminal at Fishbourne was supervised by a gentleman who charged a penny to every non-travelling person entering the terminal site, even if they were only going to wave somebody off, but apparently nobody was ever issued with a ticket!

Meanwhile the three little ferries trundled back and forth in a seemingly endless routine. The service they provided was more-or-less the same as in towboat days, the only difference being that the standard of the ships was much better. The Fishbourne ferry was specifically for the shipment of vehicles and livestock. Foot passengers were not carried except those accompanying vehicles. Livestock was normally carried on the hoof (because the tariffs were cheaper) normally on a special once weekly 'cattle boat', but the practice was discontinued

Wootton *pitching and rolling off Gilkicker Point during a rough crossing to Fishbourne, some time in the 1950s.*

George Osbon, courtesy of the World Ship Society

soon after the end of the war. One might have supposed that the ferries crews would not have been too happy about having cattle, pigs and sheep roaming around on the decks because of the inevitable mess which they would have to clear up. Far from it. No better solvent was ever found for grease and diesel stains and the wooden decking came up like new! Occasionally the crews had something more substantial to clear up. Elephants from travelling circuses also travelled over on the hoof, usually on special early morning or late evening sailings.

The fact that two services ran from Broad Street sometimes caused problems. It was not uncommon for crewmen to be asked in mid-Solent how long the ferry took to get to Gosport! No doubt many other motorists intent on travelling to the Isle of Wight found themselves on the other side of Portsmouth Harbour.

Performance and handling characteristics

The three ferries had completely different performance and handling characteristics to each other. Even the supposedly identical *Wootton* and *Hilsea* were quite different. *Hilsea* was the fastest of the three but she had extremely heavy steering. *Wootton* was the slowest vessel but she was the most controllable ship of them all. *Fishbourne* had low-geared steering, making it very light but consequently quite a lot of work was required on the wheel. *Wootton*, on the other hand, was just right – not too heavy, and a few degrees turn of the wheel in each direction to keep her on the straight and narrow. The smaller diameter wheel on *Fishbourne* was fitted with a crank to facilitate steering, but the larger wheels on the two sisters were not so fitted due to the inherent danger of a broken limb, or worse, should a wheel escape.

The ships were generally very reliable and no single vessel exhibited rogue tendencies. One problem to which they were all susceptible was big-end bearing failure on the main engines. The bearings were lubricated by a gravity feed system that could occasionally become blocked with carbon deposits. As soon as a big end was heard knocking the engine was shut down and the ship proceeded on one engine. If the ship was on passage to Fishbourne when the problem occurred repairs would sometimes be undertaken near the Island terminal, unless the weather conditions were so benign that the ship could proceed safely back to Portsmouth on her remaining engine. In order to free the Fishbourne slipway (if other ferries were in operation at the time) the ferry would anchor offshore, or perhaps tie up at one of the channel marking dolphins, and repairs would be undertaken there and then. The engine was opened up and the offending bearing removed. Molten white metal was run into the shells and then hand scraped to a precise fit before re-assembly. The whole operation took about three hours and when complete the ship could return to service.

Mechanically reliable they may have been but they were not the ferries to be on in rough weather. The First Officers (not necessarily ticketed men in those days) usually helmed the vessels. Since many of them had worked the ships man and boy they were likely to have more experience of the ships idiosyncrasies than were the fully qualified Captains, who may have joined the company from elsewhere. All their experience came into play during foul weather.

Particularly difficult conditions occurred during easterly gales when heavy seas were encountered on the approaches to Portsmouth. Such conditions would normally keep ships already at Portsmouth firmly in port but if a ferry was at Fishbourne when such a gale blew up the crew would normally try to get the ship back to Portsmouth because most crews were mainland based and they wanted to get home. They could not take the usual direct route because the beam seas made the ships roll excessively, besides which they had an irritating tendency to pay off down-sea. The only course they were able to take was to head upwind towards the eastern approaches (sometimes out as far as the forts) until they had gone far enough that they could turn round and proceed downwind back to Portsmouth. They were so directionally stable in such conditions that when the time came to make the turn, no action from the ships wheel would deviate the ship from her windward heading. Fortunately the helmsmen had developed a technique for dealing with this seemingly disastrous situation. They had to wait for the sea to become relatively quiet and then quickly go full astern whilst at the same time swinging the wheel hard to port and then hope that she would swing. Once she had, forward propulsion could be re-engaged and the ship could be steered on a roughly downwind course back to port.

Some new skippers found it hard to accept that their ships could have such bizarre handling characteristics until, that is, they were handed the wheel! Needless to say, a passage under such conditions was one of life's worst nightmares as far as the passengers on board were concerned, and it sometimes lasted for hours. Frequently, the ship would be engulfed in spray and the violent pitching and rolling motion would cause many bouts of the dreaded mal-de-mer. Lorries were lashed to the decks to keep them upright but even so a milk tanker once toppled over and had to be righted using a crane in HM Dockyard. The conditions could sometimes create such a feeling of terror that it was not unknown for the passengers to help themselves to life jackets, as they did once on *Fishbourne* as she set sail for Portsmouth during a northwesterly gale. On that occasion the crew looked on with amusement but sometimes even they were in fear for their lives.

Strong currents also played havoc with the ferries, particularly in the entrance to Portsmouth harbour. With a top speed of only about 8 knots and a tidal race of up to 5 knots or so during ebbing spring tides it can be imagined that life for the bridge crew might not have been just a bowl of cherries. The fact that the ships could not make very much headway over the ground was only a small part of the problem. The vessels also had an annoying tendency to swing if the bows

were allowed to bear too far off the tidal flow, and once the bows had begun to swing there was nothing that could be done to stop them. The helmsmen certainly needed their wits about them as they faced potential hazard after potential hazard on nearing Portsmouth. Whether the ships approached Portsmouth through the Swashway Channel or via the shorter route close to the Haslar sea wall they were going to have to break into a strong current in the Bar Channel. The tidal race had to be entered at exactly the right angle – too fine and they would not get in, not fine enough and the bow would swing and the ship would end up heading away from the harbour instead of towards it. Once in the tidal race the helmsmen still had to remain alert. The harbour entrance walls had to be avoided at all costs. Rather than take the normal course close to the starboard shore it was essential that they went straight up the middle, just in case the bow swung. An occasion was recalled when the Captain observed an inflatable dinghy heading out of the harbour whilst his ferry was struggling in on a fast-flowing ebb tide. To avoid the risk of a collision he ordered a deviation to starboard, but despite the mate's protestations that he would not be able to hold her, the order was upheld with the inevitable consequences. The bow swung round and the ferry sped straight back out of the Harbour and had travelled as far as Southsea Castle before she could be turned and brought back. Once inside the harbour the ships were gradually inched across until they were positioned in the relatively quiet water off HMS *Vernon* – now Gunwharf Quays. It was then safe to go astern up to the slipway. During windy conditions berthing at Broad Street was assisted by the motorlaunch *Alice*, which held the ship in position while the mooring lines were made fast.

Problems could sometimes occur under the benign conditions that usually existed off the Fishbourne slipway, particularly at low water. When departing from Fishbourne the sterns of the ships were turned into a swinging basin situated beyond and to the left of the mooring dolphins. To facilitate swinging, sometimes a rope was carried out from the stern of the ship, by a man in a rowing boat, and tethered to a buoy at the far end of the basin. The ship was then swung using the on-board capstan. If a rope was not used the procedure was to simply apply astern thrust and then at a critical moment swing the wheel hard to starboard.

An occasion was recalled when a ship went aground during the first trip of the day after this manoeuvre went wrong. It was normal practice for the mate to go below to have breakfast on the first crossing from Portsmouth and he would then change places with the skipper for the return trip. Meanwhile a deck hand would make up the absent place on the bridge. On this occasion the deck hand was a small fellow with short arms and he was unable to swing the wheel quickly enough with the result that the ship sped backwards into the mud bank beyond the channel where she became stuck fast. The mate sent the deck hand down to tell 'the old man' that the ship was aground. The captain was well aware of what had happened and he sent back the message "You got her stuck so you can ✱✱✱✱✱✱✱ well get her off again."

Without the benefit of radar and with no radios until the last years of the pioneer ferries the bridge crew had to rely on vision alone to avoid collisions with other ships. Coming away from the Broad Street slipway it was not easy to see traffic entering the harbour. On one occasion the skipper was confronted with a whole line of inward bound South African minesweepers immediately after the ferry had left the slipway. A quick decision was required and the captain ordered the mate to keep close to the Portsmouth side. At the time there was a strong flood tide flowing with out-flowing eddies close to Portsmouth Point. The mate was well aware of the presence of these eddies and the havoc they were going to cause but after a short debate the skipper said that his order would have to stand because there was not time for them to cross in front of the minesweepers. Inevitably, the ferry got caught in an eddy, swung round and the wheel on the prow smashed straight through a large plate glass windshield outside the Still and West public house. Prior to this little mishap a large figurehead of a dragon, which came from the coal hulk *Dragon*, had adorned the doorway of the company's office in Broad Street. It mysteriously vanished one night and subsequently reappeared in the pub, but no complaint was ever lodged about the broken windshield! *Dragon* was a former Admiralty vessel that had served as the company's hulk from 1880 until 1932, when she was replaced by C11.

As mentioned earlier, the Broad Street slipway levelled off somewhat near the high water mark. This sometimes caused minor problems because the propellers could make ground contact, which is something they were supposed to be incapable of doing. This would be one of the occasions when the engines may have been operated in reverse so that the vessel could be pulled away from the slipway using the propellers furthest from it. If the skipper was unaware that the ship was in such close proximity to the slipway and used the propellers in the usual way they sometimes dug holes in the largely cobbled slipway causing minor abrading of the screws. However this was a situation that the crews could take advantage of. Knowing that the propellers had grounded the crews often rummaged around in the vicinity of the newly dug holes when the ship arrived back at Portsmouth a couple of hours later. They were looking for booty and if they were lucky they found old coins dating back from the days when wherries serving the old naval sailing ships used this slipway.

There were other incidents that were not down to the ships troublesome handling characteristics but were of a purely deliberate nature. Although completely safe, in the wake of disasters such as the Zeebrugge incident such practices would surely be frowned upon today because they involved the lowering of a prow whilst a ship was on passage in order to pick up floating objects. Amongst the objects picked up were

dummy torpedoes. The Royal Navy used to carry out torpedo launching practice in Stokes Bay and the dummy torpedoes were fired either from the pier or from aircraft. The dummies were subsequently recovered for further use but many were lost. The crews of the ferries sometimes spotted them floating in the sea and when they did they lowered a prow and hauled them aboard. They were later off-loaded at HMS *Vernon* where a recovery fee would be paid to the crew. Other flotsam frequently hauled aboard were baulks of timber, simply because one of the skippers loved the smell of burning wood on his lounge fire. Of a somewhat more commendable nature several dinghy sailors were rescued from the sea by being pulled over the lowered prow ramps of these ships.

Modifications to Phase One fleet

During the course of their lives the three pioneer ships underwent various modifications. These were principally to *Fishbourne* in order to bring her up to a similar standard to the two sisters. As already mentioned she received an additional generator in 1928. Somewhat later her lifeboats were raised onto higher davits and she also received the improved system for charging the main engine starting plug accumulators. At an indeterminate date the saloon area was converted to a similar arrangement as *Wootton* and *Hilsea* with a single lounge and the all-important snack counter and bar.

During the war the military found that the load carrying capacity of the prow ramps (8 tons for the sisters and 6 tons for *Fishbourne*) was insufficient for supporting a number of their vehicles. Modifications were carried out to bring the capacity up to 15 tons. *Wootton* was duly modified in 1942 whilst *Hilsea* was dealt with somewhat later. By the time that the war came to an end *Fishbourne* was still fitted with her short and flimsy hand operated ramps. The Board Minutes of 22 November 1945 reported that approval had been given for an £8,000 refit for this vessel that resulted in her looking quite a different ship. The work involved the following:

1 Extension of prows by 3 feet and conversion to electrical operation to avoid risks of stranding on slipways and to facilitate mooring   £6,220
2 Replacement of three of the four hand-operated capstans by power operated ones   £1,530
3 Provision of additional buoyant apparatus to increase passenger carrying capacity from 99 to 199   £250

Total   £8,000

The work was carried out at the Southern's Marine Maintenance workshops at Southampton Docks between 8 January and 18 April 1947. After she re-emerged the profiles of the ends of the ship were similar to those on *Wootton* and *Hilsea,* as seen on the photo on page 38 and the front cover view. She was also equipped with more powerful auxiliary units – a pair of MaClaren twin-cylinder diesel powered units replacing the three-cylinder petrol/paraffin unit. The electrical power output of these units was 15kW each. The engines were initially hand started but the starting handle was situated at a very low level and after an engineer broke an arm when one kicked back they were converted to battery start. Upper cylinder heating, for starting purposes, was provided by disposable hand lit cartridges which were screwed into the cylinder heads before each start up. Without the benefit of operating instructions or drawings, the engineers got into difficulty when it was first necessary to dismantle the engines. With all bolts apparently removed it took several hours to figure out why the cylinder block would not come away from the crankcase, until it was realised that there was one more bolt hidden inside an oil gallery!

On all three ships the captain's cabin was converted into a galley complete with a coal fired stove. The flue rose from the starboard deckhouse ahead of the bridge, and can be seen on the later photographic views of these vessels. The galley was very small and there was not enough room to swing a mouse, let alone a cat! The captain's cabin was relocated in a similar position on the opposite side of the ship, in the rear corner of the saloon.

Heavy maintenance and annual surveys were usually carried out at the Southern's own facilities at Southampton. The workshops were located in the vicinity of the No 1 dry dock in the Old (Eastern) Docks. Access to this dry dock, together with the adjacent numbers 1 and 2 dry docks and the Inner Dock (all now filled in), was via the Outer Dock – Ocean Village of today. *Wootton* normally received her annual survey and overhaul first, in October / November, followed by *Hilsea* in January / March, and finally *Fishbourne*. The ships were typically in dock for a period of 4 to 6 weeks, but *Fishbourne* had another long visit between 8 April and 4 June 1948.

Late in 1946 the Docks and Marine Committee approved replacement of the four beacons and three dolphins at Fishbourne with new structures comprising lamps lit by propane gas. The previous method of illuminating the beacons is not known. The estimated cost of the work was £4350 less a contingency of £250 by the Admiralty in respect of damage caused to beacon numbers 1 and 4. The final price was somewhat more than above because the contractors original quote was on the understanding that the work would be carried out prior to the onset of winter. The beacons and dolphins were much more substantial structures than the simple posts used today and they needed to be, because they were always being knocked about by the ferries. The method for installing the propane cylinders was almost perfect! The cylinders were brought across from the mainland on board the ferries and were then stored in a small shed at the Fishbourne terminal. When the time came to replace the cylinders they were wheeled back on board a berthed ferry and through to the lowered stern ramp of the ship where they were loaded on board the launch *Alice* which was sent across from Portsmouth

for the purpose. They were then taken out to the beacons where they were lifted into position using a block and tackle. Unfortunately the fastening points for the block and tackle were not quite high enough and the men had to really struggle to get the cylinders into their final positions. They could have been positioned higher up but apparently they were never moved. If the people holding the purse strings also had to install the cylinders then things may have been different.

Also in 1946, the launch *Alice* received a new engine costing £425 10s 0d plus £100 installation costs.

An ongoing cost, not a modification, was repeated dredging works at Fishbourne. The ferries did not have the natural scouring action of the later Voith-Schneider propelled vessels and the channel required dredging every two to three years. Each dredging operation cost between £5,000 and £10,000, which was a considerable amount of money in those days. £7,500 is the equivalent of about £200,000 at today's prices, and that sort of ongoing expenditure must have been more than the Southern Railway had bargained for when they moved the service to a tidal estuary in 1926.

Unusual operations

The Fishbourne service was the exclusive domain of *Fishbourne*, *Wootton* and *Hilsea*. The route's terminal facilities were not suitable for any other ferries but the three little ships often undertook service on the Lymington to Yarmouth route. That route had continued to use towboats until as late as 1938. It would undoubtedly have been modernised earlier had there not been long running negotiations between the Southern Railway and an independent company who planned to introduce a ferry service between Keyhaven and Fort Victoria Pier, near Yarmouth. When these negotiations finally broke down the Southern Railway introduced a new car ferry between Lymington Pier and Yarmouth Quay. This was, of course, the double-ended *Lymington*. This ship was a direct descendant of the Fishbourne trio. She was of a similar basic design but she was larger and had vastly superior passenger accommodation in line with her dual-role as both a vehicle and passenger ferry. *Lymington* was a revolution in her own right, being the first ship in Britain to be fitted with Voith-Schneider propulsion, but unfortunately the original propeller installations proved unreliable and *Lymington* had a troubled first seventeen years of life until new propeller units were installed in 1955. As a result of her unreliability the Fishbourne trio often found low season employment on the western route. The first occasion that a Fishbourne ferry was sent down was in May 1938 when *Lymington* was withdrawn only four days after she had entered service and *Hilsea* provided cover during her eleven day absence. Thereafter it was not uncommon for a Fishbourne ferry (more often than not *Wootton*, it would seem) to be permanently stationed at Lymington during the winter months, when one of them could be spared, just waiting for the resident ferry to break down. The ships performed satisfactorily on the Lymington to Yarmouth route but, due to their lower speeds, they could not maintain the set timetable and no doubt foot passengers did not welcome their inferior facilities. There was also the obvious disadvantage that the ferries had to turn round in the confines of the Lymington River. They usually performed this manoeuvre without any trouble, but not always. Early in 1952 a yacht was damaged when *Wootton* was dragged against it by a falling tide. The company's own engineers subsequently repaired the yacht at Portsmouth and for their trouble the yacht's owner invited them to join him for beverages at the Royal Lymington Yacht Club!

During a period of severe winter weather, *Lymington* had to be withdrawn with propeller trouble on 4 February 1954, but due to northwesterly gales *Wootton* was unable to sail down from Portsmouth until the following day. *Wootton* took up services on 5 February, but there were cumulative delays of up to forty minutes owing to her lower speed. *Lymington* returned to service on 6th. On 4 February, services from Portsmouth were also cancelled (from 10.30 am) owing to the gales and the presence of ice at Fishbourne.

Other peacetime deviations from the normal ferry run were rare but in 1937, and again in 1953, all three vessels acted as spectator ships during the Royal Navy fleet reviews at Spithead. During the former review, on 20 May 1937, *Hilsea* even performed a public cruise from Fishbourne.

Phase One timetables

The timetables during the tenure of the pioneer ferries could not be straightforward, simply because the ferries were not fast enough to maintain an hourly schedule. The schedules may not have been as complex as they are today, but travellers needed to have a more intimate knowledge of them because if they missed a ferry they could have an extremely long wait for the next one.

Departures from Fishbourne were usually an hour and a quarter after those from Portsmouth and generally only from around breakfast time until teatime. There was never an over-night service, and there was a vast difference in the frequency of sailings between summer and winter. In 1926, when the towboat service commenced, there were only two trips on weekdays only (including Saturdays), rising in summer to three on weekdays and two on Sundays. By August 1930, when all three pioneer ships were in service, there were six trips on weekdays, ten on Saturdays and five on Sundays. The winter service lasted from late September until the end of May and comprised only two trips a day and none on Sundays. Only one boat was in service and the first departure from Portsmouth was at 09:15 and the last departure from Fishbourne at 15:30 (13:00 on Tuesdays) but there was a later boat from early April (from Portsmouth at 16:45 and 18:00

from Fishbourne) except Tuesdays.

By 1938 the winter timetable had not changed at all but the peak summer frequency had risen to fourteen trips on Saturdays between early July and mid September when the first departures of the day were 08:00 from Portsmouth and 08:30 from Fishbourne, whilst the final departures were 20:00 from Portsmouth and 19:15 from Fishbourne. Here we can see that one ship still ended her daily roster at Fishbourne. This happened every day in the summertime, including Sundays. Overnight stopovers at Fishbourne during the 'thirties were normally performed by *Hilsea*, which had an Isle of Wight crew at that time. The practice of berthing vessels at Fishbourne overnight ceased for good with the outbreak of the Second World War.

During the war, services gradually reduced and had reached their nadir by 1943 when there were only two advertised crossings in each direction, weekdays only, all year round. Following the cessation of hostilities services picked up again, but due to petrol rationing the 1948 summer timetable was back down to three trips per day, weekdays only. Thereafter, advertised sailings increased to approximately prewar levels but never substantially greater.

In 1960, the last full year of the pioneer ferries, the midwinter timetable was still for only four trips on weekdays, three on Saturdays and none on Sundays. The published timetables only ever provided for a three-ship roster on summer Saturdays, but the three pioneer ferries frequently did work simultaneously at other times, therefore a good many unadvertised trips were run. For example, in 1960 4,630 crossings were made of which only 3,996 were timetabled.

The fare structure was no less complicated than the timetables. There seemed to be a special price for everything, including a 'hearse plus corpse'. In 1926 the ordinary return fare for a car measuring 14'0" in length was £2 14s 0d (£2.70). Taking inflation into account this equates to £78 today (note 1). The 1926 ordinary return fare for persons accompanying traffic was 3/- (15p), or £4.30 (note 1) at today's prices.

Note 1 – Source: Advertised Fares, Official 'All Items' Cost of Living Index (pre-1947), 'All Items' RPI (post-1947).

The war years

The outbreak of war brought an immediate downturn in the fortunes of the Fishbourne ferry. A general restriction was imposed on travel to and from the Isle of Wight; consequently services and revenue plummeted. In the long term the ferries were to benefit from the effects of the war because the growth in car ownership was suppressed for so long that they were able to cope with the eventual increase in traffic for a much longer period than would otherwise have been the case. The war may well have extended their service lives by as much as ten years, perhaps more.

Early in the war the ships were painted in an overall grey livery. The wheelhouses were reinforced with concrete and steel and each ship was equipped with a Lewis machine gun. Machine gun practice provided the crews with a welcome break from routine, but nobody ever fired when a German bomber was seen – they were too busy trying to find cover. *Fishbourne* and *Wootton* were requisitioned by the War Department to assist in the Dunkirk evacuations, a task for which they were singularly unsuitable due to their low speed and poor handling characteristics in the prevailing conditions. During May the two vessels made their way to Ramsgate leaving *Hilsea* to run the service alone. *Fishbourne* set sail for Dunkirk on the morning of 1 June, assisted by the tugs *Duke*, *Prince* and *Princess*. After two hours the starboard rope of *Princess* was carried away in the swell. About the same time four sailing barges, towed by the tug *Sun III* had also set out, but after another hour and a half this little flotilla was missing, whereupon *Duke* turned back to look for them. After a while, contact having been made, *Duke* took over towing the sailing barge *Hasteway*, but because of poor visibility soon lost sight of the Fishbourne contingent. Then another sailing barge, *Ada Mary*, twice broke free from *Sun III* and was taken in tow by *Duke*. Five hours after setting sail from Ramsgate the little flotilla lay about two miles from the Dunkirk beaches. At 2.40 pm a violent air raid broke over the flotilla. Before long Dunkirk could not be located amid the pall of smoke from burning oil. Several hours passed by, and although the tugs picked up survivors from nearby sunken ships neither they nor *Fishbourne* reached any nearer than two miles from the beaches. After an assessment of how *Fishbourne* had behaved in the rough channel waters, a naval officer gave the order for *Prince*, *Princess* and *Fishbourne* to "turn around and get away

home as soon as possible". Both *Duke* and *Sun III* also were compelled to return, all of them arriving back off Ramsgate by 7.30 am on 2 June.

It would appear that *Wootton* may never have set sail from Ramsgate, or at least she may not have got very far. Little is known of her activities apart from an extract from *The World in Flames* (1940). Lieutenant Ian Cox, on the bridge of the destroyer HMS *Malcolm* was moved almost to tears on seeing a flotilla led by *Wootton*, which was wallowing in the Channel like a sawn off landing stage. His voice shaking with emotion, Cox burst out with the lines from Shakespeare's Henry V, which spoke of another battle in France:

> All gentlemen in England, now abed,
> shall think themselves accurs'd they were not here:
> And hold their manhoods cheap, while any speaks
> that fought with us on St Crispin's Day.

Accounts of the ferries roles in the Dunkirk evacuations are somewhat conflicting. What does seem certain was that neither reached the French beaches. Nevertheless both were awarded 'Dunkirk Evacuation' plates, which can now be found in the National Railway Museum in York. Following 'Dunkirk', both ships returned to the Solent where they apparently stayed for the remainder of the war.

It appears that *Wootton* spent much of the war at Lymington covering for the resident ferry, and at times running in tandem with her. In December 1940 these two ships provided transport during the relief of the 12th Infantry Brigade by the 214th. This operation took nine days during which 5570 men and 544 vehicles were shipped across the Solent.

Wootton undergoing a refit in the Camber Shipyard in the Inner Camber Docks during March 1945. Note the wheelhouse reinforced for wartime service. The port forward propeller is just visible beneath the staging. This entire area has now been made over to modern, luxury apartments.

Vosper Thornycroft

A poor quality shot, but it is of interest because it shows Fishbourne *on the western route, approaching Yarmouth in August 1945, still in wartime condition. The ship is still fitted with the original ramps and counterbalancing towers as well as having a reinforced wheelhouse.*
Alan Brown collection

As would be expected, the number of private cars transported across the Solent fell considerably. In 1942 a mere 2056 cars were shipped on the Fishbourne route representing less than one tenth of the prewar peak. Motorcycle combinations reached their nadir in 1943 when only seven machines made the crossing whilst solos dipped to 207 in 1945. By way of compensation the shipment of lorries, mostly due to military operations, more than quadrupled. In 1943 the number of lorries and military vehicles peaked at 8367.

During the intense preparations for the D-Day landings in 1944 the regular passenger steamers *Merstone* and *Shanklin*, with the standby vessel *Solent* from Lymington, were requisitioned to ferry troops to the transports to France, lying in Spithead. During this period civilian movements to the Island were restricted to travel on the Fishbourne car ferries with connecting buses to Ryde.

During the war the crews sometimes found a nefarious way of overcoming butter rationing. Milk was often shipped in churns at this time. From under the noses of the MoD police, they were known to scoop a jar of cream from the tops of the churns and they then spent the crossing vigorously shaking it into butter!

The three car ferries survived the war, but not completely unscathed. *Hilsea* was involved in two incidents, which are recounted in the chapter on mishaps. At the end of the war the three ferries were refitted for their usual peacetime role and it seems likely that they received new wheelhouses. They then settled back into their routine trades, which lasted for a further seventeen years.

Post-war operation

As early as 1944 the Southern Railway held discussions to consider a 'five year plan' for services and shipbuilding once the war was over. As far as the Fishbourne service was concerned there were no surprises and the Project Committee recommended the following:

Apart from a few Saturdays in the summer, the prewar fleet of three craft was sufficient to lift the traffic, and on the other days of the week much additional traffic could have been conveyed. More vessels could not be usefully employed without enlargement of the terminal facilities at Wootton Creek. There have been no losses to date, and no recommendation is made for new construction.

Indeed, it was not until 1951 that the ferries had to deal with a greater volume of traffic than had been conveyed in the peak prewar year of 1937, so the recommendation had been a wise one.

On 1 January 1948 the Southern Railway was nationalised and became the Southern Region of British Railways. As far as the ferry services were concerned nationalisation had very little impact. The only visual change on the Fishbourne ferries was the painting over of the intertwined SR logo that had embellished the outer bulkheads of the deckhouses. The old SR livery of black hull, white upperworks, teak coloured internal above-deck bulkheads and black topped yellow funnels remained unchanged; in fact it became the standard BR ship livery. The wheelhouses were finished in varnished teak once again having been painted white for some time.

During the 'fifties low unemployment and a relaxation in the post-war restrictions led to a huge increase in private car ownership. A general feeling of optimism meant more people than ever before were choosing to take their holidays on the Isle of Wight. During the peak summer weekends of July and August *Fishbourne*, *Wootton* and *Hilsea* were really struggling to cope with the traffic, though at other times there was still plenty of spare capacity. By the early 'fifties the Fishbourne service had lost its lead, in terms of traffic conveyed, to the Lymington to Yarmouth route. In 1937, the last full year of towboat operation on the western Solent, that service had only carried 10% of the volume traffic conveyed via Fishbourne. The following year *Lymington* entered service and in 1947 the capacity of the route was increased further when a second vehicle/passenger ferry was introduced, that being the gargantuan diesel-electric paddle vessel, *Farringford*. By virtue of the two Yarmouth ferries' greater vehicular capacity, higher speed and shorter crossing distance they were carrying more traffic than the eastern route. Although improvements to the Fishbourne service were in the wind no official moves were made for several more years.

In November 1957 the Isle of Wight County Council convened an Island/Mainland Travel Conference at Ryde Town Hall to seek improvements in transport facilities between the Island and the mainland. Representatives of the British Transport Commission (BR's governing body) and other transport operators were in attendance. At that time, traffic on the Portsmouth to Ryde passenger ferry was at its all time peak and the main subject of the conference was to try and find a way of doing something about the severe bottleneck that occurred on this route on about a dozen Saturdays each

At Fishbourne the uni-directional first generation ferries swung straight off the berth and sailed out of the creek bow first. Hilsea *departs for Portsmouth early on a summer's morning in 1960. To the right there is a build-up of chalk as work commenced on the new slipway.*

Ray Butcher collection

The first reconstruction of the Fishbourne terminal. The main view shows Wootton *loading on 15 August 1960, while work gets underway on the new slipway. The inset view shows* Hilsea *looking somewhat dwarfed at the new berth during the following Spring.*

Main view, British Railways. Inset view, Ray Butcher

Fishbourne *passes the training ship* Foudroyant, *formerly HMS* Trincomalee, *as she leaves Portsmouth Harbour on passage to the Isle of Wight. The pioneer ferry appeared somewhat back to front compared to her two half sisters, with the deckhouses extending forward of the bridge rather than aft of it. This view shows* Fishbourne *in her final form, with rebuilt prows and the counterbalance towers removed*

George Osbon, courtesy World Ship Society

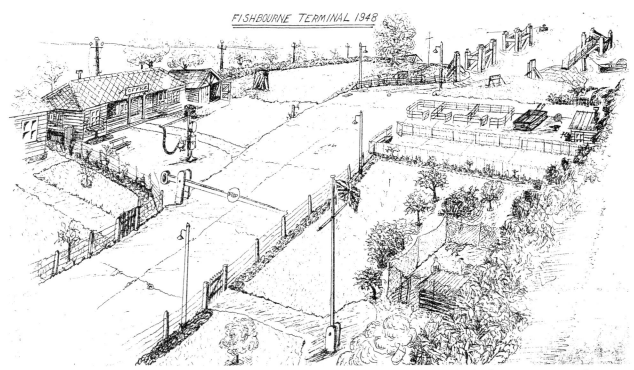

Jimmy James was an Isle of Wight railwayman with a penchant for drawing pictures. He sketched all the Island railway stations, many other railway locations and he drew many cartoons of local railway characters. The Fishbourne terminal, being Southern Railway owned, was a part of his patch. Artists' licence allowed some distortion of perspective, but all the features were present in his excellent, ink sketches.

Ray Butcher collection

A bleak winter's view from the bridge of Hilsea *looking up through the Fishbourne terminal early in 1961. The original slipway was soon obliterated as the construction work on the left spread across. The slipway on the extreme right now forms part of the Royal Victoria Yacht Club.*
Ray Butcher

summer. The inadequacies of the Fishbourne car ferry were regarded as a comparatively minor problem, however Mr G Dorley-Brown (chairman of the IW Hotels Association) mentioned during his address that the car ferries were antiquated and totally unsuitable for the demands of the day. Large numbers of bookings were refused because accommodation was not available when required. For eight years they had been asking when more up-to-date vessels were likely to be put into service, but they still had no clue of the BTC's intentions. In his reply, Mr D McKenna (Assistant General Manager, Southern Region) said that he was happy to announce that they hoped to include in the 1958 shipping programme some new ferries for the Fishbourne route, and he thought they would have a substantial increase in car-carrying capacity. He added that tenders were about to be invited for an additional vessel for the Lymington to Yarmouth route. Mr CW Gould, for the Isle of Wight Publicity Council, said they had been told that car ferries on order would take two or three years to complete. Was the Fishbourne service to be as bad for the next two or three years as at present? Mr McKenna replied

that the answer to that was negative. It would be a couple of years before a new ship came out. It was actually four, or close to it. Meanwhile the Yarmouth route received its third dual-purpose ferry in 1959. This was the company's second Voith-Schneider propelled ferry and she took the name of the paddle-steamer that she replaced, *Freshwater*.

Plans for modernisation of the Portsmouth to Fishbourne route were finally announced, not a moment too soon, in November 1958. Traffic was growing ever faster and by 1960 62,473 vehicles were conveyed on the route, including 46,990 cars. This was an increase of 16% in traffic over the previous year. Two new ships were ordered and new slipways were constructed at both ends. Work began on both slipways in the summer of 1960 and the service then entered one of its transitional phases. At Fishbourne the new slipway was placed at an angle of about 50 degrees to the original so as to preclude the new ships having to make a sharp turn as they approached the berth. The approach ramp to the slipway eventually spread across the site of the original slip so during construction it was necessary to shore up the edge of the new

Above: *Low tide at Fishbourne in 1947 with* Hilsea *loading for Portsmouth. A piling rig is present for replacement of the dolphins and installation of the fender piles on the right. The latter were installed after a bout of inter-departmental buck-passing, when marine and shore departments blamed each other for propeller damage that occurred when strong winds blew the ships into the shallows. Also of note is the dredged swinging basin to the left and on the opposite side of the creek, in front of the boathouses, a DUKW landing craft is parked. Work at Fishbourne was ongoing; in March 1952 the three terminal dolphins and one of the fender piles were replaced or repositioned in a 44-hour operation that was interrupted by only one scheduled visit by a ferry.*

Gordon Phillips collection

Right: *Something one would not see today – a convoy of vehicles promoting cigarettes. A fleet of Bedford vans, complete with rattling bumpers no doubt, is seen boarding* Hilsea *at Fishbourne on a summer's evening at the end of their visit. The ship has sprouted a radio antenna from her mast.*

Ray Butcher collection

The original Broad Street terminal was never more advanced than this. Wootton *loads vehicles for Fishbourne shortly before the old slipway was abandoned. A central window has been installed in the rear of the ship's wheelhouse. HMS* Vernon, *beyond, is now a part of the Gunwharf Quays complex.*

Ray Butcher collection

Hilsea *looking somewhat lost at the new Broad Street terminal in 1961.*

Ray Butcher

The Lymington to Yarmouth ferries were soon tried out after the second slipway at Fishbourne had been built. Here, Lymington *unloads vehicles on 11 April 1961.*
British Railways

Freshwater *was used on the Fishbourne service at about the same time. It is not clear whether or not the much larger* Farringford *was tried out at this time, but she certainly was in 1964. Unlike her compatriots she never became a reserve ferry on the Fishbourne route.*

Ray Butcher

works to allow the old ferries continued access to the original berth. Towards the end of construction the old slipway was demolished and there has been no trace of it since then. The two mooring dolphins on the south side were left to the elements and stood forlornly for the next thirty-seven years doing nothing, except causing a hazard to dinghy sailors from the adjacent Royal Victoria Yacht Club. During 1998 they once again found a useful purpose when they were incorporated into a pier and pontoon following a lottery grant to the RVYC. Apart from the construction of a large parking area at the top of the terminal no other improvements were made at Fishbourne during the 1960/61 modernisation.

At Portsmouth a new slipway was finally built at Dirty Corner. This was only a stone's throw away from the original slipway but it was on a completely different site so the pioneer ferries could continue to use their original berth unhindered. There was a good deal of disruption on shore, however. A number of properties were demolished to make way for a new ticket office and car park, about 100 yards back from the old slip. The original ticket office was knocked down as well, to make way for a new engineering workshop, therefore a temporary ticket office had to be used for a time. Once the new slipway was completed the old one was simply abandoned. It remains a public slipway to this day but it is little used and is largely covered with shingle. An old cannon that was used as a tethering point for the ferries still protrudes from the beach. The old Gosport Chain Ferry service had closed in 1959, just when car usage was about to explode. Its slipway and ticket office are long since vanished and the area has been reclaimed and converted into a cobbled promenade that provides fine views of the harbour.

The new slipways were opened for traffic early in 1961 and it would appear that *Hilsea* made the first official use of Fishbourne slip, judging from photographic evidence that shows an inordinate number of onlookers. The opportunity was soon taken to try out at least two of the three Yarmouth ferries on the eastern route. *Lymington* was in use on the route on 11 April 1961 and *Freshwater* was tested at about the same time. Both performed satisfactorily. It is not clear whether or not the much larger *Farringford* was tried out at this stage, though she certainly was later.

Meanwhile, work on the replacement resident ferries was well advanced and the faithful pioneer ships were staring retirement in the face. The names of *Fishbourne* and *Wootton* were given the suffix II in February 1961 in order to free them (for registration purposes) for the new ships, although in the event the name 'Wootton' was not revived. The pioneer ship was replaced on 7 July 1961 when the new *Fishbourne* entered traffic, but her retirement was very short and she was frequently called back into action during teething troubles with the new ship. In any case, I can remember a day when all four ships were running simultaneously. During a family visit to the foreshore at Fishbourne during July 1961 I remember one of the old ships (probably *Wootton II*) remaining berthed at the terminal for an inordinately long period of time. Clearly there must have been some sort of a problem, but at the age of just eight this did not occur to me at the time. It was a busy day and the enlarged car park at the terminal overflowed and the queue stretched back up Fishbourne Lane. Meanwhile the other two old ferries and the new *Fishbourne* all arrived and trod water at the end of the channel. Prior to 2001, this is the only time that I had witnessed more than one waiting, incoming ferry, let alone three. Eventually the stricken ferry departed and the new *Fishbourne* was allowed to proceed to the slipway, no doubt to the consternation of the occupants of the other ferries because she was not at the front of the queue! This was the first time that I had seen the new *Fishbourne* and I remember thinking how enormous she looked, and I suppose at the time, she was. The second new ship entered service at the tail end of the summer season on 29 August, but both she and her sister continued to experience technical problems and the old regime struggled on for a while longer. *Fishbourne II* was still in service on 5 September 1961 and by way of a swan song she ran aground at Fishbourne and blocked the slipway for several hours. She was withdrawn for good a few days after this incident. *Wootton* finished at about the same time and arrived at the BR Marine Department's inner dock in Southampton for lay-up on 21 September 1961. *Hilsea* followed on 5 October 1961 but *Fishbourne* did not arrive there until 26 April 1962. The old *Fishbourne* had worked the passage for 34 years, a record that will stand at least until the year 2017 when *St. Catherine* will reach that age. The pioneer ships were certainly outdated in their latter years and there can be little doubt that they would have been withdrawn much sooner had it not been for the effects of the war. But they had served their purpose admirably and no doubt lasted much longer than anyone could have expected when the radical concept was first dreamt up in the mid-twenties.

Waters new

Wootton and *Hilsea* were recorded as sold to Pounds scrapyard in February 1962, followed three months later by *Fishbourne*. *Wootton* was moved from her lay-up berth at Southampton to Pounds yard, at Tipner Lake, in the upper reaches of Portsmouth harbour, early in 1962. However, two independent sources suggest that for a while *Hilsea* was kept in a reserve capacity and was used on at least one occasion on the Lymington to Yarmouth route. One source was an engineer who worked on the ships; the other had no connection with the company but observed *Hilsea* berthed at Yarmouth slipway during the summer of 1962. It is not clear why it should have been necessary for the ship to be used on the western route when it had three resident ferries, one of which was nearly new. It is not known if *Hilsea* worked the Fishbourne route again but there seem to be no recollections of it happening. If

Engineers Ray Perry (left) and Frank Leach in the engine room of Hilsea. *An engine room, with its whirling machinery, is not an ideal place to be wearing a tie, but Ray Perry was not on duty at the time.*

Ray Butcher

it is true that *Hilsea* remained in BR ownership and use during 1962 it would seem that she was nevertheless on the market. In April of that year Denny's were requested to supply details of the ship to a company at Wormerveer, near Amsterdam, but it would appear that nothing came of this. It may be that *Hilsea's* appearance at Yarmouth was in connection with a demonstration to her potential new owners. Eventually all three vessels did find their way to Pounds scrap yard and *Fishbourne* is on record as having departed Southampton for Portsmouth harbour on 8 June 1962. All were offered for resale. *Wootton* soon departed but the only new waters she saw were on the way to a Dutch breakers yard. She left Portsmouth

on 31 May 1962 in tow of the tug *Hazelgarth*, bound for Maasluis, near Rotterdam, where she arrived three days later. *Fishbourne* and *Hilsea* remained at Tipner whilst interest was being shown in a further use for the vessels. In October 1962 Denny's were asked by agents Gristwick Ltd. of London to supply plans of both vessels for an overseas customer. In March of 1963 both ships were sold to the salvage company G Doeksen and Zonen on the Dutch island of Terschelling.

Following their sale, first *Hilsea* and later *Fishbourne* were towed to Terschelling by Doeksen's own tug *Holland* in order to be refitted for further service on the River Shannon in Ireland. At that time there were no ferries or bridges across the

Hilsea *in mid-passage towards the end of her career on the Solent. The lorry carrying Prestcold refrigerators is a tight squeeze under the bridge; the fact that it is pointing backwards indicates that this is a Portsmouth-bound passage.*

George Osbon, courtesy World Ship Society

Shannon downstream of Limerick, and the intention was to open a ferry service some 30 miles west of that town, but then another opportunity for operating the ships arose. The Dutch Oil Company Nederlandsche Aardolie Maatschappij (NAM) were about to begin exploratory drilling operations on the Dutch Wadden Isles and they had an enormous amount of plant and materials which somehow they had to get across to the islands. *Fishbourne* and *Hilsea* were in the area at exactly the right time and they were consequently leased to NAM. Operations began on 4 September 1963 using *Hilsea*, while *Fishbourne* joined the fray a couple of weeks later. *Hilsea* had already received a major overhaul for her Irish operations and the hull was painted in a silver-grey livery. *Fishbourne*, meanwhile, had merely been 'cut and shaved' to remove two years growth of seaweed and barnacles. Her general condition was not considered good enough to warrant a major overhaul and only routine maintenance was ever carried out. She was never repainted, retaining her black hull to the end. *Hilsea* on the other hand was always maintained in good order and the rather fine wheelhouse was kept well varnished. Both ships kept their original names, *Fishbourne* without the suffix II. The vessels were operated between temporary slipways at Harlingen, on the Dutch mainland, and the harbour at West Terschelling, some 16 miles distant. They were sorely overloaded in their new role, and *Hilsea* carried 96 tons on her first trip (if an oil company circular is correct). Considering the design dead weight tonnage was only about 35, a load of nearly three times that amount almost beggars belief. Such a load would not have sunk the vessel but it would have increased the waterline by close to a foot, taking it up to near

the prow hinge! It is perhaps not surprising that this load was not exceeded on subsequent trips. Due to strong currents, narrow channels and locks in the Dutch Waddensee, and presumably also due to the huge loads, the two ships always undertook their passages with tug assistance. The ferries themselves seem to have been regarded as 'enormous' by their new operators and the fact there was a bar below decks was considered something of a luxury.

The River Shannon project had not died a death due to this unscheduled new role. In 1966 there were still plans to take *Hilsea* to Ireland and run her across the river near Kilkee. Months passed by but nothing developed until another company announced their intentions to open a much shorter route between Foynes and Killadysert, some ten miles upstream from Doeksen's proposed route. They were planning to use two of the old Chepstow ferries (*Severn Queen* and *Severn Princess*), which had been rendered superfluous due to the opening of the Severn Road Bridge. Several months later Doeksen secured another long-term contract on the Waddensee and they finally abandoned their plans for the Shannon ferry, so *Fishbourne* and *Hilsea* never went to Ireland. The plans for the Foynes ferry did not come to anything either but in 1969 the present Shannon ferry between Tarbert and Killimer commenced operations with a brand new ship, *Shannon Heather*.

Fishbourne and *Hilsea* had thus ended their public service careers on the Solent but at least they were to have several more years of useful, if somewhat arduous, employment elsewhere. *Fishbourne* was eventually broken up in 1967 and *Hilsea* in 1970, when each ship was forty years old.

Assisted by the 1911-built tug Stortemelk II, Fishbourne *is seen entering the harbour at West-Terschelling (Holland) during her second life, in the spring of 1964. She and sister* Hilsea *were used to transport materials and equipment for oilrig construction between Harlingen and the Waddenisles.* Hilsea *was painted in a silver grey livery for an abortive service in Eire whilst* Fishbourne *remained in her original livery. Both were stripped of their lifeboats for their services in the Waddensea.*

Rederij Doeksen

On 4 August 1960 HMS Vanguard, *the Royal Navy's last battleship, in the company of eight tugs, ran aground at Portsmouth Point on her way to the breaker's yard. The purpose of including this interesting but seemingly irrelevant picture is that it shows the entire theatre of the mainland end of the Fishbourne service. A line of cars awaits the next ferry at the end of Broad Street (centre, above* Vanguard's *rear funnel). Beyond, the old ticket office has been demolished and work is underway on the new slipway (top left). At the top left is the site of the present terminal and towards the top right is the Camber Shipyard where* Wootton *was seen undergoing refit at the end of the war.*

The News, Portsmouth.

Chapter 3: Phase Two, 1961 to 1983

The second phase of the route's history lasted from 1961 until 1983, and was broadly the period in which the larger slipways were in use. This era was, arguably, a rather cavalier period in British history. The whole fabric of society changed in a most irrational manner. Historical character buildings were razed to the ground and replaced by some of the ugliest architectural designs ever seen. Railways were closed down and torn up in a manner that would make it very difficult to put them back again should the need arise, and two fingers were raised at public transport in general. There was a sea change in the way we lived and there appeared to be little regard for the past or the future. The motorcar ceased to be an expensive luxury and became a virtual necessity for an ever-increasing proportion of the population. People no longer needed to live close to where they worked due to the rising level of personal mobility. Retailers exploited this by building an increasing number of out of town shopping centres. The car also made people lazy, and this, together with a strongly held view that roads were too dangerous to walk or cycle along, meant that even the shortest of journeys were taken increasingly by car. More and more people tended to travel everywhere and anywhere in their cars, whatever the cost. Furthermore, an increasing quantity of goods was being transported by road, and as a 'throw away' society developed there was an ever-greater quantity of goods to transport. The end result is gridlock, noise, danger, pollution and aggression.

Of course, there were beneficiaries from all this, and amongst them were the ferry companies. Unfortunately the scale of the boom in car ownership was not anticipated and many services struggled to keep pace with it. A case in point was the Fishbourne car ferry. In 1961 a brand new pair of ferries was introduced and at first they seemed to be a sound and adequate investment. Their greater capacity and higher speed instantly eased the summer peak congestion, but within two or three years the situation was right back to square one. Additional larger boats were introduced but they, too, only eased congestion in the short term. Even an increase in the capacity of the newer ships did not provide a long-term solution. Consequently this era was sometimes less than happy for the travelling public. Summer Saturday bookings usually had to be made many months in advance. With the route operated by two completely different classes of ship, one with vastly superior facilities to the other, many people felt short changed when they arrived at the terminal and were confronted by one of the inferior variety waiting to take them across the Solent.

Another unwholesome feature, particularly of this era, was that non-booked motorists were able to bribe themselves into the queue of booked vehicles. Many people could tell of the slipping of a surreptitious fiver, although the staff were never foolish enough to ask for money. It was more a case of "Oh dear, I doubt if you will get on for several hours Sir"; no need for a nod-nod, wink-wink; people knew what was meant. Such depressing information could even be delivered on a winter Saturday afternoon, which has always been one of the quietest of times. Some members of staff were masters at persuading non-booked motorists to part with some extra money. One way they were able to do this was to simply wave on the first motorist from the non-booked queue, but a hand slipped in a pocket and a loud "Thank you sir" was often enough to convince the second and following that there was only one way to get aboard!

There was, however, at least one good feature about this era. It may be surprising to learn (it certainly surprised me) that during the late 'seventies standard vehicular fares fell to their all-time low in relation to the official inflationary indices.

The second phase not only saw a steady increase in traffic but also a rise in the status of the route. During the first phase the Fishbourne ferry was very much a secondary service, with a status similar to that afforded to a freight train as opposed to an express passenger train. Fully certified engineers were considered over-qualified for car ferries and the first officers were, in fact, leading hands. As the passenger fleet dwindled and the car ferry fleet grew, things had to change and the Fishbourne ferry became evermore important.

The 1957 Island/Mainland Travel Conference (discussed in the previous chapter) might just as well not have taken place. The principal problem discussed at that time was solved by the motorcar. Peak summer Saturday congestion at Ryde Pier and Portsmouth Harbour Station became less and less of a problem. One by one, the passenger ferries were withdrawn and not replaced. PS *Whippingham* went first, in 1962, followed three years later by PS *Sandown*. The last of the paddlers, *Ryde*, was withdrawn in 1969 and in 1980 MV *Shanklin* also went, leaving just two from a fleet of six to run the service. A whole new problem replaced it, but as far as ferry capacity on the Fishbourne route was concerned the problem was largely solved when the super ferries arrived in 1983, and that marked the end of the second phase.

The Voith-Schneider propeller

The second phase saw the introduction of Voith-Schneider propelled ferries to the Fishbourne route. The Voith-Schneider propeller is a somewhat enigmatic device so now would be a good point to delve into the history and function of this novel type of propulsion.

The Voith-Schneider propeller was developed during the 1920s by the Viennese engineer Ernst Schneider. Initially it was not intended to be a propeller but a water turbine. Herr Schneider envisaged installing whole lines of these units in free flowing rivers in order to generate electricity at low cost. The units he developed consisted of a number of vertical blades situated close to the circumference of a horizontal disc. A system of links caused the blades to feather as the disc rotated. Herr Schneider must have had a sharp engineering mind. Unlike a screw or a paddle wheel it is not particularly easy to see how the device would work, even when studying a completed design; to have come up with the idea in the first place must have needed the mind of a genius. Herr Schneider presented his design to Herr Walter Voith, the director in charge of the St Polten works (near Vienna) of Messrs JM Voith, specialists in the development and manufacture of water turbines. The initial reaction was scepticism; however, Voith eventually agreed to have some further tests carried out at the company's main works at Heidenheim in Germany. Voith's doubts about the suitability of the unit for its intended purpose proved to be well founded, however the Voith engineers found that by reversing the process and operating the turbine as a pump it was possible to obtain thrust in any desired horizontal direction, solely by adjustment of the blade oscillatory control and without having to turn the unit in azimuth. It was quickly appreciated that this device successfully eliminated all the problems that had bedevilled previous attempts to design a practical vertically-bladed propeller, and as such offered tremendous potential as a combined propulsion unit and steering system for ships. Voith thus decided to develop Schneider's invention purely as a ship propulsion unit. Thus was born the Voith-Schneider propeller.

The first Voith-Schneider propeller was installed in a small petrol-engined motorlaunch (which was christened *Torqueo*, 'I turn round') and exhaustive tests were carried out on Lake Constance. The boat's handling, manoeuvrability and reliability astounded all concerned and after two years further development Voith went ahead and marketed the propeller. The first commercial vessel to utilise the new propulsion system was a towboat named *Uhu*, built in 1931 for the Bayerische Lloyd Company of Regensburg for service on the River Danube. *Uhu* was equipped with a pair of stern mounted propellers, each driven by a 350bhp diesel engine.

Function of the Voith-Schneider propeller

As children, many of us probably noticed how a knife or a ruler behaves when it is dragged through a bowl of water. When it is sliced through the water edge on there is very little resistance and it moves freely, but when it is moved sideways it is much harder to move. The most basic form of ship propulsion, the paddle wheel or the oar, works using this side-on principle. By Newton's third law of motion every action has an equal and opposite reaction. The force of the blade pushing against the water creates a reaction that moves the vessel in the opposite direction to the paddle or the oar.

If, on the other hand, a knife or a ruler is moved through the water at some angle between edge on and side on then something quite different happens; it tries to move sideways. This is the principle by which the wing of an aircraft, the blade of a propeller, an oar moved with a sculling action, and a Voith-Schneider propeller all function. The angle of attack causes a pressure increase on one side of the blade and, again by Newton's third law, the reaction pushes the blade in the opposite direction ie sideways. As the fluid is deflected one way, the blade is deflected the other. On a wing the Bernoulli principle also has an effect. Bernoulli's theorem states that as a fluid increases in velocity so its pressure falls. A wing is curved so that air passing over the top has further to travel than that passing beneath. The pressure on top thus falls creating a pressure differential and generating lift. The blades of a Voith-Schneider propeller are of aerofoil section to create laminar (non-turbulent) flow and reduce drag, but they are not curved like the wing of an aircraft. The distance from nose to tail on each side of the blade is the same so the Bernoulli principle does not really come in to play

Although the Voith-Schneider propeller functions by the same principle as other devices it does it in its own special way. The blades of a Voith-Schneider propeller are mounted vertically and revolve around the centre of the disc on which they are mounted and as they do so they feather, as illustrated on diagram 'a' of Figure 3. As they feather the angle of attack changes and water exerts pressure on one side of the blade or the other creating hydrodynamic lift away from the high-pressure side. The resultant direction and magnitude of lift from the blade at equi-spaced points along its circumferential path is shown on diagram 'b'. The direction of the lift at any point is offset by the induced and profile drag of the blade. It can be seen that there is lift in all directions over a range of +/-90 degrees from the mean direction of lift (or thrust to put it in its true context). The components acting away from the mean direction of thrust cancel each other out, therefore the resultant thrust would be to the right in the case shown on diagram 'b'. When the blade is travelling parallel to the mean direction of thrust, ie at the top and bottom positions in diagram 'b', it generates no thrust at all. At this point it is acting like a knife or a ruler being swiped edge on through a bowl of water.

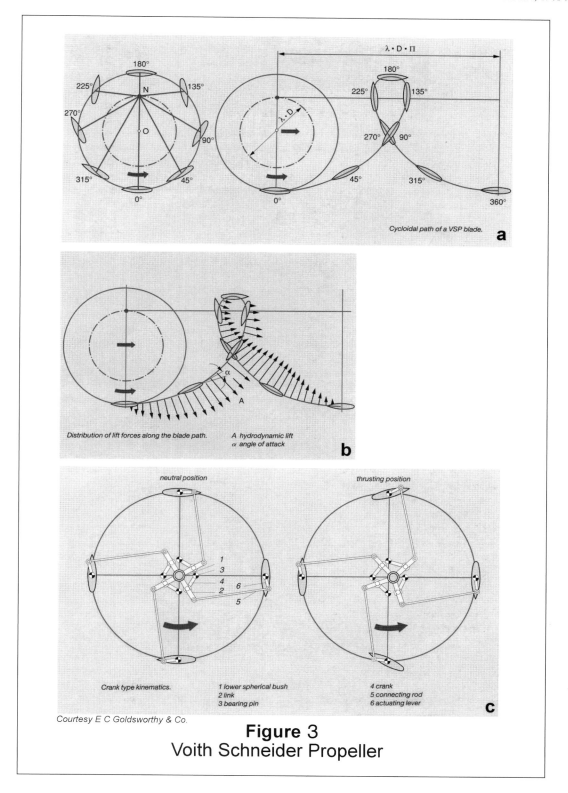

Cycloidal path of a VSP blade.

a

Distribution of lift forces along the blade path.

A hydrodynamic lift
α angle of attack

b

neutral position

thrusting position

Crank type kinematics.

1 lower spherical bush
2 link
3 bearing pin

4 crank
5 connecting rod
6 actuating lever

c

Courtesy E C Goldsworthy & Co.

Figure 3
Voith Schneider Propeller

The direction of the resultant thrust is dependent on the position of the steering centre. The steering centre governs the way that the blades feather as the disc rotates. It is labelled as the 'lower spherical bush' on diagram 'c' of Figure 3 and its function should be self-explanatory on examination of the diagram. The steering centre can be moved to any position within a small circle around the centre point of the disc. When it is moved to the right (as shown on the right hand view on diagram 'c') the direction of thrust would be towards the bottom of the paper, and when moved to the top, thrust would be to the right, etc. When it is dead centre, the neutral position, the resultant thrust is zero. The Voith-Schneider propeller thus has the supreme advantage that thrust can be reversed through the neutral position. This type of propeller therefore has the best of all worlds. Like a conventional screw or paddle driven vessel the thrust can be switched from ahead to astern without applying any side thrust, something which an azimuthing screw unit cannot do (without stopping the screws rotation), and, like an azimuthing screw unit, it can apply sideways thrust, which is something that a conventional screw or paddle cannot do.

The position of the steering centre is controlled directly from control pedestals in the wheelhouse. There is no traditional telegraph system. The controls may be linked to the propellers either with direct linkages or hydraulically. Where there is more than one pedestal they are coupled together and each has exactly the same function.

The control pedestal is equipped with a number of wheels, or alternatively wheels and levers. Athwartships thrust is applied with independent wheels situated on top of the pedestal and with their axes running vertically. With a multiple propeller ship a wheel at the forward end of the pedestal controls the side thrust on the forward propeller(s), whilst a wheel at the aft end of the pedestal controls the side thrust on the stern propeller(s). When the ship is on passage steering can be effected by using the stern side thrust wheel alone but in some cases the fore and aft wheels can be coupled together so that they steer in unison. Fore and aft thrust is controlled using levers or wheels situated on the sides of the pedestal and with their axes running athwartships. Where levers are used there may be a single or a double lever. A single lever controls ahead and astern thrust on all propeller units in unison. A double lever (there will be one on each side of the pedestal) controls thrust from the fore and aft propellers. They are normally coupled together so that the thrust from all propellers is applied in unison, but in some cases they can be uncoupled so that the bow and stern propellers can be controlled independently, although this is only done under exceptional circumstances. On more modern units the levers have been replaced by two wheels, which are normally coupled together but can be uncoupled. In a more state of the art system a single joystick may replace the wheels and levers.

A wide variety of the above options have been used on cross-Solent ferries. *Freshwater*, *Fishbourne* and *Camber Queen* used the system with the single lever. The 'C class' ships, built between 1969 and 1973, used the two lever system whilst the four 'Saint class' ferries have the four-wheel system. The pioneer VSP ship, *Lymington*, incorporated an early system in which steering could be effected by each propeller independently by means of levers, though a wheel was used when on passage. With one exception all the Fishbourne and Yarmouth ferries had the controls coupled to the propellers with direct linkages comprising shafting, bevel gears and universal joints. The Red Funnel 'Raptor class' ships and the new Fishbourne ferry *St. Clare* have a four-wheel system with four control stations and an electro/hydraulic system linking the controls to the propellers.

It can be deduced from the above that a ship fitted with Voith-Schneider propellers does not need rudders but it still has a unique level of control. A ship so equipped can very easily be made to go forwards, backwards, sideways, pirouetted on a point or held stationary, regardless of other forces acting on it. There are other advantages as well. Steering capability is completely independent of the ship's speed and any alteration in the magnitude or direction of thrust is virtually instantaneous. Furthermore, since the engines and propellers run at constant speed in a fixed direction of rotation there are no large masses to stop, restart or reverse.

Such a system was ideal for propelling the Southern Railway's 1938-built car ferry, which would have to negotiate the narrow, winding and shallow Lymington River. The original specification for the vessel was for double twin-screwed propulsion, like the pioneer Fishbourne ferries, but with double ended operation as had originally been intended for those ships. Unfortunately the manoeuvrability of the Fishbourne ferries had not proved to be all that it might have been. Certain senior members of the company's staff had experience of Voith-Schneider-propelled ships on Lake Constance, and they were prepared to risk installing this radical form of propulsion in their new vessel. Thus *Lymington* became the first ship in Britain, and the first double-ended (bidirectional) vessel in the world, to incorporate Voith-Schneider propulsion.

The company were not prepared to gamble everything however, and they decided to choose a hull form which could easily be converted to the double twin screw application if the Voith units proved unsuccessful. This was to be a fundamental mistake. EC Goldsworthy & Co (the UK Voith agency) was well aware of the potential problems, and they were not happy about the line they were being forced to take. The problem was that the fallback hull form necessitated the propeller axes being set at an angle of 22.5 degrees when they should have been vertical, or very close to it. The propellers were situated diagonally opposite each other, one at the port forward end of the ship and the other at the starboard aft. The athwartships projection of the blades meant that the blade tips protruded beyond the sides of the ship abreast of the propellers although inside the extreme hull width at half-length. The relatively large angle reduced the effective side thrust, which was necessary to control the ferry up the winding river, but her manoeuvrability was still vastly superior to the other ships on the service. When the ferry masters became used to how easily the ferry could be manoeuvred they became complacent, which on occasions resulted in the ferry shoulder or quarter being swung against the banks of the Lymington River. There was a considerable amount of heavy timber embedded in the river banks and when a propeller came into contact with it as the ship swung into the bank, with considerable momentum behind it, something had to give. The result was frequent propeller failures, which recurred over a seventeen year period. The problem was finally sorted out, with total success, in 1955 when a new set of vertically mounted propellers were installed. Since that time every new company car ferry has been Voith-Schneider-propelled. Today, all eleven cross-Solent car ferries are fitted with Voith-Schneider propellers. Red Funnel had dabbled with Voith-Schneider units briefly in 1939 when their new ferry *Vecta* became only the second British ship to be fitted with such propellers. After the war, however, she was converted to twin screw propulsion and it was to be almost half a century before they once again chose the more radical option.

MVs Fishbourne and Camber Queen – the 1961 twins

The modernisation programme initiated by British Railways in 1958 included a pair of new bidirectional Voith-Schneider propelled car ferries. Built by Philip and Son of Dartmouth, these second-generation ships cost £175,000 each to construct.

There was nothing particularly remarkable about the new vessels. They followed a formula already tried and tested on the company's Lymington to Yarmouth route. The new ferries most closely resembled the latest addition to that fleet, the 1959-built *Freshwater*, and indeed the hulls were identical. Apparently the technical manager of Philip's went away from his first meeting with British Rail carrying a brief case bulging with 'as fitted' plans of *Freshwater* and a broad smile on his face on finding that half of his design work had already been done.

The new ships differed somewhat from *Freshwater* above car deck level. The Fishbourne route was purely a car ferry service so the new ferries required far less in the way of passenger accommodation and more car-deck space than the Yarmouth vessels. The new ships were fully double-ended, though not entirely symmetrical. The Fishbourne end (they rarely turned round) was designated the bow. They were named *Fishbourne* and *Camber Queen* and were almost identical. The second ship was originally to have been named 'Wootton' but for some reason she received one of the most unorthodox names given by the company.

The ships measured 166feet in length by 43feet beam and had a draught of 6feet. Their gross tonnage was 293. The car capacity, at 34, was roughly double that of their predecessors, and they had a passenger certificate for 165 (see Figure 4 on page 52). The layout of the superstructure was most unusual for that time, with the deckhouse on the starboard side extending forward of the bridge and the port deckhouse extending aft. This layout was chosen specifically for providing sufficient space to accommodate 'Queen Mary' transporters. Queen Marys were large articulated lorries, 66ft long, used for transporting partially dismantled aircraft. They were very tall vehicles, when loaded, and would not have fitted beneath the bridge decks. Apparently the idea was that they would be parked towards one side of the ship with the tractor unit positioned beneath the bridge. It would be necessary for the ship to berth back to front at the destination terminal in order to allow the vehicle to reverse off.

The Queen Mary's would have originated from the Saunders-Roe aircraft factory at East Cowes. Saunders-Roe, traditionally a builder of seaplanes, had recently been building a larger number of land planes. These could not take to the air locally and had to be transported to airfields on the mainland. Unfortunately, by the time that *Fishbourne* and *Camber Queen* were designed the government had, in typically British tradition, already pulled the rug from under the company's last and potentially most successful aircraft project. This was the SR 177, a rocket assisted fighter aircraft. Nine foreign airforces had shown considerable interest in this aircraft, the most important being West Germany. After the Minister of Defence, Duncan Sandys, cancelled the British order on Christmas Eve (of all days) in 1957, the foreign airforces, not surprisingly, lost interest. Saunders-Roe never built a complete aircraft again and *Fishbourne* and *Camber Queen* were never to carry Queen Marys. As a point of interest, although Queen Marys would not have fitted right through, *Fishbourne* and *Camber Queen* had a very high car deck headroom. At just over 15feet this was greater than any other ship used on the route until the introduction of *St. Faith* in 1990.

The passenger accommodation was somewhat superior to that provided on the pioneer ships, although today's travellers would not think much of it. Indeed many of us will remember the two dingy below deck lounges and the single narrow lounge in one of the deckhouses. A refreshment counter and bar was provided in the bow end lower lounge. No natural light found its way into either this or the other lower lounge and people using them lost all sense of where they were. Of a more pleasing nature, seating was provided on top of the deckhouses, but in foul weather the majority of car occupants chose to remain seated in their vehicles during the crossing.

One novel feature of these ships was the method of prow ramp control. Preceding Isle of Wight car ferries had all incorporated a system comprising electric winches and chains, and Red Funnel continued to incorporate such systems until

1968. *Fishbourne* and *Camber Queen*, however, were the first local ferries to be fitted with hydraulic mechanisms. Like so many novel ideas they proved to be troublesome, and accounted for a good deal of the teething troubles experienced by these ships. Another feature of the design was a wheelhouse manufactured from aluminium alloy with curved glass corner windows. A Decca radar scanner was mounted on top.

The centrally positioned engine room comprised two main engines and two generator sets. The main engines were Crossley type EGN 8/65 unidirectional diesel engines. These eight cylinder engines were identical to those fitted in *Freshwater*. The engines were 2-stoke scavenge pump type units, meaning that air was charged into the cylinders from a piston pump situated at one end of the engine. The engines were started by compressed air on the forward four cylinders. Each engine developed 320bhp (down-rated from 375bhp) at 650rpm. The main engines were linked by shafting to Voith-Schneider propeller units situated diagonally opposite each other at each end of the ship, one on the port side towards the bow, and the other on the starboard side at the stern. Having caught a cold with the inclined nature of the propellers on *Lymington*, the company took no chances with this design and installed the VSP units on dead level sections of hull. The auxiliaries comprised 60kW Mawdsley generators, driven by

Ruston & Hornsby type 6YEZ 2-stroke diesel engines, running at 1,200rpm. Electric current was provided at 225 volts DC. All the engines ran on diesel oil.

The hard chine nature of the visible part of the hull form belied the fact that below the Plimsoll line there was a cleaner and more faired underwater shape, although it was not particularly efficient hydrodynamically and the ships did not operate at an economical speed. The hull, which being double-ended was symmetrical fore and aft, had a sharp stem and stern set at a very shallow rake in order not to foul the slipways (see Figure 17, page 154, top right).

The new navigation light regulations of 1954 demanded that vessels over 150feet in length should carry two forward facing masthead lights, the forward light being set lower than the aft light. There was some ambiguity as to whether 150ft meant length overall or waterline length. The waterline length of *Fishbourne* and *Camber Queen* was less than 150ft and they were intended to be equipped with only a single masthead light, as befitted a ship of that length. At the eleventh hour the Department of Trade insisted that that twin lights should be fitted. Gantries to support masts at each end of the ships were hastily designed and they were installed before the ships entered service. The central masts, on top of the wheelhouses, were raised in height later.

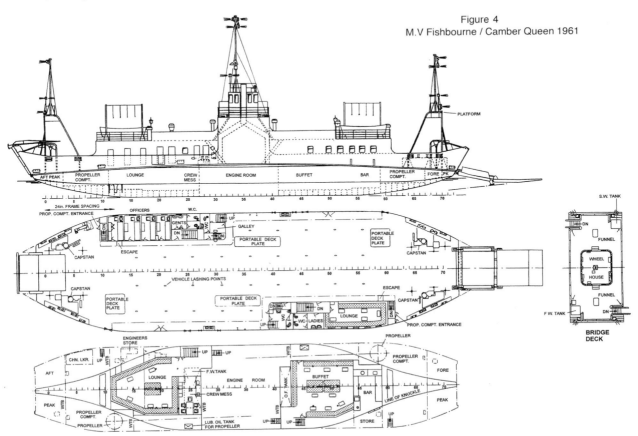

Figure 4
M.V Fishbourne / Camber Queen 1961

The new Fishbourne *undergoes a trial berthing at Fishbourne on 6 July 1961, the day before she entered service.*

Ray Butcher

The new Broad Street terminal was opened by the Mayor of Portsmouth, Mr R Bonner Pink (seen on the left, with his wife) on 7 July 1961. In the centre is Alderman Albert Johnson, whose name lives on in the Albert Johnson Quay, further up the harbour. On the right is Lord McKenna, whose wife launched the new Fishbourne, *which was about to perform her inaugural crossing. Today, the building is an estate agency and holes in the wall are the only clue to where the plaque and lettering once was.*

British Rail (Ray Butcher collection)

53

Dressed overall, the new Fishbourne *has just arrived at Fishbourne at the end of her maiden voyage on 7 July 1961. On the right is First Officer Ray Butcher, operating the already troublesome ramp controls. Behind him Lord McKenna explains a point to his wife Lady Cecilia who launched the ship. On the left is the Mayor of Portsmouth, Mr R Bonner Pink and his wife. In the background, with the striped tie, is Mr EPW Robbins, the then Marine Services Manager at Portsmouth.*

British Railways

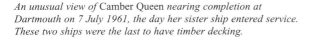

An unusual view of Camber Queen *nearing completion at Dartmouth on 7 July 1961, the day her sister ship entered service. These two ships were the last to have timber decking.*

Ray Butcher collection

Camber Queen *treading water off Fishbourne on 28 July 1973. This design of ship was a tremendous advance when introduced in 1961, but the increased vehicular capacities of her and her sister was quickly outstripped by the inexorable increase in motor traffic.*

Ambrose Greenway

Fishbourne *leaves a trail of smoke as she departs for Portsmouth on a misty morning in the mid 1970s.*

Roger Bartrum

Camber Queen gets away from Fishbourne on an autumn morning, circa 1980. The woodwork around the terminal is showing plenty of evidence of having been bashed about by the ferries, the far end of the jetty being completely unusable.

Roger Bartrum

The first of the two ships was launched at Dartmouth by Lady Cecilia McKenna on 15 March 1961 and was named *Fishbourne*. During the fitting out process, the shipyard's Technical Director warned that completion of the ships would be delayed by late delivery of the diesel generator sets. British Railways argued that this was the yard's problem and they should seriously contemplate the financial consequences of late delivery. It was quietly pointed out that the BR Board's Conditions of Contract had required that all deliveries were to be made, where practical, by rail. Embarrassingly for BR, the generators were on a wagon, lost somewhere on the neolithic freight system.

Fishbourne arrived in the Solent on 4 July 1961 and spent the next two days at BR's maintenance depot at Southampton. She then undertook some trial runs before entering service (five weeks later than scheduled) on 7 July. This was a day of much pageantry. Many civic dignitaries attended the opening of the new Broad Street terminal and crossed the Solent on the maiden voyage of the new ship. The £174,000 terminal was officially opened when the Mayor of Portsmouth, Mr R Bonnor Pink, cut a tape across the slipway. During the maiden voyage of *Fishbourne* Lady McKenna made a presentation to the master, Capt GT Dunn, the longest serving captain on the service, of an oil painting of a view of the village of Fishbourne. Mrs AW Chase, a stewardess on the ship, presented flowers to the Mayoress. Tension was high amongst the ship's crew because the hydraulic ramp mechanism had already been causing problems. By the law of Murphy, one could confidently expect something to go wrong at a time like this, but fortunately on this occasion it did not. At Fishbourne the passengers were welcomed by the Mayor of Ryde, Mr EH Castle, who was accompanied by Capt HJ Ward DL, CA, Chairman of the County Council and Mr LH Baines, Clerk. Luncheon followed at the Royal Esplanade Hotel, Ryde. Also in attendance were Lieut Col CW Brannon MC, TD, DL, JP, Isle of Wight representative of Joint Transport Consultative Committee, Mr GW Dorley-Brown, Chairman of the County Planning Committee, and Mr HFB Iles, a member of British Railways Southern Area Board. The second new ferry, *Camber Queen*, was launched by Mrs RR Barr on 13 April 1961, and entered service on 29 August. During the maiden voyage, Mrs Barr unveiled a painting of Camber Point, the area in the vicinity of the Portsmouth terminal, and presented it to the ship's master. The entry into service of *Camber Queen* marked the completion of British Rail's modernisation programme.

Camber Queen differed visually from *Fishbourne* by having her name and port of registration painted on a plate on the stern prow ramp, rather than on the sides of the ship.

Another distinguishing feature was a small cone situated on the top of the port funnel on *Camber Queen* only. This was fitted soon after the ship entered service in order to prevent a mysterious case of water ingress down one of the pipes. It remained in place for several years but was eventually removed. When *Fishbourne* was built the bulwarks either side of the prow ramps had a more rounded profile similar to her predecessors but she was modified before entering service. There was little to chose between the two ships as far as manoeuvrability was concerned, but *Camber Queen* was the greyhound of the pair.

Teething troubles apart, the new ferries were an instant success. With a maximum speed of about 10.5 knots they could make the crossing in approximately forty minutes, some fifteen minutes less than their predecessors, and they had a sufficient reserve of power to maintain a new hourly service under adverse weather conditions. The hourly timetable had been scheduled to come into effect on 3 June to coincide with the planned entry into service of *Fishbourne*. Apart from the fact that delivery of this ship was late, it was not really possible to maintain the new schedule anyway while new and old ships were operating side by side and the company had to operate as best they could until *Camber Queen* arrived on the scene. Even then the old, slower, ships had to be brought back on occasions for a month or two to cover for the inevitable breakdowns on the new vessels. The ramp mechanisms continued to cause problems from time to time until new hydraulic systems were installed when the ships were a few years old.

Traffic grew at a phenomenal rate. Despite the fact the old ferries were in service for much of the time, the year 1961 saw an increase in vehicular traffic of 49.8%, the largest annual percentage increase ever seen on the route (apart from when the figures were influenced by the effects of the Second World War). In 1962 the number of vehicles carried, at 123,791, was almost double that of two years earlier.

One unwelcome feature of the two new ships was ramp noise, which occurred during loading and unloading. The noise emanated from the plate bridging the gap between the car deck and the ramp and every axle that passed over generated a clatter that could sometimes be heard two miles away in Ryde. This was a great annoyance to the local residents but when overnight crossings commenced in 1963 it became intolerable and caused many sleepless nights. Letters of complaint went unheeded. It was only when the Fishbourne residents warned that they were about to blockade the terminal that action was taken. This was in fact a bluff, but it worked and the ramps on the two ships were modified on consecutive nights.

Competitor, Red Funnel, was in the process of modernising its own vehicular service during this period. Between 1959 and 1968 it introduced four ships of a new type. Named *Carisbrooke Castle*, *Osborne Castle*, *Cowes Castle* and *Norris Castle*, they were similar to the British Railways ships only in that they had an articulated gangway for slipway loading at the bow only. A large turntable facilitated turning of vehicles on board these single ended ships. Each with a capacity of 45 cars, these twin-screw ships were larger and faster than their competitor's and they had sumptuous passenger lounges situated above the car decks and towards the sterns. Such features were necessary in order to woo people away from the much shorter routes operated by British Railways and they were quite successful during this period.

Meanwhile *Fishbourne* and *Camber Queen* settled into an orderly and rather boring routine. Gone were all the control and handling problems experienced by the old ships, making life for the navigating crew much easier than before. Down in the engine room, more modern systems meant there was less for the engineers to occupy themselves with. Dredging of the Fishbourne channel also became less of a problem. The Voith-Schneider propellers tend to draw up water from below and have a natural scouring action, so dredging operations had to be carried out much less frequently. The deck hands occupied themselves (and raised some additional cash) by providing an on board car wash service. With a captive market of drivers who usually remained seated in their cars during the crossings there were few owners of grubby cars who escaped their attentions. One motorist, writing in the pages of an Isle of Wight newspaper, praised the efficiency of the ships' staff for their car wash service. He had observed that on approaching Fishbourne, the deck crew signalled to the bridge that they had not quite finished. On receipt of this signal the ferry was stopped whilst the crew applied the finishing touches to the writer's car after which a second signal enabled the ferry to berth!

Deviation from the usual operational route was provided by slipway groundings. Both ships became stuck on occasions, effectively blocking the slipway until the stranded ship was refloated again. The first occasion that one of these ships deviated from the regular route was on 5 September 1961, when the 1927 *Fishbourne II*, brought back into service in an emergency capacity, had her own emergency and became grounded at the Island terminal from noon until 6.30 pm. *Camber Queen* was left to operate a long service to Yarmouth only a week after her maiden voyage. The winter of 1962/63 was like no other and Wootton Creek froze over. The ferries could still reach the slipway, but ice built up around the cooling water intakes in the side of the ship and caused engine overheating. The engineers tried to overcome this problem by topping up the fore and aft peak tanks (normally used for trimming purposes) and using the supply of water to cool the engines. Eventually the Fishbourne terminal had to be abandoned for a while and services operated between Portsmouth and Yarmouth. At this time of the year the service was in the hands of only one ferry. Each of the two ferries operated during the icy weather and it is on record that *Camber Queen* undertook some long passages to Yarmouth. It is not clear whether *Fishbourne* operated to Yarmouth at this time, but there were certainly other occasions when she did so.

The Fishbourne Car Ferry

A bleak winter's scene at Fishbourne in January 1963. It was not unusual for ice to form around the slipway, but for it to extend this far out to sea was an event that has been unique to date. Fishbourne ploughs her way through a channel that has frozen over since the previous departure.

Ray Butcher

Three familiar faces at the Fishbourne terminal pause from shovelling ice in January 1963, from left to right, Bill Bastable, Ken Wilkinson and Tom 'Nobby' Clark, who always wore a cheese-cutter. Mr Bastable seems to have his fingers crossed, in hope that it will soon warm up, perhaps?

Roger Bartrum collection

Apart from incidents such as above, the 1961 twins rarely strayed from their own route. The western route now had three ships at their disposal, while the eastern route had only two. It was thus far more likely for one of the Lymington to Yarmouth trio to move routes, in a relief capacity, rather than the other way around, as had been the case in the past. *Lymington* eventually became designated 'spare' ship on both routes, although she spent the vast majority of her time 'at home'. Examples of Lymington to Yarmouth ferries operating on the Fishbourne service between 1962 and 1967 are given below:

11 to 13 August 1962
Lymington covered for *Fishbourne* after the latter suffered a disabled propeller and went to Southampton for repairs.

18 September 1962
Lymington did two trips after port engine failed on *Camber Queen*.

20 September 1962
Lymington did two trips while *Fishbourne* was undergoing repairs.

23 January to 5 February 1964
Lymington at Portsmouth as standby while *Fishbourne* was at her annual survey. *Lymington* returned to Lymington to relieve *Freshwater* for two days before returning to Portsmouth until 24 March 1964.

2 April to 12 May 1964
Freshwater at Portsmouth as standby vessel.

11 March to 5 April 1965
Lymington did occasional trips on the Fishbourne route but was disabled for much of the time due to an entangled rope damaging a propeller.

Late May 1965
Lymington operating on the Fishbourne route but became grounded on the Island slipway on 28th.

23/24 August 1965
Lymington operating the overnight sailings to Fishbourne.

22/23 July 1966
Lymington operating the overnight sailings to Fishbourne.

27 March 1967
Lymington operated on both the Fishbourne route and the Ryde to Portsmouth passenger route.

Farringford was not used on the Fishbourne service although trials were run on 19 October 1964 to test the suitability of larger vessels on the Fishbourne service. The vessel was brought from Lymington to Ryde Pier and met there by officials from London and locally, who watched gangway tests at No 2 berth. The officials then embarked and *Farringford* proceeded to Fishbourne and thence to the Camber slipway. Here, Capt Dove, the Chief Marine Superintendent at Victoria Station, insisted on taking her into the slipway himself. No difficulty at all was experienced in

making the 90 degree turn with this nonstandard ship; *Farringford* was not propelled by Voith-Schneider propellers but by independent paddle wheels. Finally, *Farringford* returned to the Harbour station where all tests were considered satisfactory and she returned to Lymington the same day. On 21 September 1964, *Freshwater* had also undertaken gangway trials at berths 2 and 3 at Ryde Pier and then at the south end of the Harbour Pier. Clearly officialdom had something up their sleeves.

Feasibility study into dual role ships

By the time the second generation of Fishbourne car ferries was only three years old British Railways were well aware that *Fishbourne* and *Camber Queen* were soon going to have insufficient capacity to lift the traffic. Meanwhile on the Portsmouth to Ryde passenger service the paddle steamers were becoming aged and increasingly uneconomic to operate. They were really only needed to clear the summer weekend traffic and otherwise saw limited employment. By this time *Whippingham* had already gone to the breakers yard and the company planned to dispose of the thirty year old *Sandown* in the near future. There was still sufficient passenger traffic in the mid 'sixties to fully load five ferries at peak summer weekends and it was therefore considered necessary to replace *Sandown*, but with what?

Confidential proposals were put forward to introduce a dual-purpose vessel which would be able to operate the purely passenger service using side loading gangways at Portsmouth and Ryde and maintain its schedule with the other passenger vessels. At other times she could be used on the Portsmouth to Fishbourne car ferry service. Suggested dimensions for the new vessel were 185'0" length x 35'0" beam (somewhat narrower than *Fishbourne* and *Camber Queen*) x 6'6" draught. It was intended to use Voith-Schneider propulsion, but with the propellers driven by 600rpm AC electric motors supplied by three diesel alternator sets. A normal service speed of 12.5 knots would be provided on the passenger service. This was a couple of knots slower than the existing passenger ferries but a couple of knots faster than *Fishbourne* and *Camber Queen*. An alternative proposal using four Z-drive screw units was put forward by Schottel, each unit (two forward and two aft) being driven by its own diesel engine. Although considerably cheaper at first cost than the diesel-electric proposal it is believed that the use of four separate engine rooms was not favourably regarded by British Railways.

The management also investigated the use of large vehicle carrying hovercraft. These would have had the considerable advantage of allowing all services, passenger and vehicular, to operate between Portsmouth and Ryde. Having separate routes for foot passengers and vehicles between Portsmouth and the Isle of Wight was not an ideal situation and the hovercraft could have changed it at a stroke. The geographical separation of the routes had been caused by the unsuitability of Ryde as a vehicular landing place for ships. Fishbourne, on the other hand, was a totally unsuitable destination for foot passengers. Ryde Sands had caused the vehicular ferry to move elsewhere but a sandy beach was no obstacle at all to an amphibious hovercraft.

Unfortunately (or perhaps fortunately on account of noise) the development of large vehicle carrying hovercraft was still in an embryonic phase and progress with the feasibility study was consequently slowed, but it was announced on 25 June 1965 that it was still hoped to have a new ferry (of one sort or another) in service during 1966. The company eventually concluded that they believed that there was no economic future for the hovercraft carrying large numbers of people and vehicles on the short run to the Isle of Wight. In their view economies would (at that time) only be favourable to hovercraft where distances of over 100 miles were involved. This does seem to be a rational conclusion. After all, the first cost and running costs of a hovercraft would have been enormous compared to a ship, and the time saved on the short crossing would have been a small proportion of the total time taken from terminal gate to terminal gate. The company did state, however, that they would be prepared to operate a hovercraft if the Government (their ultimate governing body) insisted on it and paid for it, which, of course, they did not. Meanwhile 1966 and 1967 passed by with no order for a new ship. PS *Sandown* had been withdrawn, as planned, at the end of the 1965 summer season but without replacement.

The situation regarding hovercraft at Dover makes an interesting comparison. In 1968 (just a few years after the above feasibility study) an Isle of Wight built SR.N-4 hovercraft later named *The Princess Margaret* inaugurated a vehicular ferry service on the 22 mile route to Calais. She and her younger sister *The Princess Anne* remained in service until October 2000 defying many attempts to replace them. At the time of their withdrawal they were far and away the oldest ferries on the Channel. Admittedly they were not quite the same craft as when built, having both been lengthened in 1979 and 1978 respectively, but let's not take anything away from them, their longevity was a remarkable record.

MV Cuthred, the rogue ship

The order for the long awaited new ferry eventually came in June 1968. Although she was to have passenger accommodation far superior to any preceding company car ferry, she was not intended as dual role ship for relief work on the Ryde to Portsmouth passenger link. The foot passenger / vehicular relationship was ever changing. By now the Isle of Wight had lost most of its railways and this inevitably accelerated the decline in foot passenger numbers using the ferries. At the same time vehicular traffic was steadily rising. The principal requirement in the late 'sixties was purely for an additional member of the car ferry fleet.

The design requirement for the new vessel was quite straightforward; she was to have a vehicular capacity 25% greater than the existing vessels – in broad terms a vessel with similar overall dimensions to the Yarmouth route's *Farringford*. The budget available to design and build the ship was a mere £300,000. The tight budget forced various economies, which resulted in a ship that was always troublesome, but from a historical perspective she was one of the more interesting members of the fleet. The specified capacity increase was not substantial; *Fishbourne* and *Camber Queen* had been double the size of their predecessors, but they soon became swamped by the growth in traffic. The Naval Architects' Department therefore argued that they should design the largest size of ship that could realistically use the Broad Street terminal. The local management was persuaded by this argument and a somewhat larger vessel was built. The Broad Street terminal was quite restrictive however, so the new ship was not enormous: measuring 190'0" by 51'0", her initial car capacity, at 48, was 41% greater than the 1961 twins, and the budget was only exceeded by £45,000.

The new ship was the first of an eventual quartet of cross-Solent car ferries known collectively as the 'C class'. This third generation ship was larger than any of the existing company car ferries and she offered a standard of passenger facilities hitherto unseen on either of the vehicular routes. Named *Cuthred*, she was the first Solent ship to be named under the new 'dark ages' theme, Cuthred being the king of the West Saxons between 740 and 754 AD. A diagram of the ship, as built, is shown at Figure 5.

The vessel incorporated a number of radical design features, many of which would not have been apparent to the fare-paying public. She was the first local ferry to feature a double-skinned hull. This was purely for safety purposes and could well have saved the ship from a premature demise because she was holed during her life on the route. The 1961 *Fishbourne* was also holed by a submerged object outside Portsmouth harbour, and would have sunk had the vessel not been quickly powered on to the slipway at Broad Street.

Cuthred had a more rounded hull-form than the earlier ships (Figure 17, page 154, lower left), resulting in a 30% reduction in the wave-making drag coefficient, enabling her to be propelled by VSP units no larger than those fitted in the smaller ships. On paper, this was a sensible economy because it should have allowed interchange of the propellers. Unfortunately there were features of the more modern type of propeller that did not allow this. Furthermore, their power output was not really sufficient for a ship of this size.

The propellers were driven by a pair of particularly noisy V8 Paxman 8RPCHCM 4-stroke turbo-charged diesel engines. The drive was taken via Fluidrive traction-type couplings to short cardan shafts and thence to the Voith-Schneider propellers. The engines were aligned diagonally to the ships centre-line in two physically isolated engine rooms. The main

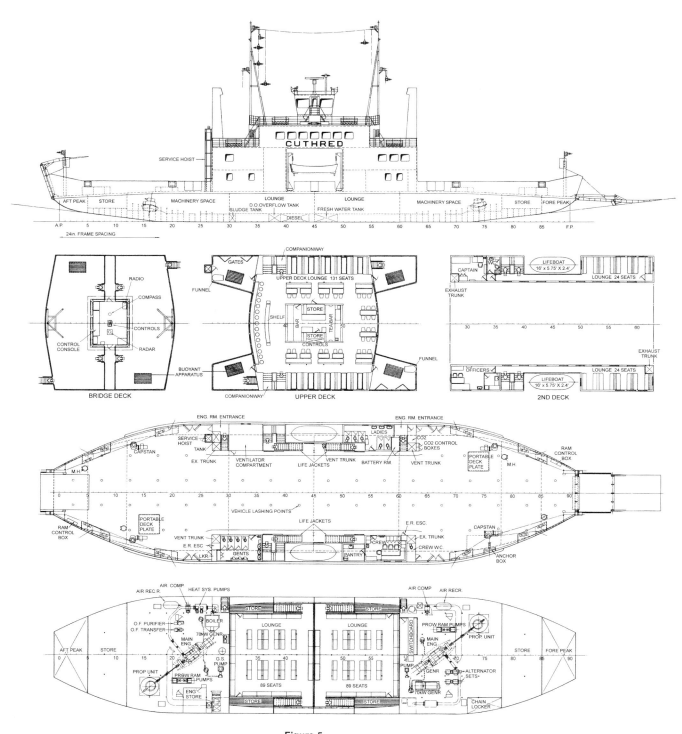

Figure 5
M.V. Cuthred (1969) as built

Destined to be the most problematical ship in the history of the service, Cuthred *is seen on the Solent on 7 July 1969, two days before her entry into service.*

Ray Butcher Collection

engines were started by compressed air but they differed from those in every other member of the fleet in that the power came from air-start motors. The system was not unlike that found in most cars but with the starter motors powered by air-turbines rather than electricity. Each main engine had an output of 378bhp, a substantial increase over the down-rated Crossleys in *Fishbourne* and *Camber Queen*, but not all of this power was available for driving the propellers. As an economy measure a 70kW generator was driven from the forward drive extension on each engine rather than by an independent auxiliary engine. When the generators were under full load they drew approximately 95bhp, leaving only 283bhp for propulsive power. This was less than the propellers could absorb and of course meant that the ship could not operate at full speed during periods of maximum electrical demand. However, it was calculated that the required 320bhp would be available when the generators were under average load. In any case there was a third 70kW diesel generator set, (a harbour generator) located in the Fishbourne end (bow) engine room. This unit was independent of the main engines, being powered by a 6-cylinder 4-stroke Ruston diesel engine. The generators themselves were dynamos rated at 225 volts DC. In order to supply alternating current for on-board domestic appliances the ship was equipped with two rotary converter sets.

The feature of *Cuthred* that was most appreciated by passengers was the large lounge completely spanning the car deck and providing seating for 131 of her 400 passengers. With its centrally positioned snack counter and bar, a lofty and well windowed position, and a virtual absence of engine noise, the accommodation was somewhat superior to that provided on the Portsmouth to Ryde passenger ferries and vastly superior to *Fishbourne* and *Camber Queen*, but it was not on a par with the Red Funnel fleet. The lounge was fully carpeted when the ship was built, although this had not originally been intended. The deep pile carpet had been ordered for the new Seaspeed cross-channel hovercraft, *The Princess Margaret* and *The Princess Anne*. Unfortunately the carpet was too heavy for those craft, because weight (or lack of it) is an all-important factor in the efficient operation of hovercraft. Luckily it was of exactly the right dimensions to fit in the main lounge on *Cuthred*. Alas it did not last long, although it was heavy-duty carpet and should have lasted for many years. It was suggested, but never proven, that the ship's crew did not welcome the task of vacuuming the carpet – much easier to slop a wet mop around on a layer of vinyl. A surprisingly large number of sticky, matted patches appeared and threads became pulled. Before long the carpet was in such a sad state that it was removed. Thereafter, carpeting did not reappear in passenger lounges until 1987.

A view inside the wheelhouse of Cuthred *as Captain Terry Monckton brings the ship into the Camber Docks at Portsmouth. On the left is Chief Engineer Ted Bache. This photograph shows the two-wheel / two-lever, Voith-Schneider control pedestal used on the 'C class' ships.*

Ray Butcher collection

Cuthred *applying reverse thrust as she approaches the Fishbourne terminal in July 1972. The ship's appearance was later improved by the addition of the open decks and a less chequered paint scheme.*

Eric Faulkner

Somewhat less sumptuous passenger accommodation was located on the second deck, either side of the car deck. The 48 seats were situated in narrow lounges that had windows along each side, overlooking both the sea and the car deck. Less sumptuous still, another 178 seats were located in two 'lounges' on the lower deck. Passengers rarely ventured into these dingy holes, many others probably did not even realise they were there. Bereft of natural light and with the engine rooms next door they were not the most pleasant of places to while away the crossing.

Cuthred was the first company car ferry to have a steel car deck rather than wood, and she was the final new Solent ferry of any type to be fitted with rigid lifeboats. The lifeboat location in wells on the side of the superstructure presented a somewhat bizarre appearance, not helped by the original paint scheme in which the dark blue colour extended up to the open deck fore and aft of the lifeboat wells. The open passenger deck was initially restricted to four small areas on top of the side casings with access via doors from each corner of the main lounge. The absence of a large open deck did nothing to improve the ships aesthetics but the embossed yellow painted ship's name above the lifeboats was a pleasing feature as were the curved fore and aft bulkheads to the main saloon. Another unusual feature of this ship was her port of registration. All previous Portsmouth based ships had been registered at that port, whilst the ships of the western route had been registered at Southampton. From now on all ships would be registered at BR Head Office, Liverpool Street. The appearance of 'London' beneath the ship's name looked most out of place when first introduced.

The contract to build the new ship was awarded to Richards of Lowestoft and construction took approximately one year. *Cuthred* was launched in a near complete condition on 3 June 1969. The launching ceremony was performed by Kathleen Rogan, the wife of the company's Chief Naval Architect, Tony Rogan, who designed the ship. During the sea trials a couple of problems became apparent. One was relatively minor; cavitation from the leading propeller was causing air to be drawn into the salt-water cooling intakes in the side of the hull and led to the pumps occasionally shutting down. The ship was slipped and the problem was cured by modifying the intake. A box shaped intake incorporating a type of weir was installed and this effectively separated the air from the water.

The second problem was more serious. As *Cuthred* was heading straight towards a sandbank a turn to port was ordered. Nothing happened! A turn to starboard was taken instead and the vessel turned normally. It was quickly realised what was causing the problem but why this ship should have been so afflicted was not fully explained. The propeller layout was the same as all previous designs, with the Voith-Schneider units situated port forward and starboard aft. When the propellers were thrusting towards the centre-line of the ship (so as to turn to port), the curved nature of the central spine of the hull was deflecting the water flow downwards, and to

some extent it was even being recirculated back through the propeller. When the propeller was thrusting in the opposite direction there was nothing in the way and there was no problem. *Fishbourne*, *Camber Queen* and *Freshwater* had flat level hull cross sections at the propeller plane but they also had central spines. One might have expected these ships to be similarly afflicted, but this was not the case. Tests could have been carried out to establish the true nature of the water flow, but the only solution was to cut away part of the hull structure adjacent to the propellers, to allow a free passage of thrust across the ship's centre line. The modified hull-form was identical to that used on the later C class ships (see Figure 6 of *Caedmon*, and the hull section diagram (Figure 17). This part of the hull was an important structural member and some major redesigning was required before modifications to *Cuthred* could be carried out. The ship thus entered service with somewhat dubious handling characteristics.

Cuthred arrived at Portsmouth less than four weeks after her launch on 28 June 1969. Her inaugural crossing took place on Wednesday 9 July. It was not a major event at the time – three American astronauts were about to take off for the first manned landing on the Moon. At Portsmouth invited guests saw the Mayor break a ribbon across the prow ramp as he drove aboard the new ship. A ceremony was performed at Fishbourne by the Mayor of Ryde. *Cuthred* settled down to operating the principal ship diagram, that being the odd hours from Portsmouth and even hours from Fishbourne and she became a very intensively used ship. Although a Portsmouth based ship there is positive photographic evidence that she visited Yarmouth in her early days.

The inability of *Cuthred* to respond satisfactorily to port helm was overcome to some extent by uncoupling the fore and aft thrust control levers on the bridge during manoeuvres, and controlling the propellers independently. Since the propellers had offset locations, a turn to port could be achieved by applying astern thrust with the bow propeller and forward thrust with the aft unit. Unfortunately, this little trick did not always keep the navigating officers out of trouble. A skipper was puzzled, and more than slightly concerned, when the ship seemed to be refusing to stop as it approached the slipway at Fishbourne one day. At the last moment he noticed that he had not released the pin that coupled the fore and aft thrust levers together and both propellers were thrusting ahead. On removing the pin he managed to bring his ship under control in the nick of time. As he mopped the sweat from his brow everybody else thought he was a hero! The hull modifications were carried out during the following winter, steering and turning being restored within design tolerances thereafter.

Soon after she had entered service it became apparent that *Cuthred* was going to be a fair-weather boat. She could achieve $10^{1}/_2$ knots in deep water on a calm day but was slowed significantly when the wind blew up. During the design phase of the ship, there had been insufficient windage data

When the Island's remaining railway was 'modernised' in 1967 the 'new' rolling stock was taken across the Solent on the Fishbourne ferry. The first London Underground 'Standard Stock' unit is seen being driven aboard Camber Queen *at the second Broad Street terminal on a wet 1 September 1966.*

Ray Butcher Collection

available for ship superstructures with large holes through their centres. The windage area of *Cuthred* soon proved to be a severe handicap and she often had trouble maintaining her schedule during foul weather. In short, she was under-powered. Although the public may not have realised it, when the ferries were running late it was more often than not this particular ship that was holding the entire fleet up. Indeed, most members of the public were probably completely unaware that there was anything problematical about the vessel. She gave the impression of being one of the superior and better appointed members of the Phase 2 fleet, but behind the scenes she often created serious headaches for the operator during windy conditions and strong tides. Her poor performance rarely prevented her from going to sea but the skippers always had to be aware that it was necessary to operate this ship within broader parameters than the rest of the fleet.

Despite her dubious performance characteristics *Cuthred* was a well-liked ship. Skippers regarded her as a challenge and some were most adept at keeping the ship on schedule

through judicious use of the wind and tide. A simple example of how this was achieved was to head to the east of Fishbourne when a west tide was running and let the current do the rest. Another trick was to use the Inner Swashway at times when the tidal height was outside the generally accepted limits. There was nothing against the rules about doing this; responsibility for the safety of a ship and its compliment rests entirely with her skipper. The Inner Swashway had the obvious advantage that it was a short cut. Additionally, on inbound passages to Portsmouth during ebbing tides, it delayed the moment when the ship had to break into the adverse current streaming out of the harbour. On the down side, there were occasional instances of what was known as 'flying with the undercarriage down', ie bottom contact. On one occasion her outer hull skin and a fuel tank were ruptured. Nobody admitted to this incident and nobody else realised it had happened until she prematurely ran out of fuel, a while after the incident. Cases of bottom contact became frequent enough for a general restriction to be placed on the use of the Inner

Throngs of people witnessed the A1X locomotive, W11 Newport, *being driven aboard* Fishbourne *at the second Broad Street terminal on 27 January 1973. The loco had previously served on the Island between 1902 and 1947 and was on her way back to the Isle of Wight Steam Railway for further service. This terminal was abandoned in 1982 but today the Corralls building in the background is the company headquarters – Wightlink House.*

John Goss (Ray Butcher collection)

Swashway. Another timesaving manoeuvre when coming off the main Swashway channel during ebbing tides was to steer to the south of the Bar Channel buoys. This kept the ship out of the worst of the current and could save ten or fifteen minutes but the skippers had to be careful; *Cuthred* was once left high and dry on the Hamilton Bank.

In benign conditions (up to about Beaufort force 5 and with no adverse currents) there was no problem and her performance was all that could have been desired. Once the hull modifications were carried out *Cuthred* proved to have fine steering qualities and she was considered to be the safest of ships during foggy conditions.

In spite of her poor foul weather performance and the shortest Solent career of any of the company car ferries, *Cuthred* was nevertheless a successful ship and she paid for herself within two years. She remains in service to this day, in Portugal.

New image

At the end of 1964 British Railways had received a new name and a new image. The railways became known as British Rail while the marine division became British Rail Shipping Services. New paint schemes were applied to all trains and ships. The principal colours were monastral blue (more commonly known as British Rail blue) and grey. This was the first change of livery on the ferries since the Southern Railway was formed in 1923. It took a while to perfect the ships livery and, after one particularly awful scheme in which the Ryde to Portsmouth passenger ferry *Brading* appeared, with an all blue hull, a good deal of white was introduced. On the car ferries the black hulls became blue and what had been a teak colour became grey. The standard BR funnel colour became red with the white 'barbed wire' logo on each side, but the funnels on the car ferries received grey paint in place of the former yellow. A red square with the white logo was painted on the ships sides instead. One car ferry, *Lymington*, later had her funnels painted red (c1968).

The new corporate identity did not last for long as by the late 'sixties it was becoming standard practice to daub company names on the sides of the ships, but something with a better ring than British Rail Shipping Services was required. In 1966 British Rail had named its hovercraft services Seaspeed so it became a natural progression to rename their ferry services Sealink. For the 1970 season all ferries, except *Cuthred*, re-emerged from their annual surveys with the new name painted on the ships sides but with an otherwise unchanged livery. *Cuthred*, ever the troublesome vessel, did not have a vacant space for the new logo. The only obvious place for it was above the lifeboat wells but she had her embossed name in this position and it was several years before the new logo was applied.

Sealink remained under the auspices of the Shipping and International Services Division of British Rail until 1 January 1979, from which date the entire shipping division was transferred to Sealink (UK) Ltd., an autonomous but wholly owned subsidiary of the British Rail Board.

Shipment of new rolling stock to the Isle of Wight

The intention of the infamous Beeching Report was to close down all the railways on the Isle of Wight. Unfortunately for Dr Beeching a good many people were still going on holidays without cars.

The majority of those heading for the Isle of Wight stayed in the southeast coastal resorts of Sandown, Shanklin and Ventnor and the only practicable way to get them there was by train. British Rail therefore closed as much of the network as they could get away with but were forced to keep the most important section open. The line from Ryde Pier Head to Cowes was closed on 21 February 1966 and the main line was truncated beyond Shanklin on 18 April of the same year, leaving the resort of Ventnor off the railway map.

British Rail decided to 'modernise', if that is the correct word, the remaining section between Ryde and Shanklin. The line was electrified and ex-London Underground standard tube stock, dating from between 1923 and 1934, was taken over to the Island. Previous stock transfers had been via Southampton and Medina Wharf (near Cowes) using the company's own floating crane. Although the new conductor rails and some wagons were transported via the traditional route it was decided to ship the entire coaching stock and one diesel shunter on the Fishbourne car ferry. A total of 43 carriages were brought over individually on the two ferries then in service (*Fishbourne* and *Camber Queen*) on normal service runs.

The first tube stock transfer, which took place on a rainy 1 September 1966, nearly went off the rails. The low-loader missed the scheduled 11.00 am departure of *Fishbourne* and then became stuck on the prow ramp as it tried to board *Camber Queen* one hour later. As the driver of the lorry tried to coax his machine forward it simply pushed the ferry away from the slipway. Eventually the driver reversed off to allow *Camber Queen* to inch in as close to the slipway as possible. The lorry eventually managed to board but departure was delayed by half an hour. In order to prevent this near disaster from being repeated it became a requirement that a portable bridge spanned between the slipways and the ships decks during loading and unloading. The bridge itself was formed from part of a low-loader unit.

The procedure for shipping the remaining stock was as follows. The low-loader comprising the bridge would drive part way on to the ferry and stop with the rear wheels still on the slipway. A beam containing two chain-hoists was lifted on to the ships lighting gantry and was used to lift the forward end of the bridge clear of the tractor unit, allowing the tractor to park elsewhere on the ship. The bridge was then lowered on to the deck. Steel channels were used to spread the load over

The launch of Caedmon *from Robb Caledon's yard at Dundee on 1 May 1973. She was the first of a trio of identical ships introduced that year, the other two for the Lymington to Yarmouth service.* Caedmon *was displaced from the Fishbourne service by the first pair of 'Saint class' vessels in 1983, when she moved west to join her sisters. Contrary to common belief, she is the only car ferry to have switched routes within the Solent on a permanent basis.*
Dundee City Archive and Record Centre

Caedmon *crosses Spithead on 29 July 1973, her third day in service. She was in every way an improved version of* Cuthred. *She was still operating the Yarmouth service in 2004 and, along with her two sisters, she remains intensively used.*

Ambrose Greenway

the deck planking. Meanwhile, the other end of the bridge was jacked up, the rear wheels were withdrawn, and the rear of the bridge was lowered on to the slipway. The low-loader carrying the carriage was then able to board over the bridge. If a heavy load, viz a motorcar, was being shipped, two tractor units were required to tow the trailer. Before the ferry could sail the whole procedure had to be repeated in reverse order in order to get the bridge back on its wheels. The bridge was carried on board to be similarly used for disembarkation.

On arrival at Fishbourne the bridge was at the wrong end of the ship so the ferry had to berth back to front to allow the bridge to be unloaded first. The ship then had to go out and turn round before the whole sequence was repeated. Obviously these operations took a significant time and could only be carried out on a rising tide to avoid the risk of a ferry being stranded on a slipway. It was unusual for a railway engineer to need tide tables in his pocket when planning stock movements!

Modernisation of Fishbourne terminal

Apart from the construction of the new slipway and an enlarged parking area the Fishbourne terminal had barely altered since 1926. With three modern ships and ever increasing traffic the facilities were hardly adequate. In the early 'seventies Sealink invested £80,000 in a modernisation programme. The new facilities incorporated an eight-lane car

loading area, capable of accommodating three ferry loads of vehicles at a time, a marshalling area, car park and 10,000 square feet of hard standing – space for 160 cars. A new concrete road for traffic disembarking from the ships was laid down along the northeastern boundary of the terminal site. Three 80 foot tall lighting towers bathed the entire terminal in perpetual light. The *Southern Evening Echo* reported:

> A ramshackle timber office in use since 1926 has been demolished and replaced with an attractive new terminal building that includes a drive-in ticket office to save drivers getting out of their cars.

The *Isle of Wight County Press* described the new building as "cream decorative brick with natural wood fascia and window frames". Put another way, a rustic pitched-roof bungalow was replaced with a flat roofed box of typically 'seventies styling. The drive-in ticket office was nothing more than a window facing directly on to the road and it turned out to be of little use. Nevertheless the new facilities were an improvement on what had gone before and included a carpeted waiting area and the first permanent refreshment rooms provided at the port. The *Isle of Wight County Press* reported:

> The refreshment rooms look out on to an attractive paved patio where tables and umbrellas in the continental style will be in use during the summer months.

Here one could sit and admire the nearby toilet block!

The new facilities, which took a year to construct, were

officially opened on 11 July 1972, when Mrs Yvonne Wheeler, wife of Sealink's Isle of Wight services manager, cut a ribbon across the entrance to the terminal building. Civic dignitaries and representatives of Island transport undertakings were among the guests at the ceremony. To mark the opening Sealink decided to give a free return ticket to the driver of the first Island-registered car to arrive at the terminal after the ceremony. Surprisingly there seemed to be a complete dearth of Island cars making the trip, and it was to be three-quarters of an hour before the first one turned up. The driver was greeted by a relieved burst of applause from the waiting guests. The deputy Mayor of Ryde, Councillor Eric Woodhouse presented the ticket to the lucky driver, Wing Commander Gordon Cradock. He had not come far, in fact only from Fishbourne Lane. Perhaps he had heard what was going on. The guests subsequently attended a reception at the Ponda Rosa, Ashey.

Three years later, on 17 November 1975, a computerised booking system known as 'Wightspace' came into use at Portsmouth. Advance bookings for either vehicular route were subsequently directed to Portsmouth rather than locally, as had been the case in the past. Non-booked motorists who bought their tickets at the terminals continued to be issued with the old-fashioned Edmondson stiff cardboard tickets, then still widespread throughout British Rail.

MV Caedmon, the second phase workhorse

Despite the introduction of the large ferry *Cuthred*, Sealink continued to struggle to accommodate the traffic. It was not long before they were once again seeking to increase the strength of the fleet. The design of the next ship was tailored for the Lymington to Yarmouth service where two of the existing ships were old and uneconomic, the company being keen to replace them. A design development of *Cuthred* was proposed but the Lymington Harbour Commissioners thought such vessels would be too large. They were not convinced that such a ship would be able to negotiate the narrow and winding Lymington River until it was demonstrated to them that *Cuthred* could do so without any problem whatsoever. Thus three new 'C class' ships were built, two for the Lymington to Yarmouth service and one as an additional member of the Fishbourne fleet. The new vessels had the same overall dimensions as *Cuthred*, the hulls were identical and the passenger lounges were broadly similar. The principal differences were in the propulsive machinery, the use of AC rather than DC electrical power generation, larger open passenger decks, an absence of rigid lifeboats, and shell doors in the ships port sides for passenger access. The latter feature was for use solely on the Lymington to Yarmouth service. Although fitted to all three ships these doors were never used on the Fishbourne route.

The order for the new ships was awarded to Robb Caledon

Shipbuilders, of Dundee, in May 1972. The first ship was due for delivery in May of the following year, but she was late partly due to overdue delivery of certain equipment. Named *Caedmon*, she was launched on 1 May 1973, by Lady Taylor of Gryfe, wife of the chairman of British Rail Scottish Board. Also present at the launching ceremony were Councillor Bruce Donald, Mayor of Ryde and Mrs Donald, Captain and Mrs LHR Wheeler, and master of the new ship, Capt B Taylor and Mrs Taylor. The ship was named after the poet Caedmon, the most famous Anglo-Saxon bard who died in the year 680. The second ship, *Cenwulf*, named after not one but two monks who lived in the late Saxon era, was launched on 1 June and the last vessel, *Cenred*, named after a seventh-century king of Wessex, went down the ways on 29 June 1973. *Caedmon* arrived at Portsmouth on her delivery voyage from Scotland on the morning of 27 July and entered service later the same day. She had arrived just in time for the summer peak. She remains in Solent service today, though not on the Fishbourne route.

Experience gained with *Cuthred* enabled the company to design a truly successful trio of ships. The three new ships were almost identical and any features of *Caedmon* described here apply equally to *Cenwulf* and *Cenred*. The most important feature that marked the success of these ships was the propulsive machinery. A pair of Mirlees Blackstone 4-stroke turbo-charged diesels was installed in place of the Paxmans on *Cuthred*. These 6-cylinder engines each developed 400bhp (down-rated from 495bhp) at 750rpm. This was not substantially more powerful than the Paxmans but unlike the engines in *Cuthred* they were not loaded by generators. The propellers, which were installed in the same locations as those on *Cuthred*, were larger diameter units but the four blades had to be cut down in length to eliminate the certainty of serious damage being caused in the likely event of a slipway grounding.

Another major improvement with the new ships was the introduction of AC power generation. Two English Electric diesel alternator sets, installed in the forward engine room, provided a 415 volt, 3-phase, 50Hz supply. The total output of the two units was 216kW.

The general arrangement of the passenger areas differed somewhat between *Cuthred* and *Caedmon* (see Figure 6 on opposite page). *Caedmon* did not have curved lounge bulkheads fore and aft, the companionways were in a central position (due to the absence of lifeboats there) and only one door was required out on to each open deck, which spanned the full width of the ship. The toilets were moved up to the second deck, closer to the main passenger lounges, while the captain's and officers' cabins were moved down to the car deck, the captain's cabin being somewhat inferior to that on *Cuthred*. Another improvement was that the service hoist for the bar and cafeteria was hidden within the superstructure rather than out on the open deck and there was an additional small lounge on the main deck (port side). The design

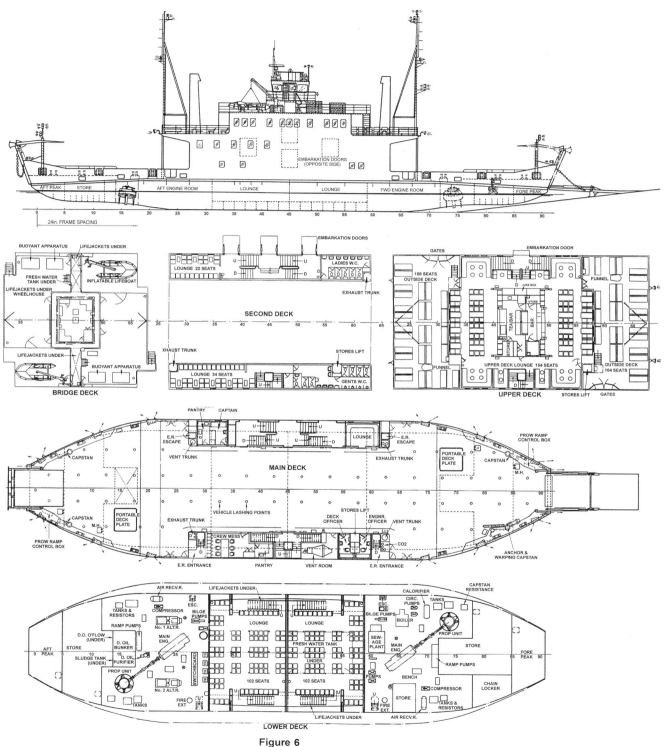

Figure 6
M.V. Caedmon (1973)

improvements were exactly what one would expect given the benefit of hindsight. Although *Caedmon* was given a passenger certificate for 756 people, as opposed to only 400 on *Cuthred*, internal seating was provided for only 414 of them – 57 more than *Cuthred*. The main lounge was marginally larger than the lounge on *Cuthred* but it was packed with more seats, giving it a less spacious feel. The second deck lounges had windows only in the side that faced the sea and once again they were equipped with more seats. Even the dingy lower lounges had more seats in them, but bottoms have rarely warmed them. These lounges were available for use until quite recently and are still fitted with the original yellow moulded plastic seating. Arsonists excepted, few people seemed to visit these lounges.

The company was exempted from the DOT requirement to carry rigid lifeboats after they argued that inflatable craft would be no less beneficial in the inshore environment in which the ships operated. Without the lifeboat wells that were present on *Cuthred*, the space saved could be put to much better use. On *Caedmon* inflatable craft were installed on the top of the passenger lounge, an area that was otherwise unused.

Caedmon could accommodate 52 cars, four more than her half sister. The deck area was the same but more compact capstans allowed the extra cars to be fitted in. The three new ships all had longer prow ramps than their older consort, and although larger they presented a neater appearance by having their outer surfaces plated over, giving the more important advantage of increased strength and load carrying capacity.

The £600,000 price tag was a massive increase over *Cuthred*. Thirty-five percent of this can be accounted for by inflation and a further proportion can be attributed to more expensive equipment, principally the propeller units and the electrical generation system. Nonetheless, the figures do not seem to square up, especially considering that *Caedmon* was one ship from a batch of three, a factor that should significantly reduce the cost per ship. However, the customer was publicly owned and the supplier was a part of the publicly owned, and struggling, British Shipbuilders. The three ships were officially owned by Passtruck (Shipping) Co Ltd, a subsidiary of British Rail, and remained as such until privatisation in 1984.

The second of the new 'C class' vessels entered service on the Lymington to Yarmouth route in October 1973, but the last was not delivered until late November and she then made her

The final member of the 'C class', Cenred, *spent her first two months of service on the Fishbourne route (December 1973/January 1974) before moving west. She is seen here about to depart from Fishbourne.*

Roger Bartrum

Caedmon, *dressed overall, passes either HMS* Fearless *or HMS* Intrepid *during the Silver Jubilee fleet review in 1977.*   World Ship Society

maiden voyage on the Fishbourne route, where she remained for the first two months of her life. *Cenred* had experienced an eventful delivery voyage from Scotland in the stormy early winter weather. Many members of the crew were not accustomed to open sea conditions in foul weather and two of them abandoned ship when the vessel took shelter at Lowestoft and continued their journey by train. When *Cenred* arrived in the Solent she had to visit Husband's Shipyard at Marchwood to have the storm damage repaired. She was then put to work on the Fishbourne service, initially to relieve *Caedmon*, which had gone off herself for repairs. *Cenred* remained on the eastern route until late January 1974, often operating the hourly services with *Caedmon*.

A minor problem associated with the 'C class' vessels was the emission of soot from the funnels during main engine start-ups. The exhaust lines were very long on these ships and soot deposits in the funnels often became unstable when the engines were shut down for any period of time only to become dislodged during start-ups. Passengers on the open deck would not be too pleased at being showered with soot so it became practice to leave the engines running continuously when the vessels were berthed at the terminals. On *Cuthred* the main engines drove two of the three generators so it was often necessary to leave the engines running anyway. *Fishbourne* and *Camber Queen* were not afflicted by soot discharges but it became standard practice to run their engines continuously as well and, like the 'C class', use side thrust to hold the ships against the jetties rather than tether them. It was also useful to have thrust instantly available during falling tides when it was necessary to adjust the position of the ships to prevent grounding.

The Fishbourne fleet had now reached its maximum Phase 2 strength. The four ships were of deeper draught than the pioneer trio but they could still use the shortest route in and out of Portsmouth harbour (the so-called Inner Swashway) approximately three hours either side of high water. At other times they used the main Swashway channel but at low water spring tides all four ships were compelled to take the much longer deep-water route around Spit Sand Fort. Rather than radio the Queens Harbour Master (QHM) for tide gauge readings, the skippers were usually able to work out the tidal height by observing the sea level relative to various coastal objects such as outfall pipes. There were many markers that they used depending on where they were and the level of the tide and the information enabled them to decide which route they needed to take.

The two 'C class' vessels on the Portsmouth to Fishbourne service normally operated the principal services, these being the hourly departures from each side, but it was still possible to find one of the 1961 twins taking the principal role. These vessels were now very much the poor relations on the route and they became rather unpopular with the travelling public by virtue of their inferior facilities. An illustration of the regard for which these ships were held could be seen on the launching plaque on *Fishbourne*. Some wag used a penknife to change the date from 1961 to 1861.

Caedmon was an additional member of the Portsmouth to Fishbourne fleet, however *Cenwulf* and *Cenred* were replacements for the two oldest ships on the western route, *Lymington* and *Farringford*, which both left the Solent for service elsewhere. The Fishbourne fleet was thus once again

Caedmon at Fishbourne, about 1980. The dip between ramp and slipway was often the cause of damage to valances and exhausts, particularly during ebbing tides when the ferries had to berth as far out as possible in order to reduce the risk of grounding.

Ray Butcher collection

larger than the Yarmouth fleet, but there was still no requirement for the former to undertake relief work at Lymington. The Fishbourne ferries only occasionally visited the western Solent, the usual exceptions being in the event of a slipway being inaccessible due to a grounded ship. The Fishbourne service was ever growing in importance and although they had four resident vessels available, the spare ship at Lymington, *Freshwater*, often acted as a relief vessel at Portsmouth, particularly in the low season.

Sealink's rival company underwent its own improvement programme shortly after the 'C class' fleet reached full strength. In 1974 Red Funnel introduced their first double-ended ferry *Netley Castle* to their Cowes to Southampton route, replacing *Carisbrooke Castle*. At almost 1200 GRT and a capacity of 80 cars she was, by some considerable margin, the largest cross-Solent ferry at that time. The advantages of the Ro-Ro system soon had the company convert the two

youngest Thornycroft 'Castles' (*Cowes Castle & Norris Castle*) to drive-through operation. The remaining unmodified ship, *Osborne Castle*, was disposed of in 1978. Extra car space was later provided on *Netley Castle* but the Red Funnel fleet never presented a serious threat to the shorter Sealink routes and in time the service began to stagnate.

Modifications to Phase Two fleet

Although the vehicular capacity of the Fishbourne car ferry fleet had been increased by almost 250% in four years, demand continued to outgrow available space. In an attempt to accommodate the ever-increasing volume of traffic intent on crossing the Solent, Sealink decided to fit mezzanine decks to their 'C class' vessels. These decks, two per ship, were capable of lifting a total of 24 cars clear of the main deck, allowing another 24 to park underneath. *Caedmon* and *Cenwulf*, one ship from each route, were fitted with the new decks during their 1976/77 winter refits. The work was earmarked to be carried out at Thames Ship Repairers at Blackwall but this yard was unable to fulfil the contractual requirements and the job was awarded to Richards of Lowestoft – builders of *Cuthred*. During the following summer season the usefulness of the new decks was assessed before a decision was taken to equip the other two ships. Although the loading and unloading time was increased somewhat, and there were inevitable teething troubles, the increased revenue gained from the extra number of vehicles carried far outweighed any disadvantages. *Cuthred* and *Cenred* were consequently fitted with mezzanine decks during the following winter surveys. On this occasion Thames Ship Repairers were successful in winning the contract for the modifications to *Cenred*, but the work on *Cuthred* was carried out locally, at Vosper Thornycroft in Southampton. Her refit was more substantial than that of her sisters. Large open decks were installed bringing her facilities up to a similar standard to the other 'C class' ships. On all four ships external companionways were installed allowing access from the car decks to the main lounge via the open decks. After conversion *Cuthred* more closely resembled her younger sisters. There was no confusing her though – the lifeboats were always a giveaway. Additionally, the wheelhouse was a somewhat different shape, the masts were stepped on top of the lounge instead of the open decks, and the funnels were situated towards the opposite corners.

Modifications were also carried out on the 1961 twins to increase their load carrying capacity. Additional watertight bulkheads were installed in each ship, one in the corner of each saloon, and arranged so as to even up the compartmentation on each side of the ship. Ten passenger seats were lost in the process. One of the bulkheads also went straight through the area occupied by the refreshment counter and bar, which was closed and replaced by a vending machine in the deck saloon. This created a further lowering of the standard of facilities compared with the 'C class' vessels. The two ships were also stripped of their lifeboats, life saving equipment regulations being met by the installation of a small inflatable lifeboat on the bridge deck. The deck structure was lengthened towards the stern to accommodate the new boat. Additional outside seating was provided where the old lifeboats had been. The modifications were carried out on *Camber Queen* first, during her survey in the spring of 1978. *Fishbourne* was similarly treated the following autumn.

Due to an increase in draught and deeper propeller immersion the performance of *Cuthred* had been improved marginally by the fitment of mezzanine decks. However, it was only a slight improvement and she still had the capacity to cause considerable embarrassment to Sealink. Since each ship visited the ports in turn, when *Cuthred* ran late then they all ran late. The inability of the company to assure a reliable

timetable led them to conduct a feasibility study into ways of increasing propulsive power of *Cuthred*.

The simplest option, and the one favoured by the Chief Naval Architect, was to release the generators from the main engines and drive them independently, thereby leaving the full 378bhp of engine power to drive each propeller. This modification would not have worked on its own because each propeller could only absorb about 320bhp. It would also have been necessary to install larger propellers and that would have involved some major structural modifications because more powerful propellers would have been a larger diameter.

Another idea put forward was to install an additional pair of Voith-Schneider propellers identical to those already fitted. They would have been positioned on the opposite sides of the ship to the existing units, so she would have had two propellers at each end. An additional pair of Paxman engines, again identical to the existing units, would be installed, although there is some argument as to whether or not there was space for them. Much shorter shafting would have connected the new engines to their propellers. Had it been possible to carry out this modification *Cuthred* would have been a real flyer.

At the end of the day nothing came of the proposals. The costs of modernisation were weighed against the estimated loss of revenue on the service had *Cuthred* carried on in her unmodified form. Since the ship was already ten years old, and design for a fourth generation of ferries was by now well advanced, it was decided not to carry out the proposed modifications.

Services on the passenger route

Although *Cuthred* was not intended as a relief passenger ferry on the Portsmouth to Ryde link, she made her first scheduled call at Ryde Pier when she was only five months old. This was on Christmas Day 1969 when she replaced the customary morning and evening trips by a passenger ship. Not

Viewed from the west side of Wootton Creek, Cuthred, *after installation of mezzanine decks and full-width open passenger decks, departing from Fishbourne on 25 May 1981.*

only was this the first car ferry service on Christmas Day, it was also the first time that a car ferry had called at Ryde Pier on a scheduled service – a taste of things to come. Thereafter these Christmas sailings became regular events, but at other times the regular passenger ferries maintained the service.

By the late 'seventies the Ryde to Portsmouth passenger service was losing money and in order to make economies Sealink decided to replace the last passenger ferry of the day with a car ferry which would call at both the Harbour station and Ryde Pier on its way to Fishbourne. Passengers departing from Ryde on the return sailing found themselves on the "00:05 Portsmouth (Broad Street) via Fishbourne" service.

The first such operation took place on 1 October 1979 using *Caedmon*. As is so often the case when something new is tried out, the first operation proved to be a bit of a fiasco. The service was rescheduled to depart from Broad Street, at 23:15, 15 minutes later than usual, before the ship sailed to the Harbour station to tie up alongside the passenger ferry berthed at the south end of the jetty. The first glitch occurred when the deck hands over-tightened the stern line, preventing *Caedmon* from swinging alongside until the rope had been slackened again. The passengers then boarded the car ferry by passing through the idle passenger ship.

Caedmon then sailed to berth 2 at Ryde Pier where the bottom hinged passenger access doors situated on the port side of the vessel were used in anger for the first time on this six-year-old ship. Unfortunately a door at too low a level was initially used, and it hit the side of the pier while only partially open. It was closed and a door on the next level higher was used instead. This one landed on one of the piles that jut up all along the edge of the pier. The door was closed again, the warping lines were slackened, and the ship was moved along to clear the pile. The door was reopened too early and it fouled on the next pile along. Once the door had been successfully lowered the end of it was left suspended approximately two feet above the level of the pier. Judging from the way the staff were staring at it in a look of apparent disbelief one couldn't help feeling that this was not what was expected to happen. The shore staff mustered a portable gangway and manhandled it up on to the edge of the door before the passengers could disembark. A good many people gathered on the open decks where they watched the proceedings with some amusement, except for one official looking gentleman wearing a deerstalker who kept shaking his head and looked anything but amused.

Such operations always experience teething troubles but once the creases had been ironed out this service operated successfully, using either *Caedmon* or *Cuthred*, until September 1983, when *Caedmon* was due to be displaced from the Fishbourne route. The regular ships were then reinstated for this final trip of the day. *Cuthred* did not have passenger access doors, so when she was used on this service boarding was made either via the car deck or the open passenger deck.

Once the service was established the ships often berthed along side the idle passenger ship at the north end of Portsmouth Harbour station and at Ryde Pier they used either berths 2, 3 or 4 depending on wind and tidal situations. Berth 4 had seen little use since Red Funnel excursions ceased using it in the late 'sixties, but it was useful as far as the car ferries were concerned by virtue of a stairway descending to low level. Low water spring tides would have made berthing difficult at Ryde Pier but fortunately they never occur at around midnight, the times when the car ferries were there.

In March 1980 the passenger ferry *Shanklin* was withdrawn from service after experiencing serious engine troubles over a long period. Her absence did not disrupt the normal passenger ferry timetable except during the early months of each year when the remaining two ferries, *Southsea* and *Brading*, had to go away in turn for their annual surveys leaving only one ship to operate a two-ship service. This problem was overcome by using car ferries on the passenger route, a practice that continued until the remaining two passenger ships were replaced in 1986, three years after the Fishbourne service had entered its next era. In early 1981 *Caedmon* was put on the service as a running mate for the remaining passenger ferry. Unfortunately, being some three knots slower than the regular vessels, she could not maintain the normal timetable, which was consequently changed for the seven-week period that she was in operation.

The following year the Yarmouth to Lymington ferry, *Freshwater*, was used instead. Due to her even lower speed and inferior passenger facilities the decision to use this ship caused a public outcry. Complaints became so vociferous that *Freshwater* sailed to Fishbourne on 28 February to load two withdrawn Southern Vectis Bristol LH single-deck buses, which were hired by Sealink for a period of four weeks as additional waiting rooms. They made more than 360 Solent crossings before being offloaded at Fishbourne once again on 28 March. *Freshwater* was not used again. *Cenred* took her place during the 1983 refit period but in the following years, until the introduction of the high-speed catamarans, *Caedmon* became the regular replacement on the Ryde to Portsmouth link.

The final days of the classic boat operation in early 1986 were sometimes chaotic due to the severe unreliability of one of the traditional ships, viz *Brading*. The third generation Fishbourne ferries sometimes had to do stints on the passenger route when they were not scheduled to do so. *Brading* was off service for emergency repairs between 14 and 20 January 1986. At the time both *Cuthred* and *Southsea* were away for refits leaving *Caedmon* to operate the Ryde route alone. Heavy seas prevented *Caedmon* from berthing at Ryde on Sunday 19 January, forcing her to berth at Fishbourne. Because of heavy delays two Southdown vehicles (a single-deck bus and a coach) were hired to convey passengers on the 17:00 Gunwharf to Fishbourne, and thence direct to Ryde Esplanade. On 27 January 1986, *Southsea* replaced *Brading*

A fully loaded Caedmon *disembarks vehicles at Fishbourne, whilst only a handful of cars await the return journey. The original concrete road can be seen running through the centre of the terminal. The pre-1961 mooring dolphins (centre bottom) are the only offshore structures to survive to this day, now part of a yacht club jetty and pontoon. This view was taken c1980.*

Peter Lamb

and operated the service jointly with *Caedmon*. On 10 February, *Brading* was put back into service to allow *Caedmon* to transfer to Fishbourne route and allow the fourth generation car ferry *St. Catherine* to depart for her survey. However, on 21 February *Brading* broke down again and this time she was taken out of service for good, leaving *Southsea* to struggle on alone for a couple of weeks. From early March until the first of the new high-speed catamarans arrived at the end of that month a two-boat Ryde to Portsmouth service was re-established using *Southsea* and either *Caedmon* or *Cuthred*. Later in the year, in July, *Cuthred* replaced the new catamaran *Our Lady Pamela* on the Ryde route for 1¹/₂ days after the new craft developed propeller troubles.

Fishbourne and *Camber Queen* were never used on the Portsmouth to Ryde route, as they were totally unsuitable for passenger work. They rarely called at Ryde Pier, but an exception was on 10 March 1973, the day after *Shanklin* had demolished a section of the promenade pier during thick fog. Thirty-six cars and vans were parked at the Pier Head and there was no way off. *Fishbourne*, carrying a 15-ton mobile telescopic crane, sailed to Ryde Pier, lifted the stranded vehicles on board one by one, and landed them at Fishbourne.

Phase Two timetables

As would be expected the service frequency increased substantially during the second phase. An hourly service was inaugurated on the introduction of the *Fishbourne* and *Camber Queen* in 1961. The summer service for that year provided for 13 crossings in each direction on Mondays to Fridays, with 14 on Saturdays and 10 on Sundays. Departures from Portsmouth were between 8.00 am (7.00 am on Saturdays) and 8.00 pm. The winter service commenced in late September and reduced to seven sailings on Mondays to Fridays, four on Saturdays and three on Sundays, the last weekend sailings from Portsmouth being as early as 2.00 pm. The year 1963 saw scheduled overnight crossings introduced on the route for the first time. On Saturdays only, a two-hourly service was introduced between midnight and 6.00 am, when it became hourly until 9.00 pm (from Portsmouth). This amounted to 19 sailings on summer Saturdays with 13 on the remaining days of the week. The winter service was also increased with nine trips on weekdays and five at the weekends. Thereafter the number of timetabled crossings generally increased. In 1966 the summer Saturday service reached the maximum possible with a two-ship operation with an hourly service around the clock. By 1968 round-the-clock sailings were taking place every day of the year except winter Sundays. Although there were three ships available from 1969, and four from 1973, intermediate departures on the half-hour were not advertised until 1977 when the summer Saturday service suddenly jumped from 24 to 35 crossings. By now the winter timetable was much more intensive with the frequency reducing to a minimum of 23 trips on Mondays to Wednesdays, 20 on Thursdays, 24 on Fridays, 10 on Saturdays and 11 on Sundays. By 1983, when the second phase drew to a close, the timetable advertised 28 crossings on summer Mondays to Thursdays, 34 on Fridays, 35 on Saturdays and 30 on Sundays. The winter service for the first part of 1983 reduced to a minimum of 28 trips on weekdays, 18 on Saturdays and 19 on Sundays. Many unadvertised crossings were made, particularly in the mid-seventies when there was only a two ship timetable but four ships were available. For example in 1976, of 16,540 single trips made only 11,670 were advertised!

The timetable was never as intensive as it is today. Even if it had been the ships and the Broad Street terminal were simply too small to accommodate the available traffic at peak periods. Sealink had long known that this would one day be the case, but in the mid-seventies an opportunity arose that enabled the company to transform the service into the third and current phase of the route's life.

Chapter 4: Phase Three, 1983 to the present

With the Fishbourne car ferry and its sister routes currently in the hands of private enterprise it is easy to forget that the massive modernisation programme of the early 'eighties was brought about by a monolithic nationalised industry. The nationalised industries were often viewed as inefficient organisations that lacked sound business sense and did not pay sufficient regard to the needs of the public. However, Sealink (the Marine Division of British Rail) displayed some inspired foresight when, in 1979, they brought about the largest and costliest modernisation programme to the Fishbourne service since the route was first opened. Four years later the modernisation was complete, the service was about to enter its third phase, and it was ripe for privatisation, along with the rest of the Sealink empire.

Clearly, the company had been struggling for over two decades to accommodate the inexorable increase in vehicular traffic and none of their considerable efforts had provided a long-term solution. The problem was that the Broad Street terminal was too small to accommodate both the volume of traffic and vessels any larger than the 'C class'. Until the company had the opportunity to move to a new site there was little they could do to improve the situation. When an opportunity did arise it was as near to perfect as it could possibly be.

Portsmouth power station, in Gunwharf Road, had closed down. Opposite the power station, in the Outer Camber Docks, was situated a former dry dock and a large yard which had been used for importing coal before the station was converted to oil firing in the early 'seventies. This redundant land presented an opportunity that was too good for Sealink to miss because it was ideally situated just inside the harbour, thus keeping the length of the passage to a minimum. Negotiations between British Rail (Sealink), Portsmouth City Council and the Central Electricity Generating Board (CEGB) commenced in January 1976 and resulted in agreement being reached for a new ferry terminal to be built on the complex. Portsmouth City Council had to raise over £3 million, in the form of loans, to purchase the site and construct the terminal. The city's investment was underwritten by Sealink with guarantees about future income from the leasehold terminal complex. A fixed rate annuity of £636,000 was to be payable until February 2002. Sealink would be responsible for all maintenance costs. The City Council estimated that the cost of construction would be recovered in twenty years after which the venture would begin to generate income for the city's rate fund. The new facilities, though undoubtedly a huge and ongoing financial burden for Sealink and its successors, paved the way to a complete revolution of the Fishbourne ferry.

In February 1979, soon after Sealink (UK) Ltd became an autonomous unit, the company announced its plans for the service. The work would involve:

1 The construction of a new terminal complex in Gunwharf Road, complete with offices, waiting room, ticket office, refreshment room, stores, car park and linkspan;
2 The building of a pair of new 130-vehicle car ferries, each costing £2.5 million, the first of which was intended to be in service by 1981 and
3 The conversion of the Fishbourne terminal to linkspan operation.

It was also planned to install a linkspan at the end of Ryde Pier. The intention was to operate one large ship between Portsmouth and Ryde during peak periods and in high summer carrying booked and pre-paid cars only. Three trips every two hours would be scheduled. This scheme was not pursued, but its revival remains a possibility. Although the company may be unwilling to admit it, their ultimate aim at that time was probably to abandon Fishbourne altogether and run all services on the shorter route to Ryde.

Work began on the new Gunwharf terminal on 11 June 1979 with the ceremonial demolition of a building on the former power station dock site. The conversion of the site actually took three years to complete. The old dry dock was simply filled in to save it for posterity. 7,000 cubic metres of dredged shingle followed by 6,000 cubic metres of chalk were used for the in-filling. Construction of the terminal proved to be a curse for the civil engineering contractors – but a joy for archaeologists. Old quay walls and dressed stone masonry dating from 1600 were uncovered during foundation works and part of an ancient cofferdam came to light during dredging operations. Seventy-three piles, each 30 metres long, were driven in to support the terminal building.

The previous practice of using slipways was abolished in favour of linkspans connecting ship to shore. Although more expensive than slipways, linkspans would have several obvious operational advantages that would far outweigh the financial outlay:

1 The problem of ferries becoming grounded on a slipway (which did happen) would become a thing of the past;
2 Vehicles would be able to embark and disembark virtually on a level run thus obviating the chance of

St. Catherine *berthed at the Gunwharf linkspan in 1983. Ship and berth fit together like two pieces of a jigsaw.*

Ray Butcher collection

vehicles being damaged due to number plates, valances, tow bars, etc, grounding in the dip between prow ramp and slipway;

3   The whole loading and unloading procedure would be vastly speeded up and

4   Less massive prow ramps would be required on the ships.

The linkspans were also made two lanes wide. This feature would dovetail with the new ships, which would have wider gangways to speed up loading even further. The Dutch-built linkspans, of the so-called 'neutral buoyancy tank type', are supported by four hydraulic rams. Sensors detect any changes in the water level and automatically adjust the height of the linkspan. An advantage of this system is that the linkspan height can be varied, simply by pressing buttons in the control room. This would be particularly useful during the transitional period when ships with different deck heights would be using the berth. After that it would still be necessary to vary the height from time to time to compensate for changes in the buoyancy level of the ships caused by their payloads, or if they berthed the wrong way round. The Portsmouth linkspan, which is also City Council property, was installed towards the end of 1981. The design of the new Gunwharf berth went hand in hand with the design of the new ships. Ship and berth would fit together like two pieces of a jigsaw puzzle. The existing ships required shortened outer ramp sections to suit the linkspans and the 'C class' ships required detachable sponsons. The 1961 twins were too small to be a good fit with the linkspans, but they were soon to be replaced anyway.

Fishbourne was the first ship to use the new linkspan

when, during trials in January 1982, Ray Butcher, the terminal supervisor, drove his own car off the ferry after a short trip of less than 100 yards across the Camber from Broad Street. The Gunwharf terminal was officially opened by Mr G Byng, Chairman of Portsmouth Council's Transportation Committee on 19 February 1982. Traffic did not start using the new facility until the first sailing of the day on Sunday 21 February 1982, Broad Street having been abandoned following the final departure on the previous day.

The Gunwharf terminal buildings were not completed until several months after traffic had commenced using it. The waiting area in the new terminal was equipped with 23 lanes for queuing traffic with a capacity for 235 cars and 17 lorries and it included a 60-ton weighbridge. All the congestion problems associated with the Broad Street terminal became a thing of the past – for the time being anyway.

Developments on the other side of the Solent went rather more slowly. Whilst the new terminal at Portsmouth was seen as a desirable improvement there was considerable hostility towards modernisation on the Island, but really only from one small group. At a packed meeting held at the Royal Victoria Yacht Club (next door to the Fishbourne terminal) in September 1979 an action group, temporarily called the Wootton Creek and District Protection Society, was formed to fight the proposals of Sealink. Protests rained fast and furious during a heated 90 minute debate. There were concerns that dredging of the channel and wash from larger ferries would cause erosion of the shoreline and perhaps structural damage to creek-side homes. It goes without saying that another major concern was the prospect of increased traffic using Fishbourne

During construction of the new berth at Fishbourne the jib of one of the cranes collapsed. Here, preparations are underway to recover the debris. Meanwhile, the area within the caisson, beyond, is almost ready for draining.

Gordon Driscoll

Concrete structures complete, the new linkspan has just arrived from its manufacturers in Holland. It sits on a small barge, which in turn sits on a submersible barge. The latter was flooded to allow the linkspan to be floated into position.

Gordon Driscoll

Fishbourne *at the new Fishbourne linkspan in June 1983, at which time this particular vessel was the only one adapted to use it. The berth was made for ships of 55ft beam;* Fishbourne *was only 43ft broad and berthed at a decided angle.*

Roger Bartrum

Lane. The yacht club issued a statement dissociating itself from the mass protest. Stephen Ross, the Island MP, while sympathising with the local residents, expressed no opposition to the proposals either. Nevertheless the vociferous opposition campaign continued and two months later the IW Services manager threatened to withdraw the concessionary fares from Island residents if the scheme did not go ahead. Later he blamed a handful of residents for jeopardising their modernisation programme. In fact, all they achieved was a delay in the necessary parliamentary approval, which went

through on 27 July 1981. Plans for terminal improvements at Fishbourne and construction of two new ferries were announced on 8 September. There was much planning to do and the improvements at Fishbourne did not get underway until several months after the new facilities at Portsmouth had come into use.

Unlike the Gunwharf terminal, Sealink own the freehold at Fishbourne and footed the £2 million bill for its reconstruction. Work began on the day after the August Bank Holiday in 1982 and lasted for eleven months. The linkspan

continued on page 89

For a while after the new linkspan came into use it was possible to see two ships berthed simultaneously at Fishbourne. The schedule dictated that it should not have happened, but on several occasions it did. On the evening of 18 June 1983 Cuthred's Fishbourne-end ramp had failed and she berthed back to front at the new berth using the ramp adapted for the Portsmouth linkspan. Unloading took longer as cars had to reverse off, allowing Caedmon *to gain time on her half sister.*

Wootton *approaching Portsmouth Harbour entrance from the Inner Swashway on 18 June 1950. She is carrying an almost customary milk tanker; one fell over during stormy conditions and was righted by a crane in HM Dockyard.*

George Osbon, courtesy World Ship Society

83

Hilsea *entering Portsmouth Harbour towards the end of her service as a Fishbourne ferry. There is much of interest in the background. On the right is the Round Tower, whilst the building behind the ship's wheelhouse was the home of the marine artist JD Wiley. The square building with the large square doorway was the Boom Yard from which a boom could be dragged across to Fort Blockhouse as part of the First World War defences. The house with the castellated roof was demolished in 2002.*

George Osbon, courtesy of the World Ship Society

An idyllic scene at Fishbourne in August 1953 with Hilsea *about to disgorge a full load of black cars. The typical Southern Railway concrete fence posts remain a familiar sight today along hundreds of miles of both extant and abandoned railway lines.*

Eric Faulkner

Wootton unloading at Fishbourne on 15 August 1960. Planks were often laid to ease the transition from ship to shore. The man on board with the black cap was Ernie Young, a long serving member of shore staff. Next to him is long-standing crewmember, Ben McDougal. Further aft, the engineer has emerged from down below to take a breather.

British Railways

Fishbourne *unloading vehicles at the ice-bound Island terminal in January 1963. The First Officer, Ray Butcher, has just taken his own photograph, which was published in Alan Brown's book 'Lymington, The Sound of Success'. Ice blockage of the cooling water inlets resulted in the Fishbourne terminal being abandoned for several days, resulting in long trips between Portsmouth and Yarmouth.*

Cliff Matthews

St. Catherine, *in her original condition, crossing to Fishbourne on her first day in service, 3 July 1983. Note the location of navigation lights on the side of the lounge rather than in the bridge wings and the mezzanine deck ramp toes stowed in a horizontal orientation. They were soon stowed vertically, thus masking parts of the ship's name.*

Hamo Thornycroft Marine Photography, Cowes

Following the advent of a fifth ferry a member of the fleet could often be spared at off-peak periods for other purposes. An example was in October 2001 when St. Cecilia *was chartered for the production of a French film called* Aime Ton Pere *starring Gerard Depardieu. The ship was supposed to be operating in the Baltic Sea between Germany and Sweden, hence the 'Norselink' branding applied on the starboard side and the forward end of the superstructure only. Viewed going astern from Fishbourne on 22 October 2001, she remained in this livery until her following annual survey. 'Isle of Wight Ferries' had been painted out on both sides and remained omitted at her next repaint.*

Andrew Cooke

A pristine St. Faith, *the final member of the 'Saint class' fleet, approaching Fishbourne four days after entering service on 20 July 1990. By this time the operator had become Wightlink and* St. Faith *was to wear the Sealink British Ferries livery for only three months. From a cursory glance the four 'Saint class' vessels appear identical. Indeed, differences between them are minor in nature, but they are not treated as equals.* St. Faith *is one of the favoured members of the quartet.*

St. Helen *in the latest Wightlink livery, introduced in 2000, approaching Fishbourne on 15 May 2002. Launched without ceremony and laid up for eighteen months between 1992 and 1994, she is a heavy ship but her long-term reliability record has been good. She has generally seen less limited use than* St. Catherine *in the years since lay-up.*

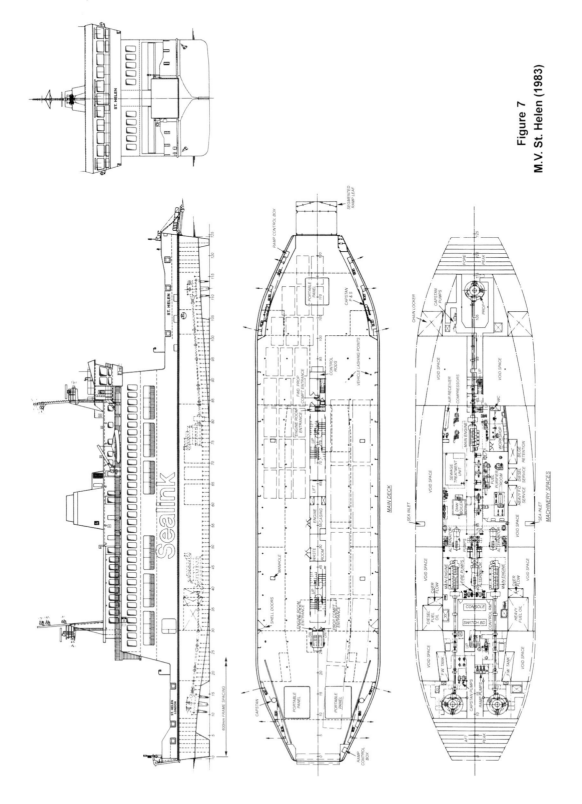

Figure 7
M.V. St. Helen (1983)

was built on the seaward side of the slipway, which continued to be used unimpeded. To facilitate construction, a chalk embankment and a temporary steel pier extended alongside the site of the new works. Disturbance during construction was considerable, particularly due to pile-driving of temporary steel caissons. The new berth comprised a reinforced concrete bridge linking the shore to the landward end of the linkspan. Further out two concrete islands provided support for the four hydraulic rams from which the new linkspan was suspended. They also formed a jawed opening to facilitate berthing and mooring of the ferries. Extending out from the easterly island was a jetty for the ships to berth against. Dredging of the channel commenced in March 1983 and lasted several months. During the operation the channel was not only made deeper, it was also straightened up, there having been a decided dogleg just outside the mouth of the creek prior to this work. A total of 78,000 tons of material, mostly mud and clay, was removed and dumped out at sea.

The improvements also saw the widening of the lower part of Fishbourne Lane to provide a filter lane for ferry traffic. At the junction with the main A3054 Ryde to Newport road more widening was carried out. Additional land was obtained on the Wootton side of Fishbourne Lane to allow left and right exit lanes to be built. The junction was also equipped with traffic lights, half the cost being footed by Sealink.

The new linkspan became available for use during June 1983. One by one the ferries had their bow ramps modified to allow them to use the new terminal. MV *Fishbourne* was converted first, although she was due for withdrawal within weeks. Several weeks elapsed before conversion of the other three ships was completed. *Caedmon* was the next ship to be converted, followed by *Camber Queen* and, finally, *Cuthred*. After that time the slipway was abandoned, but not completely. In recent years plans were made to slip one of the passenger catamarans on it to investigate the possibility of carrying out hull work without the expense of using a specialist yard. Despite lengthy preparations the operation was aborted. In 2002 and 2003 the slipway was used by the Lymington vessels to ensure it was fully operational culminating in its use for a vehicular service by *Cenwulf* on the night of Saturday/Sunday 4/5 January 2003, while maintenance work was carried out on the linkspan.

With both linkspans in place the final piece of the jigsaw was the arrival of the new ferries.

Super ferries – MVs *St Catherine* and *St Helen*

The new terminals were huge investments and were necessary in order to enable the use of substantially larger ships. The modernisation process included the design and

continued on page 91

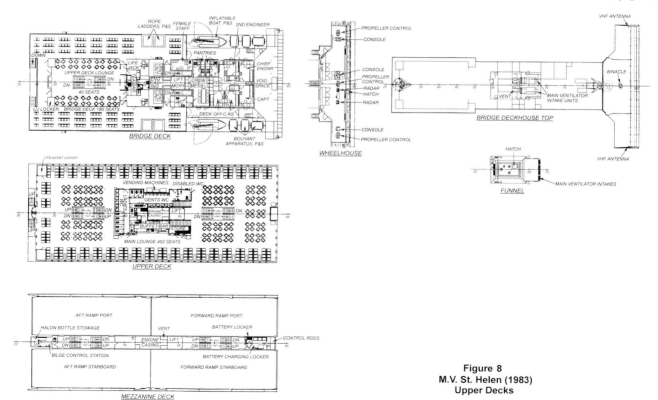

Figure 8
M.V. St. Helen (1983)
Upper Decks

The second of the Saint class ferries, St. Helen, *berthed at Fishbourne on 4 December 1983 during her first week in service. She wore the old, pre-privatisation livery for only four months.*

A heavy shower greets St. Catherine *as she enters Portsmouth Harbour on 10 September 1994. She is sporting the 'lips' livery, the first Wightlink paint scheme, applied under the tenure of Sea Containers from 1990 until 1995.*

St. Catherine *and* St. Helen, *the first of the so-called 'Super Ferries', are seen in mid-Solent during 1984. Their arrival marked the completion of the Sealink UK's massive investment in revamping the Fishbourne service. These two ships, enormous by local standards, were far and away the premier cross-Solent ferries at that time, yet a mere ten years later they were relegated from frontline service and have since been the least used of all the car ferries on the three Isle of Wight routes.*
Robert West collection

The first of the Saints, St. Catherine, *not looking her best during fitting out at Leith in the spring of 1983. Low level windows have been installed in the bridge wings, three more (amidships and adjacent to those in the wings) are yet to be fitted.*
Eddy Robson

construction of two so-called Super-Ferries. Their arrival marked the beginning of the third phase in the life of the Fishbourne car ferry. At the time of their introduction, these fourth generation ships were far and away the largest vessels ever to enter cross-Solent service. When artist's impressions were released of the new design it seemed almost inconceivable that such large vessels would ever operate to Wootton Creek. Design work on the new ships began in 1979. Captain Leonard Wheeler, Sealink's highly respected Isle of Wight Services Port Manager, who was born at sea (and also died at sea), embraced staff involvement to ensure the best possible design. The key requirements that the new ferries had to meet were, once again, quite straightforward:

1 They were to be as large as possible,
2 The hourly service was to be maintained.

The new Gunwharf terminal immediately placed a limitation on the size of ship that could be introduced. The plan was for ships capable of accommodating 130 cars each, but once the initial calculations were carried out it was found that a 142-car capacity was possible with a ship length of 77metres. Any longer than 77metres and the ships would have created an unacceptable blockage to the entrance to the Camber Docks and would have restricted access to other shipping, or so it was adjudged at that time.

continued on page 97

The brand new Caedmon *sailing out of Wootton Creek in the summer of 1973. She had the same overall size as* Cuthred *and the general layout was similar, but she had considerably more propulsive power.*

Roger Bartrum

Camber Queen *waits quietly at the abandoned slipway for the new* St. Catherine *to clear the linkspan at Fishbourne during the summer of 1983.*

St. Helen *waits for* Cuthred *to clear the Fishbourne linkspan. It has always been unusual to see a 'Saint class' ferry waiting this close to the berth, but on 23 August 1986 it happened several times, as* St. Helen *repeatedly caught up with the sluggish older ship.*

Fishbourne viewed on a busy summer Saturday, 2 August 2003, with St. Helen *disgorging cars over an hour after she should have left with the 15:05 departure for Portsmouth. The tall, acoustic fencing on the left side of the terminal was a new feature in 2003. The legs of the outermost of the pre-1961 mooring dolphins can just be made out supporting the yacht club jetty.*

Cuthred *during her final season, heading down the Bar Channel from Portsmouth on 23 July 1986.*

A study of the two Portsmouth-based 'C-class' vessels passing near Fishbourne early in 1985. By this time Caedmon *was a regular vessel on the Yarmouth route and she had returned to old waters to deputise during the 'Saint class' refit period.* Cuthred *(nearer) was permanently based at Portsmouth until her withdrawal from service in January 1987. The two ships were the same overall size but the visual differences between them are obvious.*

John Mitchell

Cuthred withdrawn *(see page 105): Following her withdrawal,* Cuthred *languished at Lymington for 21 months awaiting a new owner. She is seen here, on the left, fifteen months into that period on 22 April 1988. The Yarmouth route's* Cenwulf *is off service on the right.*

Commencing in the summer of 2001, occasional trial runs took place on the Fishbourne route using the Yarmouth ferries. Intended to assure that a service could be maintained in the event of a linkspan failure (the regular ships cannot use the slipway), they normally took place in the dead of night when they were most easily spared. However, late in 2001 some trial runs took place at around dawn on Sunday mornings. Cenwulf *approaches Fishbourne just after 8am on 25 November 2001.*

In 2001 the Fishbourne ferries started using the cheaper IFO180 fuel oil, which, being more viscous than the previously used IFO120, cannot be delivered by road tankers. At a crowded mooring St. Catherine *takes on fuel from the bunker barge* Jaynee W *on 11 September 2002. Also present are the FastCats* Our Lady Pamela *and* Our Lady Patricia.

Mishaps *(see page 143) It wasn't just the car ferries that became stranded on the Fishbourne slipway.* Camber Queen, *skippered by Don Wallace, is trying in vain to pull the stricken landing craft clear in July 1965. Passengers on board look on, seemingly oblivious to the fact that they are aligned with a rope that is transmitting the full thrust from the ship's propellers. The small cone on the ferry's port funnel was a peculiarity of this vessel. Another identifying feature is that the ship's name and port of registration was not painted on the bulwarks at the stern, but on a nameplate on the prow.*

Cliff Matthews

In order to maintain the hourly service there would have to be a quicker method of loading and unloading, the vessels would have to be faster and it would be necessary for them to be of shallow draught. The latter requirement was to limit the frequency of services having to take the longer deep-water passage around Spit Sand Fort.

With the length, breadth and draught requirements set, the Naval Architects Department could set about deciding on a suitable propulsion system. The following options were all given some consideration: -

1. 2-VSP bidirectional
2. 3-VSP unidirectional
3. 4-VSP bidirectional
4. Quadruple-screw Z-drive (asimuthing) bidirectional
5. Twin-screw unidirectional with VSP bow unit

All previous Voith-Schneider propelled company car ferries had used the two propeller arrangement, with one unit at each end. Option 1 would thus have been a continuation of previous tradition. However, the new ferries were going to be much larger and would therefore require much more powerful propeller units. (For 'more powerful' read 'deeper'.) Larger units would not only have a greater diameter; they would also be longer bladed and would have instantly exceeded the draught limitation. The 4-VSP layout, comprising a pair of less powerful units at each end, would have brought the draught within requirements, but for '4-VSP' read 'expensive'. Voith-Schneider propellers are not cheap and the cost of four units was prohibitive. Four engines would also be required, or alternatively two engines and two gearboxes.

A cheaper option would have been the quadruple-screw Z-drive layout. This was the system used on Red Funnel's *Netley Castle*, comprising four independent screw-propellers driven by shafting that turns through two bevel-geared 90 degree turns, enabling the propellers to be swivelled through 360 degrees. This would provide good manoeuvrability but not as good as a Voith-Schneider system. This option was not favoured because it was calculated that there would be a loss of efficiency and fuel economy, principally due to turbulence problems and appendage-drag from the leading propeller mounting bodies. It looked as if the usual bidirectional layout was a complete nonstarter. In fact the Chief Naval Architect, Tony Rogan, was already keen to adopt a unidirectional hull-form simply because they are more efficient. Of the two unidirectional options the twin-screw version would have been the cheapest. The ships would also have been more traditional, in the usual sense of that word. The Voith-Schneider bow unit would have offered a degree of manoeuvrability but not as much as a full VSP ship. The favoured option was always the 3-VSP layout, with two propellers at the stern and a single unit at the bow, this giving the best compromise between cost and manoeuvrability, whilst at the same time keeping the draught within the necessary requirements.

With the 3-VSP unidirectional option selected, Sealink enquired from EC Goldsworthy & Co (the UK Voith agents) whether a 3-VSP ship already existed. One did. Named Marechal de Toiras, the vessel was a bizarre looking car ferry operating between La Pallice and the Ile de Re, near La Rochelle in France. Once officials had paid a visit to La Pallice and established that the vessel operated satisfactorily the option was confirmed and design work proceeded apace.

The hull form of the completed design, though unidirectional with a faired bow and a flat transom (see 17, page 154), was hardly conventional due to the need to position a VSP unit at the bow. Ideally VSP propellers should be situated on an almost level section of the hull and in order for them not to exceed the draft limitation they must be mounted quite close to the waterline. The hull therefore has a shallow lead-in at the bow. A fin like skeg was positioned at the bow of the ship to protect the leading propeller from damage by floating objects. It was soon appreciated that the skeg would also be required to provide support for the long, cantilevered nature of the ship's bow section when the vessel was in dry dock. A skeg was subsequently fitted astern of the aft propellers, partly to improve directional stability but also to provide dry-docking support, but the first ship entered service without one. The propeller units selected were type 21GII/115, 5-bladed units weighing 13.6 tons each and measuring 8'8" in diameter. It was necessary to crop 4" from the blades to bring their depth down to 4'1½" deep and maintain the draught within limits.

The final design of the ships is shown at Figures 7 and 8. The second of the pair, which incorporated a stern skeg from new, is illustrated. Other differences between the two ships were minor.

The engine rooms, at 108 feet in length, were perhaps the longest in any UK merchant ship at that time. Such a length enabled the fore and aft main engines to be situated at opposite ends of a single chamber without the cardan shafts linking them to their respective propellers being excessively long. The original design was for a much smaller centrally positioned engine room and the hull split into a number of watertight compartments by transverse bulkheads. After the contract for construction had been signed a more radical option was chosen instead. Longitudinal bulkheads replaced the transverse versions and U-shaped, compartmented void spaces were built at the sides and continued under the machinery space to obviate flooding of the engine room in the event of grounding damage, and this allowed the engine room to be much longer. The engine rooms contain three main engines, three auxiliary engines, a well-equipped workshop and a soundproofed control cabin with an electronic illuminated push-button control panel, as well as numerous other items of auxiliary equipment. The engines chosen for propulsive power were MAN B&W 4-stroke diesels of German design, but built by Harland & Wolff in Belfast. Each engine develops 850bhp, down-rated from 900bhp. These

The vast wheelhouse on St. Helen – *Captain Brian Bowers (right) was the Senior Master of* St. Helen *before moving to* St. Faith. *Nowadays the ships do not have regular skippers, or crews.*

Brian Smith

turbo-charged units are very compact, the cubic capacity per engine being only 43% greater than those fitted to the pioneer ferries with each developing seven times the power output. The main engines run on heavy fuel oil, an unwholesome, minimally refined substance with the appearance and consistency of black treacle. It requires heating (to reduce its viscosity) and passing through a purification unit before it can be used as a fuel. Even when purified it reduces the bearing life of engine components it comes into contact with. However, such penalties are more than compensated by the low cost of the fuel, which (on the cross-Solent ferries) is used only by the post-1983 Fishbourne ships. The three auxiliary units were GEC Dorman diesel alternator sets, generating a total of 486kW, 415 volt three-phase supply. The Dorman engines, which ran on diesel oil, proved to be somewhat troublesome in service, being particularly prone to rapidly wearing tappet gear.

Since the propellers would be so remote from the wheelhouse it was considered desirable to incorporate a modern state-of-the-art electro/hydraulic system linking the controls to the propellers. The engineering department vetoed this idea. Basically, they had no experience of such systems, and insisted on the hitherto used option of very long

mechanical shafting, which has proved to be virtually trouble free. The propeller units are housed in chambers physically isolated from the engine room and accessed from the car deck. The large forward chamber contains little more than the single propeller unit whilst the smaller aft chamber includes the hydraulic power supplies for the prows and mezzanine decks.

Aesthetically pleasing but nonessential and expensive curves to the superstructure were not incorporated in the design. The ships thus present a somewhat box-shaped appearance, but from a functional point of view the design was excellent. Vehicular capacity was maximised by the adoption of a single central casing, housing companionways, lifts and services, allowing six through lanes for cars, double that on the 'C class' ships, which were only slightly narrower. Mezzanine decks are incorporated both sides, in four sections. When not in use these decks are stowed in the fully raised position rather than on the car-deck as with the 'C class'. The mezzanine decks on a single ship can hold 54 cars, which is more than could be accommodated in the entire pre-1961 fleet.

The very large, fully enclosed wheelhouse was an unusual feature in 1983, but such facilities are now almost standard on new ships.

The decision to have open car-decks was not greeted

warmly by many members of the public. Salt spray was a feature of the earlier vessels, even in moderate weather, and many motorists were not happy at the prospect of having their beloved cars covered with corrosive salt water. Sealink argued that it was just not practical to build a floating garage and claimed that salt spray would not be a serious problem. In service, the 'Saint class' ships have proved to be drier than their predecessors.

Initially, the floors within the passenger lounges were vinyl covered, as were the seats. Refreshments were served from a surprisingly small snack counter and bar on the starboard side. The small size of this facility, compared to later fleet additions, was to relegate the first two ships to a secondary status when they were a mere ten years old.

One of the provisos with the construction contract was that it must be placed with a British yard. The contract was awarded to Henry Robb, Shipbuilders, at Leith, near Edinburgh. The final contract price was set when the shipbuilder and Sealink each wrote a figure on the back of two old raffle tickets. Coincidentally, both parties both wrote down £4.75 million per ship. The eventual price crept up to close to £5 million due to the later decision to incorporate longitudinal watertight bulkheads in the hulls and to construct a lounge rather than an open shelter on the promenade deck.

The two ships were built one behind the other on the same slipway at Leith. The keel of the first ship was laid on 25 June 1982, and the second, just over a month later on 6 August. The Henry Robb yard was in dire financial straits, these ships being the last they built. The work soon fell behind schedule and in an attempt to catch up, the manufacture of large blocks of the ships hulls was subcontracted out to other yards within British Shipbuilders, this being possible due to the largely modular nature of their construction. Once built the sections were transported to Leith on barges. The work was undertaken at yards on the Tyne and Wear. Both Palmers at Hebburn, and Laings at Sunderland were contracted to build hull sections. The former was a ship repair and steel fabrication facility and the latter was a builder of larger cargo ships. The weight control factor essential for passenger ships operating in shallow water was perhaps lost in this subcontracting. The incorporation of additional steel sections to limit welding distortion contributed to escalation in lightship weight over the design criteria. The first ship ended up at least 30 tonnes above the design weight and the second was much heavier still because many more sections of this vessel were put out to sub-contract. At 1455 tonnes she was 37 tonnes heavier than her sister.

The first of the new ferries, named *St. Catherine*, was launched on 30 March 1983 by Mrs Joan Merryweather, wife of the Managing Director of Sealink UK (Mr Leonard Merryweather). Over 100 VIP guests were in attendance. The idea for the ship's name came from the late Eric Payne, the well-known Isle of Wight paddle steamer and local shipping enthusiast. He suggested a number of Island villages and

locations beginning with 'St'. Sealink approved but restricted the selection to female names. St Catherine's Point, of course, is the most southerly promontory of the Isle of Wight.

The sea trials of *St. Catherine* took place on 16 June 1983 on the Burntisland measured course. Loaded to 1702 tonnes displacement, the ship averaged 13.15 knots in smooth sea and a force 2 wind. The delivery voyage south through the North Sea was made a week later, the vessel arriving at Portsmouth on Friday 24 June.

At the end of the voyage metallic particles were discovered in the propeller units' oil filters. This was not a good omen. After inspection the following day, *St. Catherine* visited Husband's Shipyard, Marchwood, from 26 June for the problem to be investigated further. The propeller units were lifted out in turn while the ship was still afloat. It is possible to do this without dry-docking because the propellers are mounted on caisson-like structures in the hull. Heavy vehicles and a good deal of concrete were placed at the opposite end of the ship to trim her slightly and eliminate the possibility of any water spilling over the caisson. Nevertheless, with water lapping about two inches from the top of a gaping hole in the middle of the ship, it was still a somewhat nervous moment. Once the propeller units were dismantled it was found that the vertical bearing on each propeller blade was worn due to high point loading caused by a combination of blade thrust and centrifugal force. Why standard bearings fitted in standard production units should have failed so soon is not entirely clear, particularly since 4 inches had been cropped from the propeller blades. An effective repair could only be achieved by replacing the plain bearings with needle roller bearings, but this could not be done straight away. The worn bearings were thus replaced by new bearings of the same type and the ship was forced to operate at reduced power and speed until roller bearings became available. As a consequence of this problem the sister ship, still on the stocks, had her propellers equipped with roller bearings from new.

Whilst *St. Catherine* was at Husband's yard an 'old salt' pointed out that the port and starboard navigation lights, which were situated above the fifth window back along the side of the passenger lounge, would be obscured from the view of skippers of other ships by the overhanging bridge structure. Although this was true in certain situations the siting of the lights was technically legal. However, they were moved to the bridge wings in March 1984 whilst the sister ship had her lights relocated before delivery.

St. Catherine returned to Portsmouth on 1 July following her repairs. The following day several trial runs were made to Fishbourne. *St. Catherine* finally entered service with the 09:30 sailing from Portsmouth on Sunday 3 July, some four months later than intended. In fact it would have been somewhat embarrassing if she had been delivered on time because the new linkspan at Fishbourne was not usable until mid-June, and use of the old slipways by this ship was a physical impossibility. On

Thursday 14 July, an official dedication service (by the Provost of Portsmouth) and champagne reception sailing for some 264 civic dignitaries took place. The vessel was dressed overall and conveyed the Royal Marines band on board.

Being unidirectional it was necessary for *St. Catherine* to swing at the ends of the passage, just as the pioneer trio had done. With the bow ramp used at the Island terminal and the stern ramp at Portsmouth two swings are required on the Portsmouth-bound passage but none in the other direction. Despite a long run astern at a slower speed to clear the deepwater channel at Fishbourne, few people will have noticed any difference in the passage time due to this manoeuvring; therefore the unidirectional concept presented no obvious disadvantages. Occasionally, at high water, swings used to be made in the mouth of Wootton Creek. The Marine Department frowned upon such manoeuvring because it was considered to be unnecessary and skippers were forbidden from doing it. There are no restrictions today but skippers rarely swing the vessels close to the berth. At Portsmouth the supreme manoeuvrability paid dividends as the vessel was reversed into the narrow Camber entrance. With the wheelhouse situated almost the ship's length from the linkspan, judging the stern's proximity to it was easier than might be imagined. Two lines painted on the starboard side belting beneath the bridge were brought into alignment with two corresponding lines on the quay as the vessel inched up to the berth.

The new ship was immediately barred from using the short Inner Swashway route in and out of Portsmouth Harbour. The Queen's Harbour Master considered that she was too large to use this passage, but in any case a small boat channel was being established close to the Haslar shore.

She was soon labelled a noise nuisance, too. With the wheelhouse positioned at the bow, and a more restricted view astern, it became standard practice to sound a precautionary three blasts on the ship's whistle every time the vessel left Fishbourne. The ear-shattering noise could be heard for miles around. The view astern from the bridge wings was adjudged to be satisfactory and in any case a viewing port was provided beside the stern ramp so use of the whistle ceased unless other boats were in the channel.

Meanwhile, work on the second new ferry was running further and further behind. She was finally launched on 14 September. There was no ceremony, no civic dignitaries were there, just the shipyard workers who quietly slid their last vessel into the water. Due to her long slide down from the top of the slipway, she achieved the greatest speed of any 'Saint class' vessel at the moment of her launch! The shipyard was by now running down its operations and they attempted to persuade Sealink to accept the ship unpainted. Needless to say the request was turned down and the yard was forced to bus in a team of painters from Glasgow. Trials took place during mid-November, after which the vessel headed south, arriving at Portsmouth on 24 November. She carried on board a stern skeg for fitment to her sister.

The new addition entered service with the 06:00 sailing from Portsmouth on Monday 28 November, still not christened. In lieu of an official launching, a special naming and inauguration ceremony was performed on 8 December when Mrs Yvonne Wheeler, wife of the Divisional Shipping Manager, Capt Leonard Wheeler, named the ship *St. Helen,* after the patron saint of travellers. The Venerable Freddie Carpenter, Archdeacon of the Isle of Wight, conducted a dedication ceremony on the car deck. At Fishbourne, a cavalcade of vintage cars boarded, led by a 1920 Star saloon carrying Mr Leonard Merryweather, managing director of Sealink UK, and his wife. Mr Merryweather said "It is a great day for all those concerned with the sea link between the Isle of Wight and Portsmouth. It is a day of pride for those who built the ship and the new linkspan at Fishbourne." In praise of the Henry Robb yard Mr Merryweather continued "They have done a tremendous job – the workmanship is absolutely superb." This must have been cold comfort for the shipyard workers, who were now facing redundancy. Some of the first passengers on board were the pupils and staff of St. Helens Primary School. They travelled across to Portsmouth on *St. Catherine*, and were given Sealink hats, badges and flags before making the return journey aboard *St. Helen*. Local dignitaries were among the 300 invited guests on board. Captain Wheeler performed the opening ceremony of the new linkspan while *St. Helen* was berthed at Fishbourne.

Visually, there were (and still are) some minor differences between the two ships, the most obvious being the colour coding of the seating; green on *St. Catherine* and red on *St. Helen* (initially both externally and internally). Additional windows at a low level had been fitted in the wheelhouses to improve visibility from the control pedestals. A single deep window was installed amidships on *St. Helen* only while the additional windows in the bridge wings are of staggered heights on *St. Catherine* but level on *St. Helen*. A pair of small ventilator cowls is situated on the top deck near the funnel on *St. Helen* only. Inside, a mural of St Catherine's Lighthouse adorns the bulkhead at the forward end of the main lounge of *St. Catherine*, while *St. Helen* has a mural of the remains of the old church in her namesake village. Both murals are the work of the Bembridge artist Peter Wright.

The new ships were soon nicknamed 'Hoovers' owing to their ability to clear a vast area of the marshalling yards at the terminals. Their introduction was rewarded by another surge in traffic and they gave the Fishbourne route a clear lead in the cross-Solent vehicular transportation market. Red Funnel did not react at all; probably they could not afford to. The improved facilities on the Fishbourne route bit deep and one could not help feeling that the rival company was really feeling the pinch.

Camber Queen *departing for Portsmouth on 18 June 1983. This view shows the staggered deckhouse layout clearly.*

Fishbourne and Camber Queen sail away

MV *Fishbourne* had continued operating for two weeks after *St. Catherine* joined the fleet but was withdrawn after the 18:30 sailing from Fishbourne on 18 July. Thereafter she languished in Portsmouth harbour until 4 September when she was pressed back into service to cover for the failure of *Caedmon*, which had to visit Husband's Shipyard due to engine trouble. The following day saw *Fishbourne* on her final passage. *Camber Queen* soldiered on until the end of the summer timetable, making her final sailing on 2 October. When *St. Helen* entered service, MV *Caedmon* was transferred to the Lymington to Yarmouth passage where she replaced *Freshwater*, leaving *Cuthred* as the sole member of the previous fleet still based at Portsmouth. *Cuthred* became the spare ship at Portsmouth and was used for the intensive summer service and during the annual survey periods of the 'Saint class' vessels.

Fishbourne and *Camber Queen* were tied up at the Odds-and-Evens pontoons in Portsmouth Harbour, initially berthed end to end and later side by side. Odds and Evens were the names given to the pair of pontoons that in April 1981 replaced the last of the hulks, the 1918 built *Bressuire*, a French coal barge and later a salvage vessel, which had replaced the earlier hulk C11. Some consideration was given to using the ferries to reactivate the vehicular link from Portsmouth to Gosport but it came to nothing. Both ferries were put up for sale and a purchaser was quickly found for *Camber Queen*. She was sold on 6 January 1984 for £67,750 to Transado-Transportes Fluvias do Sado of Setubal in Portugal. She left Portsmouth on 11 January 1984 and was slipped at Husband's Shipyard at Marchwood prior to leaving during March on her long voyage south. Renamed *Mira Troia* her appearance was altered significantly by various modifications, but she remained recognisable. The prow ramps and the adjacent structure were modified considerably and the end masts and their gantries were taken down. She was also equipped with a new pair of funnels placed much closer to the sides of the ship. Her new route was the two and a half-mile passage across the Sado Estuary between Setubal with Troia.

Following her withdrawal from the Fishbourne service, Camber Queen *went to Portugal, where she operated on the 2½-mile crossing of the Sado Estuary, south of Lisbon. As* Mira Troia *she is seen departing from Setubal on 24 November 1990.*

Tim Cooper

She became surplus to requirements when her operator acquired *Marechal de Toiras* (qv), which had been made redundant by the opening of the Ile de Re bridge and she was broken up a few miles from Setubal in 1998.

Sister ship, *Fishbourne*, was less fortunate, as was the redundant Lymington ferry *Freshwater*. Both were sold to HG Pounds, Shipbreakers of Tipner, Portsmouth, each for £20,000. Both ships sailed to Tipner Lake under their own power on 2 February 1984. Captain Wheeler, the Divisional Shipping Manager, was quoted as saying that he could have sold *Camber Queen* ten times over, but apparently the same could not be said for *Fishbourne*. Although *Fishbourne* had undoubtedly become a 'smoker', the general consensus amongst those who should know was that there was little to choose between the two sisters, so why one was sold to a scrapyard while the other was awash with potential buyers remains a mystery. Whatever the case, Pounds soon found a new buyer for *Fishbourne*. She was sold to Seagull Marine Ltd., of Kyrenia in the Turkish Republic of Northern Cyprus. Prior to her final departure *Fishbourne* made various appearances in the Solent and the Camber before

leaving on 7 May 1984 painted in a white livery with blue relief and carrying her new name *Kibris I*. Her structure remained unaltered but she carried a red wooden shed on the car deck. Registered in Famagusta, her base was Kyrenia on the north coast of Cyprus. From here she operated a twice-weekly service to Mersin on the Turkish mainland, an almost unbelievable passage for a ship of her type. The route was approximately 125 miles in length and the crossing was scheduled to take eighteen hours, although it could be done in much less. The main deck planking was replaced for her new role and canvas awnings were located above the deckhouses to protect passengers from the fierce Mediterranean sun. Alas, she did not last long in her new operation. At about 4.00 am on 5 February 1985, while berthed at the end of a mechanical ore-loading facility in Morphou Bay (Cyprus), a north-northwesterly gale blew up. It is said that the ship was lifted on to a breakwater where she balanced for about an hour before sliding off, tearing open her hull and sinking. Fortunately there was nobody on board at the time but it was a sad end for the ship.

Kibris I, *formerly* Fishbourne, *at the Albert Johnston Quay prior to her June 1984 departure to take up service on a 125-mile route between Cyprus and Turkey! Alas, she was wrecked only eight months later.*
Malcolm Palmer

Privatisation

Back in home waters, both of the new ships had been introduced with the standard Sealink livery of monastral blue hull and white upper works, but in readiness for privatisation, the BR double arrow logo was omitted from the sides of the red funnels. *St. Helen* was to carry this livery for a mere four months. As privatisation loomed larger the press were invited, at the end of March 1984, to the unveiling of a completely new livery on *St. Helen*. A new shade of blue was applied to the hull. The funnel was painted in the same blue colour and finished with a distinctive gold logo suggestive of an officer's arm braid. The upper of the two bands was curved into a symbol representing the fused letters 'S' and 'L'. Along the sides of the ship a pale blue band was applied, with the word SEALINK amidships. At this time *St. Catherine* was already

partially repainted in the new livery. For a few days she could be seen running with the new coloured hull but with the funnel still painted red and no logo whatsoever on the ship's side. *Cuthred* remained in the old livery during 1984.

Privatisation was mooted from 1979, but did not take off until 1981 when the Monopolies and Mergers Commission ruled that Townsend Thoresen could not bid. From then on a number of other companies showed an interest but many failed to make the list of bidders approved by the Secretary of State for Transport on 21 May 1984. Approval to bid was granted to the Sealink Consortium, Trafalgar House plc, Sea Containers Limited and Ellerman Lines plc. P&O Ferries were excluded at this time. The Sealink Consortium comprised Charterhouse J Rothschild, Globe Investment Trust, National Freight Consortium, Sealink UK Limited and James Fisher & Sons Limited. By far the highest bid (double any of the others) was from Sea Containers, a Bermuda registered company chaired

In 1990 Sea Containers sold the greater part of Sealink British Ferries, along with the name, to Stena Line. The Isle of Wight services then became known as Wightlink. St. Faith *sports the new livery, while* St. Catherine *still wears the old Sealink BF colours on 11 December 1990.*

For a few days only St. Catherine *operated in this form, partially re-liveried for privatisation. Meanwhile the full new livery was unveiled a few days later on* St. Helen *with a press launch at the end of March 1984.*

by the American, James Sherwood. On 18 July 1984 it was announced that Sea Containers bid of £66 million had been successful. The sale involved 37 ships, 10 harbours and 24 routes. On 27 July 1984 control of Sealink (UK) Limited, together with all of its subsidiaries, passed to the English registered British Ferries Limited, a wholly owned subsidiary of Sea Containers Limited.

The Fishbourne service was already prospering following the introduction of the new ships and there was no visible evidence that privatisation made any difference. In 1985 the livery was modified slightly to display the name of the new owners, SEALINK British Ferries. *Cuthred*, along with the remainder of the fleet, was now repainted in the new guise. The presence of the lifeboats on *Cuthred* meant that the company logo had to be awkwardly applied towards one end of the superstructure.

After years of stability as part of a nationalised monolith, Sealink was now in an unstable world. In June 1989 Sealink British Ferries was embroiled in a fierce and most bizarre takeover battle. An unsolicited tender offer was made by Temple Holdings Ltd, a company owned jointly by Stena AB and Tiphook plc, to buy the whole of the Sea Containers group. Two months later Sea Containers stated that it was then considering a £100 million sale of the IW routes as part of its defence against the £648 million bid. Various groups bid for the IW services, including a local consortium, Sally Holdings (who had already made an unsuccessful bid to obtain Red Funnel) and Michael Aiken, currently Wightlink's Chairman, who as a director of Sealink British Ferries, led a management buyout proposal.

At the end of November 1989 the issue appeared to be settled when it was announced that Sealink IW Ferries was to be sold to a consortium of Solent businessmen in a deal worth £107 million. Managers and all 520 employees were to take a large stake in Radiant Shipping, a limited company chaired by Mr Dick Hedger of Shalfleet Manor on the Isle of Wight. Within two weeks the deal seemed less certain after Temple Holdings decreased its bid. The deal was thrown into further doubt when in early January 1990 share-holders of Sea Containers were asked to vote at a special meeting on 25 February on plans by the company to sell off assets in a major re-capitalisation programme. This meeting never took place because a fortnight later the shock announcement was made that Sea Containers had sold most of its container business to Tiphook and the bulk of Sealink British Ferries to Stena. But it retained the Isle of Wight services, along with Hoverspeed, the ports of Folkestone, Heysham, Newhaven, part of the port of Harwich and a 42% minority share in the Isle of Man Steam Packet Company, as well as the five SeaCat programme and Venice Simplon Orient Express Company.

Along with the bulk of the ferry services the SEALINK British Ferries name was also sold to Stena. As an interim measure the Solent services came under the auspices of Passro (Shipping) Co Ltd, one of the British Ferries subsidiaries,

although the company continued to trade as Sealink until a new identity was found. The public was asked to choose a new name in a competition launched by the *Isle of Wight County Press*. Several people came up with the selected new identity, the name of winning entrant being drawn from a hat. The new name 'Wightlink' was officially adopted on 1 June 1990 and a new livery was launched on 7 November 1990. This comprised a deep blue hull with a red band just below the belting. Upper works remained white and the funnel was blue to match the hull. The name WIGHTlink was painted on the ships sides, repeated with a row of signal flags. The first letter and the main funnel logo were a bastardised signal flag W. The central red square was converted into a shape that was supposed to look like a map of the Isle of Wight, but in fact looked as much like Marlene Dietrich's lips as the Island that it was supposed to represent.

During March 1995 the future ownership of Wightlink was again the subject of speculation. Sea Containers needed to sell off assets in order to raise capital to pay down high interest debt and retire high dividend preferred shares and it announced that it thus intended to raise $250m through the sale of one ferry unit and one hotel. Michael Aiken, previously with the Group as Sea Containers Vice President responsible for their F&P interests became aware of this and with the support of CINVen and the Royal Bank of Scotland bought Wightlink for £107.5m. CINVen was Europe's second largest venture capital company and manager of pension funds for British Rail and British Coal. Mr Michael Aiken was appointed the new Chairman of Wightlink and became the largest individual shareholder. The management of Wightlink acquired shares in the company at the same time. A new livery to reflect the change in ownership was applied during the ships 1996 annual refits. The signal flag symbols were dispensed with, except for the funnel logo, which was converted to form a wavy flag, but it was a rather feeble effort compared to the P&O flag logo, for example. The WIGHTlink branding became larger with 'link' painted in red.

In 2001 Wightlink management bought out CINVen's stake in the company. In 1999 the bulk of the initial Finance for the 'Buy-In' had been repaid with a £135m investment Grade Bond Issue, but CINVen had remained as the majority shareholder. In October 2001 their equity stake was acquired by Wightlink's management via a loan of £21m from the Royal Bank of Scotland, which acquired an equity stake of 35% with Wightlink's management team owning 65%.

Cuthred withdrawn

From 1983 *Cuthred* operated an additional third diagram during the summer. In 1985 and 1986 the timing was advanced by 15 minutes to leave Portsmouth at 15 minutes past the odd hours on weekdays and the even hours at weekends, daytime only. This arrangement gave scope for the

Cuthred letting go prior to moving away from the Gunwharf lay-by berth in Portsmouth on 12 September 1986.

sluggish *Cuthred* to lose more time before she affected the schedule of the following 'Saint class' vessel. During the annual survey season, when each ship has to be drydocked, *Caedmon* always came back from Lymington to operate the No 2 diagram, whilst *Cuthred* normally operated an unscheduled relief service half an hour ahead of her half sister. Before *Caedmon* could be put back into service on the Fishbourne route she first had to have the sponsons and short ramp sections fitted so that she could use the linkspans on the eastern route. This routine was repeated over four winters but in 1986 the company ordered a third 'Saint class' ferry, and this signalled the end for *Cuthred*.

Cuthred normally received her annual survey during February, after *St. Helen* had returned from hers. With her DOT passenger certificate due for expiry at the end of January 1987 and with the new ship due in March, it was not considered worth extending *Cuthred's* certificate to cover for the later absence of *St. Catherine*. The latter ship thus had her passenger certificate extended until the new ship arrived, allowing *Cuthred* to be withdrawn. Her last day in service was Friday 30 January 1987. On her final day, apart from a decided lack of provisions in the snack bar, there was no

indication that the ship was about to go out of service. Passengers on her last sailing were probably unaware that they were on a rather special trip. Skippered by Captain Bill Frampton, *Cuthred's* final service run was a mid-afternoon sailing from Portsmouth to Fishbourne. She never entered Portsmouth Harbour again. After unloading at Fishbourne, *Cuthred* sailed light to Lymington, where she languished for the next twenty-one months, lying beside the old slipway upstream from the new terminal there.

An interesting proposal for further use for the vessel was as a 'people mover' in Dover Harbour. At that time, proposals were being examined to transfer foot passengers from the Marine station to the Eastern Docks to obviate the ferries berthing at the Western Docks to coincide with the Boat Trains. It was suggested that *Cuthred* could be used as a cross-harbour ferry between the dockside at the Marine station and the sides of ferries berthed at the Eastern Docks. By coincidence, the upper deck of *Cuthred* was almost exactly on the same level as the main shell doors on *St. Anselm* and could provide easy and safe access for passengers transferring between the vessels. The proposal was evaluated but was not finally acceptable. Instead *Cuthred* remained at Lymington visibly deteriorating as she awaited a new owner.

Eventually *Cuthred* was sold to Mr Jim Pepper, of Newcastle, who intended to use her as a floating restaurant on the River Tyne. A £1.3 million facelift was to see her converted into a Mississippi style steamer, complete with a stern paddle wheel! After nearly two years of disuse one engine had seized. A tug sent to tow her away in the middle of November 1988 was found to be too large to negotiate the Lymington River so two small launches were used to move the dead ship down to the sea. *Cuthred's* new owners ran into financial difficulties and the ship spent a further fifteen months languishing at South Shields on the River Tyne. She was placed back on the market and was sold to Portugal as a running mate to her former compatriot, *Camber Queen*. She left the Tyne on 11 February 1990 under the tow of the tug *Towing Chieftain*. The pair made a call at Newhaven on the 16 February during the long journey to Setubal. Renamed *Mira Praia*, alterations were carried out to her ramps and the adjacent structure and the lifeboats were removed but otherwise her external appearance was little altered. She was put to work on the crossing between Setubal and Troia, where she remains in service to this day. Although apparently regarded as the main unit she is currently in a rundown state. The bar and buffet has been stripped out, her accommodation is filled with uncomfortable plastic seating and all her saloons are covered in graffiti.

Meanwhile, back on the Solent, *Caedmon* had remained on the Fishbourne link for a further two days following *Cuthred's* final departure. *Caedmon* left Fishbourne for the last time with the 19:00 departure for Portsmouth on Sunday 2 February 1987. *St. Helen* returned to service the next morning

Cuthred eventually joined the former *Camber Queen* in Portugal, where she was renamed *Mira Praia.* Unlike her fleet-mate she remains in service and is seen departing from Setubal in October 2000. Although she is regarded as the major unit in a fleet of four and her external appearance is reasonable, she is rather shabby internally.
Frank Lose collection

following her annual survey, and with three 'Saint class' ships available in future there would no longer be a requirement for 'C class' vessels to stand in at Portsmouth.

MV St. Cecilia, the thoroughbred Saint

When the modernisation programme was first initiated in 1979, project planning always indicated a need for three ships, but only two were authorised for Sealink (UK) Ltd under British Rail. Released from the shackles of Government, Sealink British Ferries published the tender document for the third ferry on 18 January 1985. The following negotiations were rather protracted. The favoured bidder was Richards of Lowestoft but the final terms could not be agreed. Tenders were also received from yards in Holland, Germany, Denmark and Hong Kong. Eventually, in December 1985, the contract was placed with the small independent yard, Cochrane Shipbuilders Ltd, of Selby in North Yorkshire. Cochrane's yard was intriguingly sited well inland, about 35 miles upstream from the Humber Bridge, on a narrow and meandering section of the River Ouse. The new vessel was the widest ship the

yard had then built. The contract price with the yard was £4.76m, although the total bill for the ship (including various miscellaneous expenses) was £5.14m. The keel of yard number 135 was laid on 23 January 1986 and construction then proceeded apace. The vessel was launched sideways into the River Ouse on Tuesday 4 November 1986 by Lady Mottistone, wife of the Lord Lieutenant of the Isle of Wight and was named *St. Cecilia.*

A number of modifications were made to the existing design. One of the more important, but least apparent, was the design of the hull at the stern. The rake was increased, reducing transom immersion and turbulence, gaining approximately $\frac{1}{2}$ knot in speed for the same power output. The engines were of the same type as the earlier ships but they were manufactured by MAN B&W at Augsberg (Germany) rather than by a sub-contractor. Auxiliary engines manufactured by Gardner were used in place of the troublesome GEC Dorman units.

A unique feature of *St. Cecilia* was a waste heat boiler, powered by the exhaust from the forward main engine and used for services such as liquefying the heavy fuel oil. Although additional maintenance was required, the ship was more fuel-

A view showing the aft propellers and skeg on St. Cecilia *moments before she was launched. The aft skeg was a feature initially omitted from the first ship,* St. Catherine. *Also evident in this view, around the propellers and on the skeg, are sacrificial anodes; blocks of zinc alloy that, due to galvanic action, protect the steel structure from corrosion.*

Eddy Robson

efficient because a diesel-fired boiler was not always required. But whilst the ship was berthed at a terminal with the engines stopped the waste heat boiler was non-functional and such a unit was not incorporated on any of the other vessels.

Above deck, the most noticeable difference was in the prow gangway design. The design of the hinges was altered, with only three hinges instead of five, and the main section did not have a plated outer face. Although less aesthetically pleasing, the design offered certain operational advantages over *St. Catherine* and *St. Helen*. The fluted nature of the outer face allowed any waves washed up over the prows to be dispersed freely. A more important factor was that it allowed a noise problem associated with the earlier ships to be virtually eliminated. On *St. Catherine* and *St. Helen* the outer ramp sections were made up of three triangular segments. The smaller outer segments were hinged between the outboard corners of the main ramp section and the central extremity of the central outer ramp segment. This meant that the tip of the ramps would lie flat on the linkspan if the ships were rolled, and thus reduce stress. Unfortunately the segments tended to bounce as the wheels of vehicles passed over them, and this created a lot of noise. Understandably, the residents of Fishbourne did not appreciate this, especially when the clatter

was generated in the dead of night. On *St. Cecilia* the main ramp sections were more elastic, which allowed the single outer leaves to lay flat against the linkspans. This meant that bouncing and noise were much reduced. The design was such that the load carrying capacity was unaffected.

Another important but barely noticeable change with the new ship was a significant increase in car deck headroom. On *St. Cecilia* the passenger lounge was placed higher up, increasing the headroom to 14'9". Although more steelwork was required for the taller support structure, the ship was actually lighter than her older sisters, this being due to the high quality standard demanded by Cochrane's yard of their steel supplies and their own workmanship.

Of minor interest, the car deck clearances differed slightly between the first two ships: 13'11" on *St. Catherine* and 14'2" on *St. Helen*. This was due to wide dimensional tolerances, mostly due to unequal distortion in the mezzanine decks that had proved difficult to eliminate during manufacture. Both the mezzanine decks and prow ramps were a much better job on *St. Cecilia*, mainly due to the skills of their manufacturer, Navire, who had taken over the original contractor, MacGregor. The quoted headroom is the minimum clearance found anywhere on the car deck, plus an allowance, and it is measured quite simply by a man walking around with a telescopic stick looking for the lowest point.

There were several variations to the layout of the central structure within the main lounge, principally the forward companionways up to the open deck were further outboard and, most noticeably, the refreshment counter was substantially larger and extended right across the rear of the central casing. Nicely finished in stainless steel and lightweight ceramic tiling it gave a more welcoming feel and allowed a far greater throughput of customers. The passenger accommodation on board *St. Cecilia* was far more sumptuous than on the earlier ships. Wall to wall blue carpeting was laid in the main lounge and to prevent dirty shoes spoiling it coconut matting was installed at the bottoms of the companionways. Internal seating was vinyl covered and coloured blue to match the carpeting.

The plating on the open passenger deck on *St. Cecilia* was made from heavier gauge steel in order to obviate welding distortion that had occurred with the lighter gauge material used on the earlier ships. There were numerous other minor differences. The outboard windows on the forward side of the wheelhouse were made from one deep pane of glass instead of two panes as previously, and the rear bulkheads on the upper part of the wheelhouse were canted instead of vertical. The promenade deck at the sides extended slightly further aft, there was an additional window in the upper lounge, and the deck seats were coloured yellow. The doors out on to the open deck were flush with the bulkheads rather than recessed, as on the earlier ships. There were many more external visual variations, far too many to mention here, and mostly on the open deck or above. *St. Cecilia* also has one very obvious

A bow view of St. Cecilia *during construction at Selby, Yorkshire. One end of the prow ramp has been jacked up to check that it will have sufficient flexibility to lie flat on the linkspan when the ship is rolled.*

Eddy Robson

audible difference from the rest of the fleet; the ship's whistle has a completely different tone, being higher pitched.

Unlike *St. Catherine* and *St. Helen*, which were fitted out in a wet dock, *St. Cecilia* was fitted out in a tidal river and at each low tide she sat in the mud. Towards completion it was necessary to check and clear the VS propellers. Sadly a diver lost his life during this exercise.

St. Cecilia *at the moment of launch, on 4 November 1986, showing the single forward propeller and the bow skeg.*

Eddy Robson

By the late 1980s the remaining 'Standard stock' brought over for the Island's railway in 1966 was worn out. Replacement '1938 stock' two-car units were separated from their bogies at Fratton and shipped on three-lorry convoys, which simply drove on and off the Fishbourne ferry without any of the fuss that was involved in the earlier operation. Carriages and wheels were reunited at Sandown station before the old stock was returned to the mainland, mostly for scrap, by the same means. Most units were shipped on St. Cecilia, *which had the greatest headroom at that time. Car 225 is seen coming off that ship at Fishbourne on 15 March 1990.*

St. Cecilia made a spectacular sight when she sailed under her own power through the lowlands of Yorkshire on her way to the King George Dock at Hull where she was based for her trials. Due to the meandering nature of the Ouse the river was closed to all other traffic and a tug was positioned ahead and astern of the new ship in case assistance was required on some very tight bends. *St. Cecilia* arrived at Portsmouth at the end of her delivery voyage on 18 March 1987 and made a trial run to Fishbourne at midday on 21 March. An inaugural cruise took place on 23 March with a compliment of 300 invited guests from the Isle of Wight and the mainland on board. A service of dedication was led by the Venerable Tony Turner, Archdeacon of the Isle of Wight, and the IW Symphony Orchestra provided the music for the occasion. Lady Mottistone presented another painting by the Bembridge artist Peter Wright, to Capt G Saunders, senior master of the *St. Cecilia*, before the ceremonial cake was cut to mark the first sailing of the vessel. The painting was displayed at the forward end of the main lounge, and depicted a Ryde seascape as viewed from St Cecilia's Abbey (the nunnery at Ryde), after which the ship was named.

St. Cecilia entered revenue-earning service with the 06:00 sailing from Portsmouth on a wet and stormy Friday 27 March 1987. By late afternoon that day the weather had become so bad that the Fishbourne ferry was the one and only route to

the Island that was still operating and the passenger lounges were full to capacity.

The galley was equipped with a PA system. As the catering staff played with this new toy, passengers on the first Portsmouth-bound sailing were treated to the following; "Bing Bong" (spoken) "Number 12, your toast is ready," – pause – "Bing Bong. NUMBER 12, YOUR TOAST IS READY". Following an encounter with some particularly large waves, during which the sound of breaking crockery echoed around the lounge – "Bing Bong. Number 12, your toast is all shook up"!

Once *St. Cecilia* had entered service, *St. Catherine* was released for her belated annual survey. For her first few weeks in service, while teething troubles were sorted out, *St. Cecilia* was used on the less intensive No 2 diagram. During the summer the three ships rotated on a three-diagram system.

Initially *St. Cecilia* was not owned by the operating company, but by the Eurolease Corporation Ltd, of Chester. Basically, the ship was owned by a bank and leased to the operator. The company still had exclusive use of the ship and was liable for insurance. The arrangement saved tax payments for the operating company. Today Wightlink wholly owns all its ships.

St. Cecilia soon gained a reputation for being a fast ship and by 2002 she had become the most intensively used member of the 'Saint class' fleet. By the end of her first 15 years of service she had undoubtedly crossed between Portsmouth and

The mezzanine decks, which can accommodate 27 cars each side, are seen being tested on St. Cecilia *during commissioning of the ship at Hull. When not in use they are stowed in the fully raised position, beneath the passenger lounge.*

Eddy Robson

Fishbourne more often than any other ship in the route's history.

At the time of the inauguration of *St. Cecilia*, *Herald of Free Enterprise* was lying on her side just outside Zebrugge harbour, having shipped water through an open bow door. Quite naturally there was public concern about the safety of all car ferries. The ramps on the Island ferries are always locked and a signal of confirmation sent to the bridge before the skipper will set sail. Since 1980 indicator lights have been installed on the bridges to indicate when the prow is locked. Additionally, the ships had always been equipped with freeing-ports to allow shipped water to escape and they were thus safe from that particular danger. Nevertheless the company was required to carry out dead weight surveys on each car ferry with the exception of the nearly new *St. Cecilia*, which had a lightweight of 1,400 tonnes. The surveys on the rest of the fleet were carried out on 24 & 25 February 1988. The results were as follows:

Ship	Lightship As built/modified	Lightship Feb 1988	Increase
St Catherine	1418t (1983)	1429t	11t (0.78%)
St Helen	1455t (1983)	1480t	25t (1.72%)
Caedmon	668t (1977)	677t	9t (1.35%)
Cenwulf	668t (1977)	675t	7t (1.05%)
Cenred	673t (1978)	679t	6t (0.89%)

There were some curious differences in weight growth (mostly due to layers of paint), and it was unfortunate that the already heavy *St. Helen* had gained the most. However, due to the relatively small increases in weight coupled with the substantial metacentric heights (GM) values it was considered unnecessary to take any action. A ship's displacement is calculated after moving a known mass a known distance across the deck and measuring the change in the ship's angle of heel.

MV St. Faith, the final sister

With the Fishbourne service equipped with a fleet of three modern vessels Sealink British Ferries next turned their attentions to the needs of the Lymington to Yarmouth route. In December 1988 they announced that they were planning to introduce a pair of large ferries, each costing £5m and capable of carrying 118 cars and 850 passengers. They were intended to be smaller, bidirectional versions of the Portsmouth-based 'Saint class' vessels. One of the existing 'C class' ships was to be retained to work alongside the new tonnage. Whilst Yarmouth Harbour Commissioners were enthusiastic about the proposals, their counterparts at Lymington were not. At a special meeting held on 12 December the Lymington Commissioners vetoed the proposals. They claimed that larger ferries would reduce navigation rights for local sailors on the

Construction of St. Faith *at Selby, North Yorkshire, early in 1990. This view is looking aft along the starboard side.*

Brian Smith

Lymington River, lead to increased traffic congestion on local roads, have a far-reaching environmental impact and lead to unwanted applications for increased shore facilities.

Within weeks of this setback (at the beginning of January 1989) Sealink British Ferries announced that they were to introduce a fourth 'Saint class' ferry on the Fishbourne route. Whether or not the Lymington setback had any influence on this decision remains to be seen, but with a surplus of ships over the following few years, it could be argued that a fourth vessel was not really justified at that time. Nevertheless the proposals went ahead and an order for construction was placed with Cochrane's of Selby at the end of April 1989. The contract price with the shipyard was £6.4m but the overall price, including various miscellaneous items was £6.95m.

The principal requirement for the new ship was a further increase in car deck clearance because Sealink was unable to accommodate some loads without turning the ships at one terminal or the other, usually Portsmouth. Turning the ships enables high vehicles to reverse on board and then drive straight off at the other end without having to drive beneath the superstructure. The increase in headroom on the new ship was substantial enough to make it quite noticeable when compared to *St. Catherine* and *St. Helen*. Several other modifications were made as the result of a company suggestion scheme. The most obvious of these was the

incorporation of seating on the funnel deck. Hidden from public view, an overhead beam was incorporated in the engine-room to facilitate the removal and replacement of the engines turbochargers. The ship also had her own individual décor. Fixed seating was fabric covered in deep blue-ish green with matching patterned carpeting. Outside deck seating was blue.

The new ship was launched into the River Ouse on 28 February 1990 and named *St. Faith* by Mrs Jackie Field, wife of the Island MP Barry Field. An exceptionally high tide, which caused flooding 14 miles upstream in York, delayed the launch by approximately two hours because the shipyard workers could not gain access underneath *St. Faith* to knock out the final chocks. By the time the river level was back down to a reasonable level it was touch and go whether the launch would take place at all that day because the ebbing current was becoming too rapid.

The ship was named after the church in Cowes dedicated to the child saint of Aquitaine. There had been some speculation beforehand as to what the name would be. 'St. Mary' and 'St. Theresa' (or Teresa) had also been short-listed but *St. Faith* was chosen because three other ships were introduced by Sealink British Ferries in 1990, all with names beginning with F, these being *Fantasia*, *Fiesta* and *Felicity*. Like her sister, *St. Faith* was initially owned by Eurolease Corporation Ltd.

Following sea trials *St. Faith* left Goole at 2.00 pm on 2

July 1990 and arrived at Portsmouth at 7.00 pm on the following day. She was met with a welcoming blast from *St. Catherine*, which had deviated from her route to greet her new sister. Over the next few days *St. Faith* undertook trial runs between Portsmouth and Fishbourne, during which it was found that the mezzanine decks were fouling the main structure during raising and lowering. Some butchery was required to cut the decks back by an inch or so and this work took some time to complete.

The inaugural cruise took place on Wednesday 11 July. A spectacular departure was made at noon, being marked by fireworks, balloons and streamers. During the cruise the retired Bishop of Carlisle performed a formal dedication ceremony. *St. Faith* returned to Portsmouth at 3.00 pm and later performed an evening cruise in the eastern Solent. With the pageantry over, work continued to get the mezzanine decks in working order. The first commercial crossing of *St. Faith* was the 09:30 from Portsmouth on Monday 16 July 1990. After one round trip some further adjustments were required to the mezzanine decks before the ship resumed service during the afternoon. At 13:00 the following day *St. Faith* took over the most intensive No 1 diagram from *St. Helen*.

Essentially *St. Faith* is a sister ship to *St. Cecilia*. Apart from the differences already mentioned the two ships are visually very similar. In order to accommodate the companionways up to the top deck the main open deck was extended aft a few inches amidships. Seating was omitted from the forward end of the open deck in order to allow access gates in this position. These were to be used in conjunction with planned new passenger access facilities at the terminals. The three other ships were similarly modified in this respect at their following refits but the terminals have never been equipped to allow their intended use. It was planned to equip the other ships with seating on the funnel deck but in the event this was not done either. *St. Faith* sported the old Sealink British Ferries livery for only three months. On 7 November 1990 she was used as part of the press launch of the new Wightlink livery, along with *Caedmon* and the Portsmouth to Ryde catamaran *Our Lady Pamela*.

Following the introduction of *St. Faith* a four ship service operated with services every half-hour during busy periods. The ships were treated with equal status and they rotated in the schedule so that each spent a week on each diagram and they all did the same amount of work. This situation did not last for long.

The laying-up of St. Helen and a further intervention by Stena

During the early 'nineties Britain was in the grip of a recession and a mere fourteen months after the four-ship operation began, the company (by now Wightlink) announced that one of the 'Saint class' ships would be withdrawn from service and laid up until the economic climate improved. *St. Helen* was selected for this ignominy. Being one of the older pair of ships this particular vessel was chosen because *St.*

The wheelhouse is lifted aboard St. Faith *on 24 February 1990, five days before her launch.*

Brian Smith

113

Catherine had recently received a major refit (including shot blasting of the hull) while the generally more reliable *St. Helen* remained due for such treatment.

St. Helen was withdrawn from regular traffic on 13 September 1992, but while her passenger certificate remained valid she continued to be used on occasions. Her final day in service was 16 December 1992 after which she was moored beside the 'Odds & Evens' pontoon facing an uncertain future. Her bunkers were drained down and she became a completely dead ship. To cover for possible problems during the annual survey period Wightlink planned to bring *Cenwulf* down from Lymington to act as a standby, but in the event this did not happen.

Sea Containers had not bargained on their old adversaries, Stena-Sealink, making a bid to charter *St. Helen* and operate her independently on the Portsmouth to Fishbourne route. Needless to say Sea Containers refused this request, made in February 1993. Stena were studying the possibility of operating from two other unspecified Island sites, whether or not they got a slice of the Fishbourne cake. Sea Containers claimed that Stena's approach was a political ploy to foil their own proposals for a route from Holyhead. Stena denied that this was the case. Speaking at a public meeting, at the Riverside Centre in Newport, Mr Jim Hannah, Stena Director of Communications, stated that they had been looking into the feasibility of operating an Island service for some time and were confident that they could capture about 10% of the cross-Solent market. Also present at the meeting was Mr Bill Gibbons, who resigned as general manager of Sealink IW services after Wightlink was formed, and became a consultant for Stena. He was also critical of the stance of Wightlink in refusing to charter *St. Helen*. Mr Rod Stewart, Wightlink marketing manager, confirmed that *St. Helen* was being advertised as available for charter but "that was an exercise to test her value on the market". After the meeting Mr Hannah threatened that if agreement on the proposal could not be reached, Sea Containers would be reported to the Office of Fair Trading.

Although the plans to charter *St. Helen* faded into the background, Stena reiterated its intention to establish an Isle of Wight service. In July the board announced that it was considering three options for a cross-Solent ferry route. The objective was to get the matter signed and sealed with a view to getting the operation started by the 1994 holiday season. The Isle of Wight County Council was in support of a third operator being introduced but the County Surveyor advised caution and warned that people had to be aware that an existing operator could go out of business and that a worse situation than at present could be a possible outcome. The majority of Stena's Board visited the Isle of Wight during Cowes Week in 1993 to look at options for an Island terminal.

Meanwhile, *St. Helen* continued to languish in Portsmouth harbour. Stena excepted, no other company made an offer to charter the ship. In June 1993 the faded high-visibility band was painted out and as time went on the ship visibly

deteriorated. In places the original red paint on the funnel began to show through and mildew started growing on the carpets. Various fixtures and fittings were removed and transferred to the three operational ships. During 1993 the other ships continued to rotate equally on a three-ship roster. Fortunately they behaved themselves during the 1993 summer and the absence of *St. Helen* did not cause any undue problems. Wightlink planned to bring *St. Helen* back during 1994 and lay up *St. Catherine* instead in order to even up wear and tear and prevent any one ship from deteriorating unduly. However, financial arrangements originating from the highest levels within Sea Containers prevented *St. Catherine* from being taken out of traffic. *St. Helen* thus faced a second year laid-up.

By January 1994 the prospect of Stena Sealink starting up a ferry service on the Solent was fading. A company spokesman said "The project has been put lower down in our list of priorities because of the amount of work required to establish terminals on each side of the Solent and because of other major ferry schemes we are involved in elsewhere." Stena realised that the only way it was going to break into the Solent market was by building new terminals and not having dual use of existing facilities. He stated that Stena had not abandoned its hopes for a Solent route. Stena has more recently been involved in various amalgamations and buyouts and nothing more has been heard of its interest in the Isle of Wight services.

Happily, in February 1994 an 11% increase in bookings led to Wightlink announcing that *St. Helen* would be restored to service for the 1994 summer season. However, a new car deck drenching system being installed on the other ships was not included on *St. Helen*. The new system allowed the ships to operate safely with two less crewmembers. Since *St. Helen* required a larger crew she was less economic to operate and was restricted to the fourth boat diagram. *St. Helen* received a refit during April and returned to traffic with the 11:30 sailing from Portsmouth on Friday 27 May 1994. A Folkestone family, Trevor and Pauline Francis and their three children, were greeted with champagne and flowers when they became the first passengers to board *St. Helen* at Portsmouth. During 1994 the other ships experienced a number of reliability problems and *St. Helen* was frequently switched to her sisters' diagrams. Although out of use for the whole of October 1994, *St. Helen* was frequently used thereafter while maintenance work was carried out on the other ships.

During her survey in March 1995 *St. Helen* was fitted with the car deck drenching system, bringing her up to the same standard as *St. Catherine*. Both *St. Catherine* and *St. Helen*, however, were relegated to a secondary status due to alterations (costing £90,000) to the refreshment facilities on *St. Cecilia* and *St. Faith*. Gone were the separate bars, with their draught beers, and in their places facsimiles of the snack counters, selling the complete range of sandwiches, soft drinks, canned beers and beverages. This meant that the complete catering range was duplicated, allowing one half to

St. Cecilia *in full Sealink British Ferries livery on 29 March 1987, six days after entering service. This livery, which was used from 1985 until 1990, was jovially described as the 'cigarette packet livery' by one of the skippers.*

be closed during quiet periods and a far greater throughput of customers during busy times. Since refreshment sales are a lucrative source of additional revenue the newer ships alternated the intensive round-the-clock operations while the older ships alternated the half-past-the-hour 'dawn to dusk' services, a situation that would remain all the while that the older ships had inferior refreshment facilities. For a while, however, *St. Helen* made up for some lost time by being used more intensively than *St. Catherine*.

'Saint class' characteristics

St. Catherine is a cantankerous old dowager, *St. Helen* is a WI matron in pearls and sensible shoes, *St. Cecilia* is a power-dressing yuppie in stockings and high heels and *St. Faith* is something you would find on a street corner at King's Cross. This colourful analogy was given by one of the skippers and from it one can deduce that the performance of the four ships differs markedly. Naval architects claim that this cannot be the case but navigating officers say otherwise. It is not easy to be objective about the ships characteristics because skippers views sometimes differ. There is no doubt, however, that *St. Cecilia* is the fastest ship and *St. Catherine*

is the slowest. There is no doubt, either, that *St. Cecilia* has a curious and seemingly inexplicable tendency to drag water in a channel. Stern waves often follow *St. Cecilia* down the channel at Fishbourne. The officers instruction book even orders that at low water *St. Cecilia* should be taken across the Swashway at reduced speed because of her tendency to 'squat'. In June 1987 a cadet dinghy sailor received injuries to his hands after two boats were knocked together at Fishbourne by the wake from *St. Cecilia*. On another occasion I witnessed a sailing instructor beach his rubber dinghy on the old slipway and stride aboard the berthed *St. Cecilia* with great purpose. Clearly, the incident had nearly been repeated. Many passengers on board may have noticed that *St. Cecilia* tends to vibrate, particularly during turns; transmission of vibration into the passenger lounges has always been a feature of this vessel.

St. Catherine's perceived cantankerous nature is reinforced by the fact that she lacks power from her forward propeller, affecting manoeuvrability. This idiosyncrasy cannot be related to the propeller unit itself because they are changed from time to time without significant effect. It is probably related to the hull form. It has been hypothesised, but never proven, that this peculiar characteristic is related to her early propeller problems. It is thought possible that her hull may have hogged while she was heavily ballasted at one end in order to remove propeller units from the other. It is more likely due to hull deformation that occurred during her first dry-docking in Leith, when the support blocks locally deformed the hull. *St. Catherine* also suffers from vibration but of a lower frequency than *St. Cecilia*. In addition to being slower and less manoeuvrable than the rest of the fleet, she also has poor acceleration.

Her twin sister, *St. Helen*, is better, but it took many years to get her over problems caused by her languishing out of use for eighteen months. Disuse is not conducive to the longevity of any machine unless it is properly mothballed because everything becomes cold and damp. Condensation causes corrosion of metallic parts and it plays havoc with electrical systems. Before her laying up *St. Helen* was regarded by some skippers, not by others, as having the best all round performance and currently she is perhaps the most vibration-free member of the 'Saint class'.

St. Faith is the best presented of the ships, but she has some curious characteristics. She is slow to react to the application of reverse thrust, as if bereft of brakes. She also has a tendency to 'skid' ie her stern continues to swing at the end of turns. Although the hull of *St. Faith* is supposedly identical to that of *St. Cecilia* she seems, by contrast, to have a small wake profile, though this clearly does not make her any faster. Speed differences are not large, perhaps $1/2$ knot or so, and theoretically the younger pair should be faster than the older pair due to the different hull designs at the stern. This is true when comparing *St. Cecilia* and *St. Catherine* but there is little to chose between *St. Faith* and *St. Helen*.

Some of the above characteristics may seem rather alarming but there is no reason for public concern, the skippers know what they are up against.

The 'Saint class' ships are usually reliable. When compared to the high-speed catamarans operating between Portsmouth and Ryde the number of breakdowns that occur is minuscule, but they are more problematic than cross-channel ferries, many of which operate continuously from one survey to the next with barely a hiccup. From a number of unofficial records it can be deduced that *St. Catherine* and *St. Faith* have apparently been the least reliable members of the quartet. However, most of the breakdowns of *St. Catherine* occurred during the first half of her life to date, often due to alternator problems, and many of those with *St. Faith* have been due to trouble from the hydraulic prow ramp systems plus a spate of propeller problems. *St. Helen* was generally the most reliable ship until she increasingly suffered from power generator or other electrical faults. On 6 September 2000 she became completely disabled off Clarence Pier when all three diesel alternator sets failed. As a consequence of ongoing problems in this respect, a portable auxiliary Aggreco power unit resided at the aft end

of the car deck for much of the time and she became the least used ship until the vessel's own auxiliary diesels were replaced. Since then *St. Helen* appears to have, once again, become a very reliable ship.

The 'Saints' have proved to be very good sea boats. Occasionally foul weather can cause some disruption to the service but it rarely prevents the ferries from going to sea. However, the ships are not as directionally stable as conventional screw propelled vessels in as much that they will not maintain a straight course if the helm is set dead centre. Anybody standing at the ships sterns will have noticed that the ships' wakes do not remain straight for very long. Frequent adjustments are required by the helmsman to maintain a direct heading but this is of little consequence on a short crossing in crowded waters in which deviations to avoid other traffic are frequent anyway.

Annual surveys

Traditionally, the mandatory annual surveys have been carried out at Southampton. Until the 'sixties the work was carried out in British Rail's own facility and, since its closure, at independent yards such as Vosper's, on the River Itchen and Husband's, at Marchwood. These yards had slipways, which allowed the ships to be hauled up on special cradles. Unlike the earlier ships, the 'Saint class' vessels are unsuitable for slipping and they thus require dry-docking, with both the Trafalgar and King George V dry docks at Southampton having been used. In the event of the non-availability of these docks some long excursions away from the Solent have taken place. In 1987, immediately following the entry into service of *St. Cecilia*, *St. Catherine* was sent to Falmouth in Cornwall for her annual dry-docking. In 1990 the Thew yard in Southampton was unable to carry out the surveys there as the company was in the hands of the receivers. The three 'Saint class' vessels in existence at that time were thus sent to the subsidiary yard of Blundell and Compton, at Tilbury on the River Thames.

During 1993, the 'Saint class' ships were surveyed in the Royal Naval Dockyard at Portsmouth. For the next two years the surveys reverted to A&P Appledore at Southampton. During January 1995, *St. Cecilia* shared Appledore's King George V dry dock with the rival Red Funnel ship *Red Falcon*. It goes without saying that the engineers from the rival companies had a look over each other's vessels. In 1996 the 'Saints' returned to the RN Dockyard, where Wightlink staff carried out the work. In 1997 the 'C class' vessels joined the 'Saints' in the RN Dockyard and in 1998 the high-speed catamarans were there too. On two occasions a ship from each route could be found dry-docked together.

In 2000 Wightlink closed its marine workshops at the end of Broad Street in Portsmouth. Wightlink have stated that the objective was to give the responsibility for ship maintenance to the individual ships under the management of the Chief Engineers. A&P in Southampton was initially subcontracted to do the work previously undertaken by the Wightlink fitters, but the remoteness of their base was a handicap. Nonetheless, in 2001, reliability and standards improved with the route achieving a constant 99.5% reliability factor. Trips lost in 2001 amounted to 0.46% or 102 out of 23,990 planned sailings.

In 2001 A&P regained the contract for annual surveys until at least 2003/4. Wightlink claimed to have been disappointed with the new contractors, Fleet Support Limited, who had taken over the Dockyard in Portsmouth, saying they seemed to be preoccupied with defence work.

'Saint class' modifications and usage

Modifications to the 'Saint class' vessels have not been substantial. During her 1988 survey *St. Catherine* was equipped with fitted carpet in her passenger lounge, bringing her up to a similar standard to *St. Cecilia*. The carpet was a maroon colour and the lounge seating was re-upholstered with matching vinyl. *St. Helen* was carpeted during the following winter, in pale green, and with matching fabric-covered seats. *St. Catherine* and *St. Cecilia* were later re-upholstered with fabric-covered seating.

As a result of crewing reductions, revised SOLAS regulations concerning life-saving equipment were imposed, seeing new inflatable life rafts and ship evacuation systems installed on the four 'Saint class' ships. *St. Catherine* and *St.*

Helen were so equipped during their 1997 annual surveys and *St. Cecilia* and *St. Faith* the following year. Three life rafts were installed on each side of the ships, with associated shute systems to facilitate passenger evacuation from the upper decks into the inflated rafts. The control systems are situated in the areas previously occupied by the old life rafts.

The year 1998 saw the old refreshment counter on *St. Helen* replaced by a full-width facility at the rear of the central casing, bringing her up to the same standard as the two newer ships. The work involved moving the ladies' toilet to the position where the old refreshment facility had been. Inferior catering facilities had relegated the two older ships to a secondary status in the first place; now new circumstances conspired to keep *St. Helen* largely off the principal rosters.

Commercial vehicles were becoming higher and Wightlink were increasingly unable to accommodate some vehicles on the 1983-built sisters without the time wasting manoeuvre of turning the ships at one terminal or the other. It was thus decided to keep the two younger ships, with their greater headroom, on the running and second boat duties, with *St. Helen* on third and *St. Catherine* on the least intensive fourth boat duty until the latter also had her snack counter upgraded two years later. Only during the annual survey season, during main engine maintenance periods or in the event of a breakdown were *St. Catherine* and *St. Helen* likely to find themselves back on the round-the-clock services.

This policy meant that the ships had vastly differing operational hours, which lead to maintenance problems from which the older pair suffered the most. General maintenance

For several years, annual surveys were carried out by Fleet Support Limited in the Royal Navy's Dockyard in Portsmouth. St. Catherine shares the dry-dock with the Yarmouth route's Cenwulf on 4 February 1999. The livery, which was the first Wightlink scheme under CINVen ownership, was first applied in 1996 and was replaced in 2000. The ship looks like new, but vehicle-deck paint-work seems to rapidly deteriorate nowadays, which can give a first impression of a fleet that is rather older than it is. The vehicle deck paintwork on the ships of the rival fleet often make a striking comparison.

Andrew Cooke

work is principally carried out while the ships are in service, but *St. Catherine* and *St. Helen* spent far more of their time tied up out of use. Manning arrangements had become less than ideal with crewmembers likely to serve on any of the four ships, and some on the passenger catamarans as well. Each ship used to have a senior master and regular crews later amended to crews serving two ships – *St. Catherine* / *St. Cecilia* and *St. Helen* / *St. Faith*. In order to improve reliability the four ship rotation was restored during October 2000, but it lasted only until the end of the following annual survey period and regular crewing arrangements have not been reinstated, except for engineers who were allotted to single ships from the autumn of 2002. Eight regular engineers were allotted to each of the newer ships and four to the older pair.

From the latter part of 2001 until the end of the 2002 summer timetable *St. Cecilia* operated the round-the-clock service almost exclusively. *St. Faith* more often than not operated the less intensive third ship diagram, whilst *St. Catherine* and *St. Helen* were normally used on the least intensive 4th and 5th ship diagrams. (By this time the second ship diagram was the exclusive domain if the new and larger *St. Clare*.) The reason for the above disparity was down to differing facilities once again. A shop (stocking a curious selection of bric-a-brac, magazines and snacks) had been constructed at the forward end of the main lounge on *St. Cecilia* during 2001. *St. Faith* was similarly fitted in 2002 but at the same time *St. Cecilia* was further upgraded by the incorporation of a coffee bar in the upper lounge. Meanwhile *St. Helen* and *St. Catherine* incorporated neither such revenue generating facilities. Over a long period the rostering arrangements have somewhat evened out the overall usage of the four ships, which at the time of writing (2004) varied in age between 14 and 21 years. By the end of 2003 they had all probably undertaken between 80,000 and 100,000 Solent crossings. There can be little doubt that *St. Cecilia* has crossed the most (well over half a million miles), followed by *St. Catherine*, *St. Helen* and finally *St. Faith*. If current utilisation continues, *St. Faith* will soon overtake the seven-year-older *St. Helen*.

All four 'Saint class' ships were extensively refurbished internally during the 2000 annual overhauls. New carpets were installed (including the hitherto uncarpeted upper lounges), the fixed seating was re-upholstered and all other furniture was replaced. The carpeting, seat coverings and furniture became identical in each ship, taking away some of the individuality previously seen. Fixed seating was upholstered in two shades of blue whilst the carpets were multicoloured. The improvements were accompanied by yet another minor revision to the livery – the inclusion of the company's website address on the face of the bridge being a sign of the times.

During the 2002 overhauls, following repeated and sometimes embarrassing breakdowns of *St. Helen*, brand new Scania diesel engines replaced the unreliable GEC Dorman prime movers on the alternator sets in both the older ships.

The total cost of the new installations was £118,000.

As part of the program to phase out ozone destroying chemicals, December 2003 was the date set for the outlawing of halon fire extinguishant. Halon reacts chemically with a fire; the alternative carbon dioxide (CO_2) merely smothers it. Consequently a lot more CO_2 is required to do the same job; in fact 24 cylinders in place of five, too many to fit in the old halon compartment on mezzanine deck level. There is insufficient ventilation to permit fire extinguishant to be housed in an engine room or the void spaces around it, therefore new chambers were installed on top of the bridge deck, starting with *St. Cecilia* and *St. Catherine* early in 2003.

In the summer of 2003 *St. Cecilia*'s tatty yellow deck seats were renewed in white (the previous yellow being unavailable) and the promenade deck was covered with blue plastic matting.

Terminal developments

In February 1987 Sealink British Ferries applied for planning permission to considerably enlarge the Fishbourne terminal. Despite inevitable opposition from The Fishbourne and Wootton Creek Protection Association, and Fishbourne residents in general, the plans were approved in early May. The plan involved the demolition of 99 Fishbourne Lane, as a site for traffic marshalling and parking and the conversion of 101 Fishbourne Lane into a buffet and office. The scheme would provide 170 extra vehicle spaces over the existing 255. The proposed felling of 16 trees on the site also caused concern to the scheme's opponents. The work did not commence until the end of April the following year. The £1/4million contract was undertaken by Bardon Vectis and was completed in just seven weeks. The resulting improvements were somewhat different to the proposed scheme. Both of the properties purchased by Sealink British Ferries were demolished and a new exit road was constructed several lanes to the northeast of the previous road. 135 additional car spaces were created. Island MP Barry Field officially opened the terminal extension on 12 August 1988.

On the other side of the Solent an area of land on the old power station site (on the opposite side of Gunwharf Road from the terminal) was earmarked for use to relieve peak summer congestion. Although this land was turned into a car parking area, and was purchased freehold by the company, it became a 'pay and display' park and has only been used occasionally as a vehicle marshalling area.

An abortive scheme that would have had a great impact was initiated in April 1989. A local developer, Mr. Peter Rogers, offered to build a relief road at Fishbourne as a private venture in return for permission for a new industrial/housing development at the Ranelagh Works site, just upstream from the Fishbourne terminal. The proposed road was to run from opposite the terminal gates to a point midway along Elenors Grove on the main A3054 Ryde to Newport road. The road, which would have passed through a 200-acre farm owned by Quarr Abbey, included a marshalling area halfway along its length. Although Mr Rogers claimed that the abbey's mainland agent had warmed to the plan, Brother Francis, the procurator, had other views. He said he would need convincing that the road would be of real benefit to the Island before allowing the farm to be cut in two. The resident's watchdog group, the Wootton Creek Protection Association, were also opposed to the proposals, claiming the plan would merely move the noise nuisance elsewhere and spoil a piece of countryside in the process. They claimed that widening of Fishbourne Lane was the only answer, but neither the developer nor the council were keen on that idea. Obviously the developer would have lost his bargaining lever but in the event it did not do any good anyway. Planning permission at Ranelagh was refused and the road was never built.

The road would have had some advantages; apart from giving the Fishbourne residents a more peaceful life it would have helped to ease congestion that sometimes occurs when traffic turns up at the terminal gate at a higher rate than the staff can admit it. This often occurred on Saturdays in late summer when departing tourists flocked to the terminals in their droves, hoping to catch earlier sailings. Once a queue reached the main road total chaos ensued because through traffic between Ryde and Newport became snarled up with the ferry traffic. On 24 September 1988 the problem was exacerbated by the passenger service being cancelled due to foul weather, placing a further burden on the Fishbourne ferry. Queues stretched to Binstead in one direction and Wootton in the other. As a consequence, a football match between Newport FC and Portsmouth RN was delayed and wedding guests missed a service. With time, long queues have become more frequent. On Saturday 3 June 2000, at the end of the school half term break, traffic queues snarled up the main Ryde to Newport Road for eight hours after *St. Helen* missed one round trip due to an electrical failure. In recent times, Wightlink has employed traffic wardens to forbid vehicles from entering Fishbourne Lane more than an hour before their booked departures.

In order to allow ferries to improve turnaround times and avoid unnecessary delays, a fifteen day dredging operation of the Fishbourne channel was carried out by the MV *Volvox Anglia* during July 1989. Two additional dolphins were installed on the port side of the channel. The passing place was rarely used until a five-ship timetable was introduced in 2002.

At Fishbourne, two passenger reception booths were installed during the autumn of 1995 and knocked down again in early 2002. The booths were placed adjacent to the existing booking office on its southern side, one right across the original 1926 concrete road. This facility allowed passengers to purchase tickets without having to leave their vehicles, but like an earlier scheme it was abolished.

At about the same time an unaccompanied drop trailer facility was also introduced at each terminal. This system allows hauliers to leave trailer units at the terminals and have them shipped when there is space on board, often overnight. An added benefit is that space is freed up for domestic users to travel on popular services. Three Tugmaster tractor units are shared between the terminals for hauling trailers on and off the ships, the tractors being moved between the terminals to suit demand. The drop trailer facility has been a great success and has enabled freight customers to reduce their overheads and helped Wightlink to retain its freight market share at improved rates. The operation was enhanced by a new trailer park on the 1/3 acre so-called 'Island Link' site, which was located to the left of the Gunwharf terminal vehicular entrance. Red Funnel adopted a similar drop trailer system and in 2003 the two companies announced plans to open trailer parks on adjacent sites on the Island, several miles from the respective terminals.

A further improvement programme at Fishbourne was officially opened on 28 April 1998. Wightlink had spent £60,000 refurbishing the booking office in January 1991 but seven years later spent a further £200,000 completely revamping it. The glass screens in the booking office were considered to be rather forbidding and in order to present a friendlier image they were dispensed with. The refurbished terminal building incorporates a new passenger waiting area, angled ticket office counter, a purpose-built disabled persons/mother and baby room and a low-fitted telephone suitable for wheelchair use. Included in the overall cost was the construction of a new colonial-style 'timber-built' buffet pleasantly situated on the waterside on the downstream side of the terminal.

During the 'nineties there was considerable housing and leisure development in the vicinity of the Gunwharf terminal. This included luxury housing to the south of the Inner Camber Dock (where Vosper Thorycroft's yard had once been) and the massive redevelopment of the former HM Gunwharf site to the north of the terminal. The terminal was such an important asset to Wightlink that in 1998 it negotiated with the City Council to secure it against possible redevelopment. The result was a new sixty year lease. The new contract was signed on 18 September 1998 to take effect from 1 February 2002 (the expiry date of the original lease), although there were some transitional effects due to the overlap. The new terms have not been divulged.

In the early months of 2002 yet another redevelopment programme at Fishbourne saw the portable gatekeeper's hut replaced by an octagonal structure whilst the unsightly toilet block was replaced by facilities within the main building. Later in the year a 4 metre-high acoustic fence was installed along part of the terminal's northeast boundary.

Renewed competition from Red Funnel

For many years the Fishbourne ferry had it easy. Even before the introduction of the 'Saint class' ships it was the dominant route and as the 'eighties progressed its position was simply reinforced. The rival company offered no threat at all, and eventually made losses on its car ferry service from Southampton to Cowes. During 1989 Red Funnel had to fend off a hostile takeover bid from Sally Holdings, an issue that was only resolved when the group was taken over in October of that year by Associated British Ports. With sound financial backing Red Funnel could begin to rebuild its business, but new tonnage remained off the agenda until an impending MMC audit was out of the way. In order to provide a regular hourly service, calls by car ferries at West Cowes were abolished in 1991. The most significant impact occurred three years later when Red Funnel introduced its first new car ferry tonnage in twenty years. Their two new ships *Red Falcon* and *Red Osprey* are larger than the 'Saint class' ships in every respect except Gross Register Tonnage. They are longer, broader, heavier, more powerful, faster and have considerably more car deck headroom. Their vehicular capacity is double that of their predecessors but, in fact no more than the 'Saint class' ships, despite their greater size. Passenger facilities are sumptuous and cooked meals are available from walk-in buffets more akin to those found on continental ferries. The new ships regularly make their long crossing in 55 minutes, only about 20 minutes more than on the Fishbourne route. Their introduction immediately made an impact and Red Funnel reported record increases in traffic. Although not originally intended, a third ship was added in 1996. Named *Red Eagle*, additional passenger accommodation pushed her GRT slightly higher than *St. Faith*, making her larger than the 'Saint class' in every respect.

There is little doubt that the management at Wightlink viewed their opposition's re-emergence with some concern, although it may not have worried them unduly. Wightlink is in an inherently strong position owing to its shorter routes; the ship cycle time is 1 hour 30 minutes on the western route and 2 hours from Portsmouth to Fishbourne compared with up to 3 hours on Red Funnel. Some of the working conditions within Red Funnel, however, gave their rivals certain operational advantages, and this was a matter that Wightlink decided to address.

After the management buy-in of Wightlink in 1995 the new management stated that it was not anticipated that there would be any job cuts under the new regime. Less than a year later this view changed. Wightlink advised that the key factor in deciding that working practices had to change was their inability to meet demand with sufficient scheduled services due to old-fashioned restrictive trade unions collective agreements. As a result of changing these collective agreements – introducing flexible rosters, modal manning and annualised hours – Wightlink has increased its scheduled sailings of existing ships by 50%. It was decided to call the project 'Industry Standard' to indicate that the company was not being over radical but endeavouring to match working practices in the rest of the UK ferry industry. In order to introduce the more flexible arrangements that already existed throughout the industry Wightlink gave notice to staff and recognised Trades Unions of a variation to the existing terms and conditions of service and bargaining arrangements. This announcement, made at the beginning of January 1996, was also linked to a plan to make 69 posts redundant (later increased to 80).

It was proposed that the Fishbourne ferry would provide the bulk of the staff reductions because of the impact of the additional hours that would be worked and a reduction in the base crew on each ship from 13 to 10. In future, the crew levels would be varied according to passenger numbers rather than fixed at a higher base. With little progress being made within the negotiations, or a deadline for these to be completed, the RMT union called for an industrial action ballot by staff, leading to the spectre of Easter strikes. Nonetheless, the negotiations continued and eventually the strike threat was lifted. It became clear during the negotiations that sufficient staff were coming forward to enquire about severance terms so the company was able to announce that there would be no need for compulsory redundancies to achieve the required reduction in staff numbers. The dispute was settled in May 1996 after compromises from both sides. Redundancies amounted to between 50 and 60. Improvements in sick pay, leave and manning levels, when compared to the company's original proposals, were also agreed. The new system, known as 'modal manning', was introduced in September 1996 on all the company's ships. Crew numbers would henceforth be quickly varied according to passenger numbers. The crew would normally be at its base level but should, for example, a fully loaded coach arrive for shipment then shore staff would immediately be put on board the ship in order that evacuation procedures could be complied with. Wightlink claims that the new system has enabled the company to reduce some of its operating costs and enabled it to operate more services, giving greater choice to its customers.

Disputes

Disputes such as the above are bound to occur from time to time. Squabbles also occur between the public and the operator. Most people complain about the fares but take it no further. The people that seem to be most likely to take some sort of action are the residents of Fishbourne. Various watchdog groups such as the Fishbourne Residents Action Committee and the Wootton Creek Protection Association have been set up and they keep the operating company on its toes.

The Fishbourne resident's opposition to the introduction of the so-called 'Super Ferries' is documented earlier in this chapter. In the summer of 1989 the Fishbourne Residents Action Committee presented a 200-signature petition to the Isle of Wight County Council and Medina Borough Council, objecting to the introduction of a fourth ferry. The ship was already under construction and their opposition had no effect.

Not deterred, the Fishbourne residents registered another objection to Medina Borough Council in the following July, complaining about noise. Their complaints concerned the noise from vehicles boarding the ships, lorry tractor units coupling up with trailers, Tannoy announcements and on board safety announcements. On this occasion the Council arranged a meeting with Wightlink to thrash out the problems, many concessions being made. As a result of this meeting passengers are requested to return to their cars earlier than they need to. The noise from vehicles boarding the ships mostly emanated from the ramps on *St. Catherine* and *St. Helen*. Modifications were made to the ships including the fitting of nylon bushes to the hinges, although this particular modification proved to be unsuccessful.

A very long running dispute, which still rumbles on, concerned coastal erosion at the mouth of Wootton Creek. There is no doubt that erosion has taken place; the dispute was over the cause. In April 1989 Sealink made a voluntary donation of £5,000 to the IW Archaeological Committee after a Roman site had become uncovered on the eastern shore of the creek. Other finds uncovered at that time dated back to 8000 BC. A few days after this event the Isle of Wight County Council called for an 'independent study' into the cause of the erosion but it was not until 1996 that the Council really began shaking the big stick. On 1 May that year the Council agreed to seek £30,000 from the operator (by then Wightlink) for beach nourishment works. Their consultants, Posford Duvivier, identified dredging of the channel as one of the causes of erosion on the eastern shore, adding that the activities of ferries also had a contributory effect on the western shore. Wightlink did not agree. In late September 1996, an IW councillor threatened the possibility of legal action when Wightlink decided to carry out its own 'independent survey', by consultants Gifford and Partners. Things became more heated and in mid October the Council gave an ultimatum to Wightlink that unless it attended a meeting within 21 days, to discuss the alleged damage, it would consider taking legal action against it. Wightlink responded by saying that it could provide no further comment until its own report was ready at the end of November. A meeting did take place in early November when the IW Council asked Mr Michael Aiken, the Wightlink Chairman, to make an interim payment to preserve the archaeological remains, a matter that he would give proper consideration to after publication of Gifford and Partner's report.

Eventually Wightlink managed to persuade all parties to sit around the same table, after which the proceedings continued in a less confrontational manner. After Gifford & Partners concluded that natural wave and tide action was the main cause

of erosion at Fishbourne, in February 1997 Wightlink said they would be "offering to make a contribution to the Council to aid with the general protection of the Island's heritage". A donation of £20,000 was subsequently paid without prejudice. It would appear that honour had been at stake. The donation was to cover the cost of the protection of the archaeological finds, not to fund coastal defence works. A modest rock protection beyond the old boathouse at Fishbourne, a timber groyne constructed in the same area during the summer of 1998 and the depositing of a quantity of coarse shingle (removed from the beach between Shanklin and Luccombe) were funded from the Council's coastal protection budget.

Since that time there has been evidence of erosion of the shingle spit upstream from the terminal and new channels have been opening up in the silt near to the ferry channel, which itself has become deeper. Meanwhile, there has been a build up of shingle on the offshore shingle bank to the east of the creek. A further survey, commissioned by Portsmouth University, was carried out by English Nature in 2003, the report being awaited at the time of writing. This one looks set to run and run.

Following clandestine observations from adjacent properties, 14 Sealink employees were suspended after a police swoop at the Fishbourne terminal on 17 January 1990. Thirteen of them were charged with conspiracy to defraud the company. During a court appearance in the following November eight of the accused were each fined £100 after pleading guilty to accepting bribes to let drivers on board the ferries without tickets. Six others were committed for trial by jury after pleading not guilty. Of those, four were acquitted of the charges at Southampton Crown Court in April 1991 and the case against a fifth was ordered to be left on court files. The charges against the sixth were dropped before the case came to court.

These convictions did not deter several members of staff at the Gunwharf terminal from later defrauding their employers. Four were sacked in September 2000 after more clandestine observations and dawn raids exposed a ticket counterfeiting racket.

An unfortunate set of circumstances during 1997 very nearly resulted in a strike being called. One of the busiest early season days, Easter Monday, was disrupted by thick fog. To make matters worse, *St. Catherine* ran aground just outside Portsmouth Harbour. She was soon re-floated but thereafter ran late. With a heavy build up of traffic on both sides of the Solent, four crew members were suspended after they refused to return to sea on the ship later in the day claiming it would have pushed them over their rostered turn of duty. During May more than 300 RMT union members were balloted on taking industrial action over the suspensions. A strike threat was only averted after the management decided to reinstate the crew, although the complaints were upheld.

In August 2002 industrial action was threatened once again

after Wightlink gave notice that its employees final salary pension schemes were to be withdrawn. These schemes had not been available for new employees since earlier in the year. After talks with the RMT union the company agreed to withdraw their proposals for long-term employees and to seek a mutually acceptable alternative for new starters. An interim fares increase soon followed – coincidental, of course.

Phase Three timetables

With a fleet of two large ships and one medium sized one, instead of two medium and two small ships, the service frequency fell at the beginning of Phase 3. From 35 summer Saturday sailings in 1983 the number fell to 28 in 1984. On other days throughout the year the number of services also fell except for the least intensive service (winter Saturdays), which remained unaltered at 17 per day. *St. Catherine* and *St. Helen* alternated the two principal operating diagrams week and week about. The No 1 diagram (or running boat) operated every two hours from 3.00 am until 11.00 pm (ex-Portsmouth) throughout the year. The No 2 diagram (or second boat) was less intensive and operated from 6.00 am until 6.00 pm in winter but was extended in summer. On summer Friday nights through Saturday mornings the service was hourly. The Sunday timetable was such that there was a natural changeover between the two ships, enabling them to swap diagrams without any awkward shuffling.

When *St. Cecilia* replaced *Cuthred* in 1987 the service frequency remained virtually unaltered but with the arrival of *St. Faith* a four ship timetable was introduced for the summer of 1990, but only for that and the following summer season. Although four ships operated during 1992 they were not scheduled as such. It was to be two years after the restoration of *St. Helen* to traffic before a four-ship operation reappeared on the published timetables. Its reintroduction was no doubt a response to the renewed threat from Red Funnel, who, though gaining trade hand over fist, could not offer much better than an hourly frequency with their three ships on the longest cross-Solent route.

Year by year the service has become more intensive, in 1997 passing the frequency offered at the end of Phase 2 and with several times the vehicular capacity. The second boat now operated an around-the-clock service throughout the year (except winter weekends) with only one weekday round trip missed in each 24 hours. The first boat operated a continuous service around the clock, with the 5.00 am from Portsmouth and the 2.00 am from Fishbourne being the hazardous cargo runs.

Hazardous cargo services began operating on the Fishbourne route on 1 January 1988 when new government legislation came into force limiting the carriage of hazardous cargoes on ships that also carried passengers. However, after eight months of negotiations with the Department of Transport, the Isle of Wight County Council, with the help of the Island MP, won special exemptions allowing certain chemicals and other hazardous goods to be carried aboard passenger sailings, provided certain extra safeguards were put in place. The exemptions included the carriage of liquefied petroleum gas but not bulk tanker supplies. To cater for the latter's shipment Sealink British Ferries agreed to run a freight-only sailing from Portsmouth at 1.00 am and Fishbourne at 2.00 am. From 1 January 1990 the mainland departure was rescheduled for 5.00 am. The service ran each weekday and when no hazardous traffic used the service normal traffic was allowed on board. During the early days of this operation there were stories of LPG tankers being turned away because normal traffic had already gone aboard, and this would have caused a certain amount of consternation.

Following the introduction of an additional, larger vessel a five-ship timetable was offered at peak periods. Operating on Fridays from late March to early November and Fridays to Mondays inclusive in high summer, the straightforward clock-face timetable was replaced by a broadly 25 minute service interval between breakfast and teatime, but with a 30 minute break for the new ship, which takes longer to load. After some tuning of the service times, and with the benefit of experience, the five-ship schedule was operating reasonably well by 2003, except during very busy periods when slips of over an hour were not uncommon. The fifth vessel itself performed four round trips, but since the other four ships were scheduled to slip one hour the net gain was only two additional round trips. However, with one ship being larger, an 18% increase in capacity was available during the period of 5-ship operation.

In 2004 the 5-ship service was reduced from 78 days throughout the year to just eight peak Saturdays. With a few services pruned out elsewhere, there were approximately 1.5% fewer crossings scheduled for 2004.

Apart from the effects of the occasional breakdown, bad weather or heavy traffic, the timetables can be occasionally disrupted for other reasons, as will be seen below.

Services on the passenger route and other operations

A timing trial was conducted using *St. Catherine* on 1 November 1988, when a scheduled Fishbourne to Portsmouth service called at Ryde Pier en route, no passengers being disembarked. This was a portent of things to come. On 26 February 1989, the 21:00 sailing of *St. Helen* from Portsmouth to Fishbourne diverted to Ryde following the failure of the catamaran *Our Lady Patricia*. With sister-ship, *Our Lady Pamela*, away for survey *St. Helen* became the first 'Saint class' vessel used to ferry passengers between Portsmouth and Ryde. Henceforth calls at Ryde Pier by car ferries became a regular feature whenever the catamaran service was disrupted. Later, it became standard practice for mainland bound car ferries to call at Ryde Pier during the morning commuter period and Island

Nowadays it is unusual to find people queuing along Ryde Pier to catch a ferry. It is also unusual to find a Fishbourne ferry there on a calm summer's day, but it happened on Sunday 14 July 2002 when a large open-air service was held at Portsmouth as part of the celebrations of the 75th anniversary of the diocese. St. Helen was chartered to transport the Isle of Wight contingent to the mainland as there were far too many passengers to squeeze into the regular catamarans. The same ship brought the worshippers back again in the late afternoon.

A P&O flag waving to the left, a second linkspan above and HMS Bristol to the right tells us that St. Catherine is disembarking vehicles at Portsmouth's Continental Ferry Port while work was being carried out on the Gunwharf linkspan on 8 September 1999. The extended passage assured that the services were soon running very late.

During the Gunwharf linkspan's maintenance closure on 8 September 1999 the ferries berthed bow in at the Continental Ferry Port. This gave the unique site of all four ships berthing stern in at Fishbourne. By the time this photograph of St. Cecilia *was taken the Gunwharf terminal had just reopened and the ship turned round before reloading so that services could revert to normal.*

bound ships to call there in the early evening. At other times buses were provided between Ryde and Fishbourne, and between the Gunwharf and the Harbour station.

The demise of the traditional passenger ferries has led to the car ferries being used occasionally as cruise ships. Nowadays *St. Faith* is the vessel most likely to be used for cruise work on account of her additional seating on the funnel deck. She sometimes worked the traditional Cowes fireworks cruise, although this was discontinued after 1994, but was restored in 2003 by the new *St. Clare*. *St. Faith* has been chartered three times as a spectator ship at the start of major yacht races and on 5 June 1994 she was similarly used during the review in Spithead marking the 50th anniversary of the D-day landings. Many Islanders appreciated that the regular noon sailing from Fishbourne that day was likely to be an excellent, and cheaper, platform from which to witness the review itself. This indeed turned out to be the case and passengers were treated to a running commentary from the captain of the ship (*St. Cecilia*).

The ships have also been used in pop video productions, TV commercials and even in feature films. Such activities have become more frequent since a fifth ship was added to the fleet, rendering a ship surplus to service requirements for more of the time.

St. Helen underwent berthing trials at Portsmouth Continental Ferry Port (CFP) on 8 July 1992. This turned out to be a worthwhile exercise. While *St. Helen* herself was laid up, a valve failure at the Gunwharf terminal on 29 December 1993, prevented the linkspan from rising and falling with the tide, necessitating the three operational ships being diverted to berth 4 at the Continental Port for a few hours.

This procedure was repeated on 8 September 1999 during maintenance work on the piling at the Gunwharf terminal. On this occasion the four ships berthed bow in at berth 4 at the CFP giving the unique sight of all vessels berthing stern in at Fishbourne. It so happened that a TV commercial was being filmed that morning. It was one hell of a day to choose; one of the catamarans was out of action due to mechanical failure, the Gunwharf terminal out of use and all ferries were berthing back to front at Fishbourne for the only time in the 'Saint class' era. Two similar operations took place during April 2003, but with the ships berthing stern first at berths 4 or 5 at the CFP.

At the turn of the new millennium a ferry was stabled overnight at Fishbourne for perhaps the first time since before the war. The IW Council, police, health authority and health care trust footed the £11,500 bill for the operation, for which the principal requirement was to allow ambulances to transfer

St. Helen *departs from the Gunwharf terminal on 16 July 2001. No photograph can portray the racket of car burglar alarms, which accompany almost every departure in the present day.*

Andrew Cooke

patients to mainland hospitals had an emergency arisen during this night of extreme revelry. At 21:00 on 31 December *St. Helen*, sailed light to Fishbourne and her Island-based crew remained on standby. Fortunately their services were not required and she slipped away again at 08:00 on New Year's Day.

In January 1987 the Southern Vectis Bus Company proposed to start up the first ever bus service to the Fishbourne terminal, hoping to cash in on the increasing number of foot passengers using the car ferry. The scheme failed, principally for two reasons – the Isle of Wight County Council policy as contained in the Structure Plan was to discourage passenger interchange facilities at Fishbourne and Sealink British Ferries was either unable or unwilling to allow a bus turn round facility on their terminal property. Ryde, with its good interchange facilities, has always been the natural terminal for foot passengers and Sealink was hardly likely to discourage passengers from using their new catamaran service from there to Portsmouth.

However, in January 2000, Wightlink introduced its own minibus service linking the Island's county town of Newport with both the Ryde to Portsmouth passenger ferry and the Fishbourne car ferry. A flat single bus fare of £1 was accompanied by the reintroduction of the day return passenger fare on the Fishbourne ferry. This was the first occasion in the route's history that foot passengers had actually been encouraged to use this car ferry service. During the first phase of the route's life foot passengers were not permitted; thereafter they were carried but hardly encouraged, day return passenger fares having been abolished in 1953. Before 2000, there had never been a regular public transport connection at Fishbourne, parking spaces for cars being somewhat limited and expensive (the latter being to discourage people from using a marshalling area as a car park), and all passengers had to pay the full return fare. The small independent operator, the 'Traditional Motor Bus Company', better known as Fountain Coaches, was contracted to operate two services, one from Newport town centre to Ryde Pier, and the other from St Mary's Hospital to Fishbourne. The buses on each route were painted in the same liveries as the ferries with which they connected. The services were quick (limited stops), cheap and convenient, since they connected directly with the ferries. Although the public had said they would use the services if they offered cheap travel, only the Ryde Pier route developed anything approaching promising passenger numbers and then only during the morning and evening commuter periods. Wightlink lost heavily on the operations, which were withdrawn (regrettably without notice) after only five months. Sadly, this may be a fair indication that integrated transport policies are not going to work. If people have cars they will use them, no matter how much it hurts. The perceived convenience of the motorcar appears to be something for which the public is prepared to pay a premium and it has led to a further dramatic development in the history of the Fishbourne Ferry.

MV St. Clare, the new flagship

With four large ferries operating a half-hourly service, sometimes struggling to do so, rumours in early 2000 that a fifth ship was likely to be added to the service were dismissed by many as fanciful speculation. However, Wightlink were determined that there was space for an additional, larger ship. At the beginning of 2000 a detailed brief and plan was submitted to 23 shipyards, four of them British. None of the yards that built the previous ships of the Fishbourne fleet were in the running because, without exception, they had closed. Wightlink broke with tradition by awarding the contract for the construction of a conventional ship to a foreign yard for the first time. The Remontowa yard of Gdansk in Poland was selected from a shortlist of three on the basis of cost, experience, quality and the ability to meet the required delivery date of July 2001. The new ship was required to meet

St. Clare *dwarfs* St. Catherine *at the end of her delivery voyage from Gdansk on 16 July 2001. At £11.5 million the innovative new ship was a huge investment in what was already a well stocked route. Although she serves her purpose, sadly she does not appear to have been greeted as warmly as many previous additions to the Isle of Wight car ferry fleets.*

the following broad specification:

1 Maximum length that could be accommodated in the Camber Docks
2 Increased capacity
3 Increased freight capacity without losing car capacity
4 Must dovetail with the existing linkspans
5 Draft similar to existing 'Saint class' vessels
6 Two-hour cycle to be maintained

The ship was designed by the Portsmouth based naval architects Hart Fenton, who are made up from the former Sealink's own design department. A length increase of 9m over the 'Saint class' ships was made. This provided an initial gain in capacity. The third requirement (above) was achieved by incorporating a fixed upper car deck allowing cars to be accommodated above freight vehicles – not hitherto possible on any other cross Solent ferry. To restore stability lost by situating a deck load of cars at high level, with a corresponding increase in height of the passenger accommodation above, the upper passenger lounge and the bridge structure were fabricated from lightweight aluminium alloy. Further stability was gained by increasing the beam by 1.8metres over the existing ships. An untidy, but unavoidable means of making a broader ship fit the existing berths was to set the prow ramps and the superstructure off centre. This is clearly illustrated in the hull sections diagram (lower right view at Figure 17) and the general arrangement diagrams (Figures 9 and 10).

There appear to be commonly held beliefs that the ship was either an existing completed ship or the design was completed around an existing hull. Wightlink are emphatic that the design was bespoke. Indeed, there would be little chance of finding an existing ship with a laterally asymmetric layout extending right up to the upper decks, which just happened to fit berths peculiar to the Fishbourne service. Similarly there would be scant chance of finding an existing, shallow-draft hull of this format, or one where the format could be adapted more easily than building a new one from scratch.

To gain access to the upper car deck, side casings were chosen instead of the previous single central casing arrangement, but the port one was offset inboard allowing access ramps to be situated outside of it. The two ramps, each hinged at the ship's mid-length end, would swing down to the main deck and up to the upper car deck. Cars stowed on the upper deck face in the opposite direction to those below. In their stowed, level position at mid-height, the ramps were designed for use as additional mezzanine decks, although they are rarely used as such. The main four-lane wide mezzanine decks were incorporated in three sections on the main through deck.

For propulsion the choice of a four VSP layout was a logical one for a number of reasons. A larger ship would require more power, and more still if the two-hour cycle was to be maintained because loading time would be increased with the higher vehicular capacity. Deeper propellers were not an option if the toughest specification of them all (a shallow draft) was to be complied with, therefore there would have to be more of them. Four propellers would also allow bidirectional operation, saving time otherwise spent swinging on passage. Additionally there would be sufficient reserve of power for the ship to virtually maintain full service at up to Beaufort 6-7 with one engine shut down. The propeller units are the same size as those in the 'Saint class', but differ by having oil coolers incorporated and also reduction gearboxes with shaft/propeller step down ratios of 10:1 rather than 7.5:1

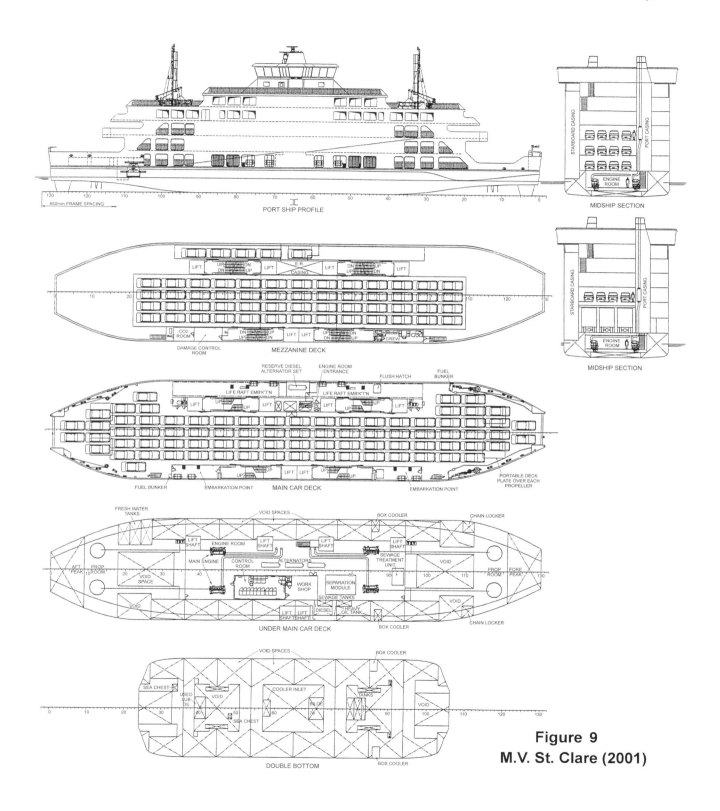

Figure 9
M.V. St. Clare (2001)

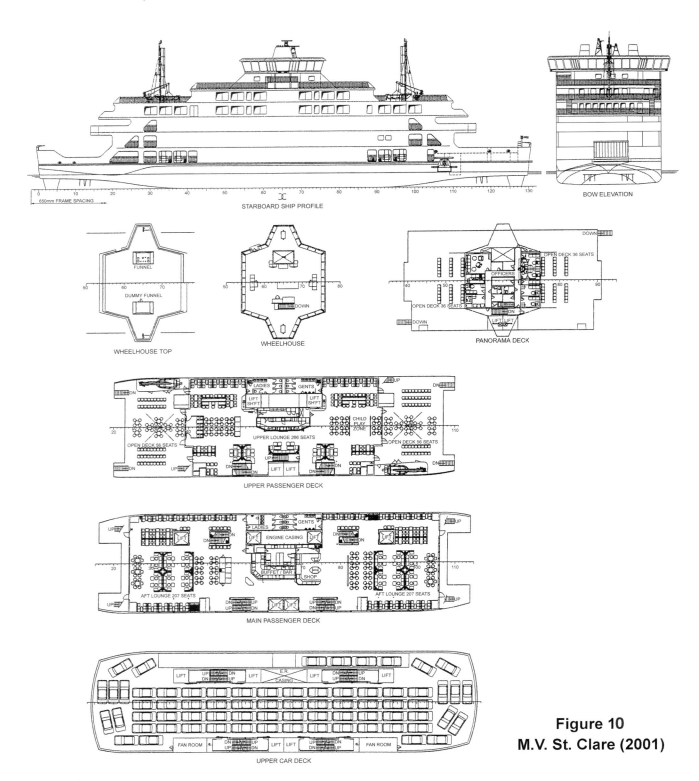

Figure 10
M.V. St. Clare (2001)

because of a higher engine speed. The engines are 5-cylinder Wartsila W5L20C 4-stroke heavy oil engines producing a total of 3860bhp. This may sound like a lot of power, it is in fact only 28% of the output of the former SR.N-4 hovercraft and less than 4% of the Stena HSS catamarans!

Although a bidirectional ship, the layout is asymmetric, with the Fishbourne end designated the bow. Because the distances between the wheelhouse and the propeller units are so great, and due to a more enlightened view on modern systems, an electro-hydraulic system was chosen to link the propellers to the wheelhouse controls, like the Red Funnel 'Raptor class' ferries.

For electrical generation the ship is equipped with three diesel alternator sets, all of which are required in service to provide a massive increase in power demand over the 'Saint class' ships. A useful design feature of the new ship is a standby diesel alternator set installed on main deck level in a chamber beneath

the upper deck access ramps. It is identical to the main generator units, but it is part of an independent system. In the event of a total failure of the regular electrical supply this unit will fire up and provide an emergency supply to power the main engine alarm systems and provide limited lighting, allowing the ship to continue to navigate. Thus, incidents such as that which occurred with *St. Helen* on 6 September 2000 should be avoidable.

Passenger facilities are provided by spacious lounges on two decks, each with beverage facilities. The upper lounge incorporates a pets corner and children's play area and the main lounge, a shop. Luxuriously furnished, the extensive use of large mirrors made the lounges appear even larger. As many as six hydraulic lifts and four internal companionways are provided for access between the decks. Copious open deck space is also available on three levels, connected by companionways which were initially rather steep.

The engine room in St. Clare, *viewed just after completion of her delivery voyage, is large enough and spacious enough to hold a rave. The port aft main engine is to the left, the port forward unit is in the far distance and the exhaust trunking from the starboard aft unit comes in from the right. The auxiliary engines are in the centre distance and the engine room control room window can be seen to the right.*

Wightlink's Senior Master, Captain Geoff Meadway who brought St. Clare *to Portsmouth from the builders at Gdänsk in Poland, makes his address during the inaugural cruise of the ship on 26 September 2001. Under the spotlight is the Wightlink Group Chief Executive, Mr Michael Aiken and in profile, on the top table, is Mr Christopher Bland, Lord Lieutenant of the Isle of Wight and the Chairman of Hovertravel.*

Placed above the lounges is an officer's accommodation deck topped off with a wheelhouse akin to a vast penthouse suite – the floor area being almost 40% of the entire main deck area on the first ferry *Fishbourne*. Inside, control consoles are positioned at both ends and in each bridge wing. Despite the bridge's lofty position the prow ramps are obscured from the navigating officers' view, no more a problem than the view astern on the existing 'Saint class' ships however. Engine room exhaust uptakes are channelled through the port casing and the wheelhouse to a single active funnel, a dummy being positioned on the opposite site for aesthetic purposes only.

The official vehicular capacity of the ship is 186 cars (CEUs) although a shipyard drawing quotes 204 and Figure 9 shows 205.

The keel of the new ship was laid on 17 November 2000 and construction was very rapid indeed with a 24 hour a day, 3 shift rota in operation. She was launched, or rather floated in the dry dock in which she was built, on 26 April 2001 when she was named *St. Clare* by Mrs Sigi Aiken, the wife of Wightlink's

chief executive. The name has a rather tenuous link with the history of Appuldurcombe House on the Isle of Wight. In 1399 Henry IV assigned the former Abbey of Appuldurcombe to the Minories of St Clare, a religious order based at Aldgate in the City of London, to stop the flow of money to its French Mother House during the Hundred Years War.

The contracted delivery date of the new ship was scheduled and written in the contract for 27 June 2001. In the event, MCA checks carried out at Gdansk delayed delivery until mid July. Officially handed over on 9 July, *St. Clare* set sail from Poland on the evening of the 12 July, her passage taking her through the Kiel Canal. Commanded by Captain Geoff Meadway, Wightlink's Route Company Senior Master, and achieving as much as 16 knots during the passage, she arrived in Sandown Bay in the early hours of Monday 16 July before making her grand first entry into her home port at 11.00 am. On a bright summer's morning the new flagship was greeted in the eastern approaches by the catamaran *FastCat Shanklin* and on approaching the harbour mouth, amongst much whistle blasting, she passed the outbound *St. Cecilia* and was followed by the inbound *St. Catherine*. Like most car ferries she is no oil painting (although there are two paintings of her on board), but the overwhelming first impression was the sheer size of the new vessel. At 5359 her GRT was 77% greater than the then largest cross-Solent ferry, Red Funnel's *Red Eagle*. Although *St. Clare* is 9m above the length limit previously set for ships using the Gunwharf linkspan, and she does protrude further out into the open space when berthed, she does not appear to seriously impede the passage of most other vessels that use the Camber Docks.

The first and only trial run of *St. Clare* to Fishbourne took place in foul conditions at 1.30 pm the following day. Her maiden voyage took place only three days later with the 2.30 pm departure from Portsmouth to Fishbourne on Friday 20 July 2001. The first trip was not an overwhelming success. With the first day of the school holidays being chosen for this momentous event it did not turn out to be a public relations coup for Wightlink. It was known from the single trial run that the prow ramp toes were a poor fit with the linkspans. At Fishbourne this problem was still being temporarily overcome by a team of carpenters as the ship approached. Lack of familiarity with the hydraulic systems resulted in a power trip out of the access ramps to the upper car deck when the ship arrived back at Portsmouth. After a single round trip she was taken out of service.

On her first trip *St. Clare* travelled in a unidirectional mode, swinging off Wootton Beacon and again inside the harbour, just like her fleet mates, it being said that she travels best bow first in certain sea conditions. However, she has since normally operated as a true bidirectional ship, bow first operation being restricted to heavy weather when the extra freeboard at the bow provides additional protection.

St. Clare returned to service on 23 July working an occasional third boat roster until more crews had been trained to operate this innovative ship. It was not until early October that she was moved to the second boat diagram (Saturdays only) and 22 October before she began operating this service seven days per week, maintenance periods excluded. This even hours service from Portsmouth operates around the clock missing one trip in the early hours (three on Sundays).

A formal inaugural ceremony for 86 invited guests, including the Polish Ambassador and the Lord Lieutenant of the Isle of Wight, took place on Wednesday 26 September 2001. A service of dedication was performed by the Venerable Mervyn Banting, Archdeacon of the Isle of Wight, and the Royal Marines Band played on board. A cruise of the Solent followed, the ship sailing as far as Newtown Creek.

With numerous Portsmouth-based P&O cross-channel ferries with names such as *Pride of Portsmouth* (a fanciful idea if ever there was one), the new Wightlink ferry was quickly nicknamed the 'Pride of Poland' by the crews and public alike.

Although the sumptuous and extensive lounge facilities are welcomed, the public does not appear to have warmed to *St. Clare* to the same extent as to many previous new ships. Access to the fixed, upper car deck has been one bone of contention. The access ramps are narrow and sighting over cars bonnets is impaired, making some motorists nervous of, or even hostile towards, using them. Furthermore, cars with large turning circles can have trouble manoeuvring once aloft.

The new St. Clare *fires up at Fishbourne on the evening of 15 May 2002. Modifications were carried out to prevent the engines being loaded by the propellers while they were starting up, thereby reducing such soot emissions.*

Consequently loading can be time-consuming and there have been a number of claims for damage to cars. Another less than welcome feature has been machinery vibration transmitted into the passenger lounges. Vibration is more evident than on any of the 'Saint class' ships. Being high-sided and relatively narrow, the new ship can be very uncomfortable in beam seas; in easterly gales she takes a similar deviated route to the pioneer ferries and in stormy weather she remains in port.

Needless-to-say the Fishbourne residents did not warm to *St. Clare* either. Soon after details of the new ship were released to the press a new organisation, known as the Fishbourne Residents Group, circulated a glossy leaflet to all households in the Wootton Creek area. The leaflet highlighted problems that the group considered had been caused by Wightlink, principally noise, excess traffic and coastal erosion. It objected to plans to carry out extra dredging close to the Fishbourne terminal and the installation of a raised walkway allowing passenger access directly to the lounges on the ships. Wightlink stated that the dredging was to allow the Yarmouth ferries to use the old slipway, thus enabling some sort of a service to be maintained in the event of a linkspan failure. The group considered that it was more than a coincidence that the plans were announced at the same time as the introduction of a fifth ship. Clearly an inbound ferry would be able to heave-to adjacent to the linkspan, in the channel to the slipway, and

wait for a berthed ferry to depart, allowing a faster turnaround. Although periodic trial runs to Fishbourne were carried out over a period of about a year with each of the 'C class' ferries, the plans for both the walkway and the dredging were officially dropped. The Yarmouth ferries trials usually took place in the dead of night (when one of them could be spared from their own route), initially at high water, but later at lower states of the tide when the silted up slipway was inaccessible. Once again, suspicions were aroused. Voith-Schneider propelled ferries do stir up the seabed and during their sorties the Yarmouth ferries passed through an area where the service ferries would ideally wait. Nonetheless, the service ferries have not used this area (quite). Instead (when tidal conditions permit) they usually wait reasonably close to the terminal on the east side of the channel where it was widened in 1989. The 'C class' sorties were in fact clearing the way for their intended purpose, culminating with *Cenwulf* being used in overnight service on the route on 4 and 5 January 2003 while maintenance work was carried out on the linkspan. However, such an operation would be impossible at low water without first dredging the channel.

A few modifications have been carried to *St. Clare* since she entered service. New prow ramp outer leaves that fitted the linkspans better were soon installed. In order to reduce heavy smoke emissions a system was installed that inhibited

Following a number of trial runs, on 4 January 2003 Cenwulf *was brought down from Lymington to operate the night-time service while work was carried out on the Fishbourne linkspan. She is seen disgorging cars over the old slipway at the end of her first trip. It is believed that this was the very first occasion that the 1973-built* Cenwulf *had been used in commercial service on the Fishbourne route.*

the engines from being loaded by the propellers as soon as they were started. Although the MCA had approved the design of the outer deck companionways and all drawings when the ship was in build in Poland, a letter was written to Wightlink six months into the ship's service regarding their steepness. The MCA expressed concern to Wightlink who replaced them with less steep versions.

Despite some shortcomings *St. Clare* is an illustration of Wightlink's commitment to this route above all others. She may well be a sign of the way ahead and should confirm the Fishbourne car ferry as the premier service to the Isle of Wight for the foreseeable future.

Recent developments

St. Clare was introduced in response to the ever-increasing demand for space on the service. With the best will in the world, there is not really room for five ships on the Portsmouth to Fishbourne route. The operator has been faced with the same dilemma as in the late 'fifties and late 'seventies ie the service has reached its throughput limit at peak periods, largely due to the restrictive, bottlenecking nature of the terminals. Amongst a number of options that could ease the situation would be the following:

1 Increasing the throughput capacity of the terminals by
   a) Reducing periods when a berth is vacant
   b) Loading and unloading two ships simultaneously
   c) Loading and unloading single ships on two levels
2 Operating a completely different route, or
3 Introducing a supplementary route

Option 1a would be relatively simple but of limited benefit and it would not provide a long-term solution. It could be achieved by dredging an area close to the terminals to allow incoming ferries to wait next to the berth for outgoing ferries to depart. There is scope to do this at Fishbourne, but not at Portsmouth. Another way to reduce the period when a linkspan is empty would be to have a fewer number of larger ships, but the cost would be massive and four ships like *St. Clare* (the maximum size that can be accommodated in the Camber Docks) would have room for only ten more cars than the present fleet of five. Furthermore, a fleet of 'St Clare class' ships would be less capable of maintaining an all-weather service than the standard ships.

Option 1b could only be achieved effectively if a second linkspan was constructed at each terminal. At Fishbourne this would be reasonably straightforward; Portsmouth would be more problematical. Side-loading facilities could be provided at the lay-by berth, but a vessel berthed at the present linkspan would block access. Of course, two ships could sail together, bound for adjacent linkspans at Fishbourne, but they would

have to keep pace with each other at all times in order to avoid snarl ups.

Option 1c, similar to that adopted by Red Funnel in 2003, would perhaps be more viable because it should hasten loading and unloading and reduce the length of time that a ferry is at a berth. However, any of options 1 would further despoil the estuary of Wootton Creek, the subject of ongoing environmental studies, and heap more congestion and misery on the long-suffering residents of Fishbourne. Wightlink has already dropped plans for additional dredged areas and the installation of a high-level passenger access walkway at Fishbourne.

It is unlikely that a completely different route would be a suitable option. To be fully viable the route would have to be no longer than between the Gunwharf and Fishbourne. The Gunwharf is the perfect terminal site, being just inside the harbour mouth and Wightlink has no intention of vacating it. On the other side of the Solent there is no possible nearby site apart from Ryde or Fishbourne. An over-ambitious reclamation proposal at Ryde during the 1980s did include a car ferry berth, but this scheme never got further than the drawing board. Ryde Sands are vast and would impose the same restrictions today as they did when Ryde was abandoned as a vehicular landing place in 1926. Ryde Pier extends beyond the sands but it is an old structure, which without prohibitive financial outlay would be unsuitable for heavy commercial transport and the volume of private cars that uses the Fishbourne service today. Nor would it be easy to provide a suitable all-weather berth at the end of an exposed pier.

Reinvigoration of the old scheme to build a supplementary car ferry berth at Ryde Pier has now emerged as the preferred option. It is proposed to use the old tramway pier (disused since 1969) for access and for accommodating waiting cars. Though still an expensive option, it would be cheaper and more practicable than building an all-weather facility for all traffic and should ease the summer weekend bottleneck problem at Fishbourne. The proposed mainland terminal arrangements were not clear at the time of writing. The Continental Ferry Port would be one possible site. The length of passage from there to Ryde Pier is almost the same as from the Gunwharf to Fishbourne, so theoretically the convenient two-hour cycle could be maintained, but additional staffing costs would probably be prohibitive. More likely, an additional berth at the Gunwharf lay-by would be used. A ship could only get in and out when the present linkspan is vacant, but if two ships departed one after the other there would be no problem with queuing at the other end because they would have different destinations. A drawback of using the Gunwharf terminal would be less easing of congestion in that vicinity.

Needless to say, the announcement of this scheme was greeted with hostility amongst residents of Ryde, but presumably not by those in Fishbourne!

And so, the story continues. Where it will lead next?

Chapter 5: Traffic

Traffic is shown graphically on Figures 11 to 15 and, by and large, the charts speak for themselves. The Phase One data for cars and lorries is so dwarfed by the subsequent figures that a separate graph has been compiled for this period (Figure 12). The opposing effect that the Second World War had on domestic traffic and lorries is obvious. Not so clear is the ratio of passenger numbers for each car carried. The ratio has always been between 2.5 and 3.7, except during the war when it rose to over ten, indicating that many foot passengers were using the route at that time. Motorcycle traffic has not been recorded since 1987 and the data for solo and combination motorcycles have been combined on figure 11. Combinations accounted for a mere 0.5% of the total by the mid 'eighties, having peaked at 33% in the mid 'fifties. Records for coaches commenced in 1962 with only 202 vehicles carried. By 2002 the number had increased eighty-two-fold!

Figure 13 shows how the fleet capacity and the number of crossings have changed over the years. The dip in the capacity in 1993 was due to *St. Helen* being laid up. Unfortunately there is a gap in the data for the number of single trips, but the trend is clear.

Figure 14 gives a clear indication of the general passenger trends between 1973 and 1998. Over this period overall passenger numbers crossing the Solent via Portsmouth or Southsea rose by about 18% but an ever-increasing proportion of them were accompanying road vehicles. Assuming very few foot passengers use the Fishbourne Ferry, then only about 19% of passengers crossed in vehicles during 1973, rising to 55% by 1998. It is interesting that while passenger numbers using the Portsmouth Harbour to Ryde Pier service have dwindled (they have increased slightly since 1998) the Southsea to Ryde hovercraft has flourished.

Figure 15 illustrates how the three cross-Solent car ferry services have fared since 1986. Red Funnel has been increasing its market share of domestic car traffic since 1986 but the rate of increase slowed once their new ships were introduced in 1994 while their freight traffic figures began to take off when their new tonnage arrived. There are some curious annual blips in the figures for coach traffic, but the general trend for all types of traffic up until the introduction of *St. Clare* is clear. 2002 was the first full year that *St. Clare* was in service and in that year and 2003 the Fishbourne service significantly gained the share of coach traffic. It is still too early to predict long term trends due to *St. Clare*'s introduction, especially as Red Funnel is currently enlarging its fleet. One might logically predict that Red Funnel will continue to close the gap on its competitor.

Although the annual number of freight vehicles has been somewhat erratic of late, the general trend in the volume of all traffic on the Fishbourne Ferry remains upwards. During 2003 there were 25,046 crossings between Portsmouth / Fishbourne. The average numbers of passengers and vehicles per trip can be calculated to be as follows: 112 passengers, 34 cars, five lorries and 0.7 coaches. Assuming that the average lorry or coach occupies the same space as $3\frac{3}{4}$ CPUs (cars) it can be calculated that the average vehicular loading is currently running at approximately 37% of deck space. With many services full to capacity there must be many more that are very lightly loaded and some that are totally uneconomic. There remains plenty of scope for traffic levels to rise still further.

The Saturday at the end of the spring half-term break is always a busy time at Fishbourne, but on 5 June 2004 the Queen's Harbour Master at Portsmouth closed the harbour for a while, allowing the procession of ships taking part in the D-Day commemoration to leave port. This delayed services on the Fishbourne route by 45 minutes, resulting in a choked marshalling area. Compare this view of Fishbourne with the one on page 27.

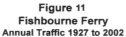

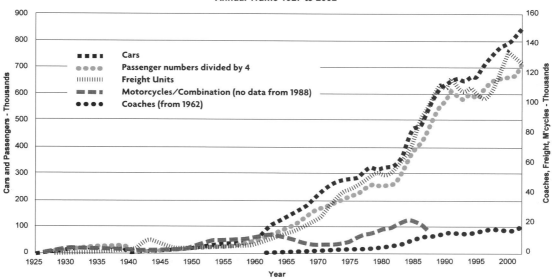

Figure 11
Fishbourne Ferry
Annual Traffic 1927 to 2002

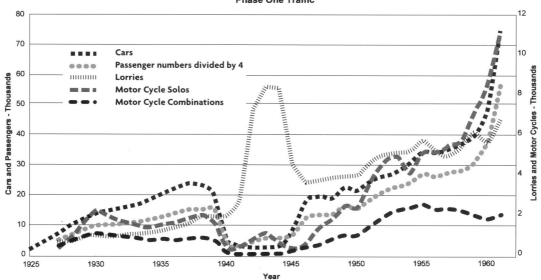

Figure 12
Fishbourne Ferry
Phase One Traffic

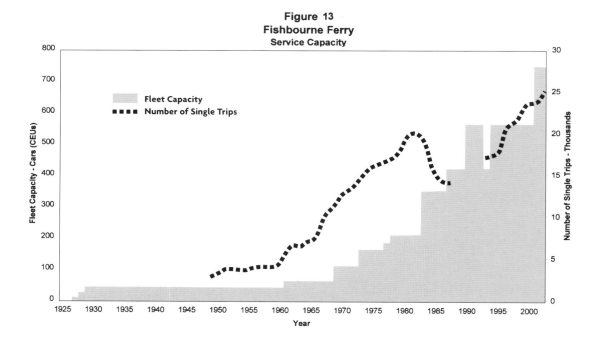

Figure 13
Fishbourne Ferry
Service Capacity

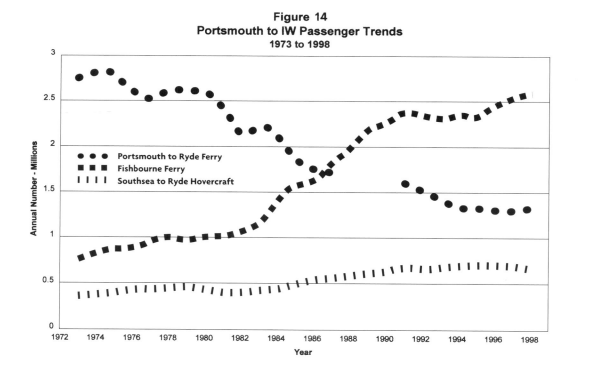

Figure 14
Portsmouth to IW Passenger Trends
1973 to 1998

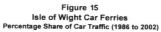

Figure 15
Isle of Wight Car Ferries
Percentage Share of Car Traffic (1986 to 2002)

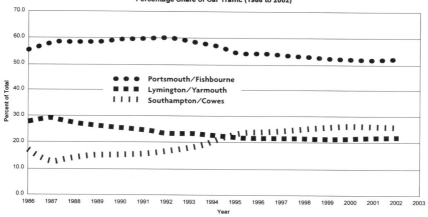

Percentage Share of Freight Units (1986 to 2002)

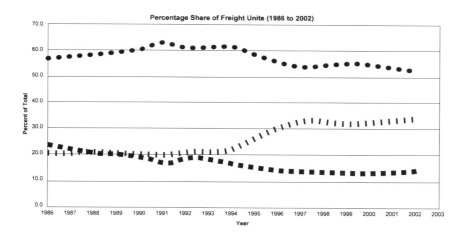

Percentage Share of Coach Traffic (1986 to 2002)

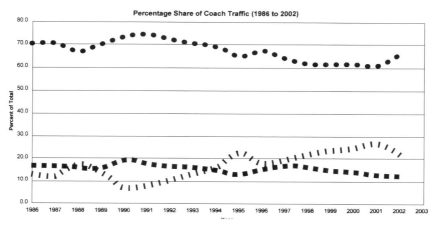

Chapter 6: Fares and Monopolies and Mergers Commission Audit

Cross-Solent fares, particularly vehicular fares, have long been a bone of contention with the travelling public; and let's make no bones about it – they are dear; the last General Manager of Sealink Isle of Wight, Bill Gibbons, admitted as much during a TV interview many years ago. People from all walks of life have always complained about the fares and will probably continue to do so. "This is the most expensive stretch of water in the world" was (and remains) one of the most common claims made about cross-Solent travel. Objections to the fare structures became so vociferous that in 1990 a Monopolies and Mergers Commission audit was carried out on all cross-Solent ferry operations. Early in 1992 their 124-page document was finally published, but it did not bring much joy to the travelling public. The auditors concluded that whilst Wightlink's profits, and in particular those of the Fishbourne car ferry, were high, there were insufficient grounds to impose any controls. The Commission came to the following broad conclusions:

1 Whilst the concerns of Island residents were understandable, the smaller companies were making losses or small profits; with Wightlink's main competitor operating old and uneconomical ships. In contrast, Wightlink had the major market share and enjoyed substantial profits based on efficient operation of modern ships on a prime route. In the Commission's view, neither its level of profitability nor its level of fares was sufficient under the circumstances to be regarded as against the public interest.

2 It was felt that the interests of Islanders and other users were best served by an increase in competition, which may then put pressure on fare levels, rather than artificially imposed fares reductions that might drive out existing competition.

3 At that time it was considered too early to say whether the recent increase in competition [referring to the emergence of the short-lived 'Cowes Express' service] would prove sustainable or develop further. Competition with Wightlink could not be regarded as strong and it remained the dominant provider of reference services, a position that could be open to abuse. This was a matter of some concern and would require further monitoring.

4 Other aspects of recent performance had clearly been to the benefit of the users of the services, in particular the increase in the capacity and usage of most ferry services and the availability of cheap promotional fares. The operators would no doubt recognise it as in their own interests to continue to improve their services to meet user needs and thus alleviate some of the criticism. There would be particular benefits from greater transparency of freight charges.

5 Having considered the matters, the Commission concluded that;
   a No steps were being taken by Wightlink or the parent company, Sea Containers, for the purpose of exploiting or maintaining a monopoly situation.
   b There was no action or omission on the part of Wightlink or Sea Containers attributable to the existence of that monopoly situation, and
   c There were no facts that operated, or may have been expected to operate, against the public interest.

The auditors had examined the accounts of the various operators and listened to the views of users, the operators and other interested parties. For the first time, the accounts for individual routes were laid bare for public examination, something that Wightlink (and before them Sealink) had hitherto steadfastly refused to allow. It was found that the Fishbourne ferry was by far the most profitable route. Based on the 1990 figures the route made a net profit (after depreciation) of £5,237,000 on a turnover of £19,041,000. The profit per CPU (the standard car unit) was £4.50 and the profit per trip was £295. The other routes did not fare as well, with the Wightlink passenger ferry making a profit of only 1p per passenger trip. Red Funnel's car ferry service came off worst of all with a net loss of £415,000 on a turnover of £5,613,000; they had actually been subsidising car drivers to the tune of £1.30 per trip! Wightlink's profits may have been 'towards the limit of acceptability' but what could the Commission do? If they had imposed fare reductions on the Wightlink car ferries Red Funnel would have been forced to follow suit if it were not to lose more customers. With Red Funnel already making a loss it is easy to see what the likely outcome would have been and the Solent probably would have had a monopoly. This may not have been very pleasing news to cross-Solent travellers but the fact that the competing Companies have vastly different lengths of route is probably the factor, more than any other, that is holding fares up. The Commission's report did not appear to be a sham, as some people suggested, but a comprehensive and subjective analysis. Distressing as it may have been, it would seem that the Commission was justified in not penalising Wightlink.

But was the Solent the most expensive stretch of water in the world? The Commission assessed the cost per mile of many ferry routes around our shores. As a rule of thumb: the longer the route, the cheaper the cost per mile, but life's never that straightforward. Even within the confines of the Solent the situation is confused because the routes are of differing lengths, while the fares are similar. The Lymington to Yarmouth route was (mile for mile) over $2^{1}/_{2}$ times more expensive than the Red Funnel route from Southampton to Cowes and almost twice as expensive as the Fishbourne ferry. Of course, one could not expect the fares to be pro-rata on route distance, because the Isle of Wight would end up with only one very intensely used service. In a survey of 54 car-carrying routes around the coast of Britain (clockwise from Dover to John O'Groats), Lymington to Yarmouth was the 5th most expensive in terms of the peak-period return fare for a 4 metre car – the most expensive four were all very short routes in Western Scotland. The Fishbourne ferry was 18th in the table: the major routes of Dover to Calais, Folkestone to Boulogne, Stranraer to Larne, Fishguard to Rosslare and Holyhead to Dun Laoghaire and Dublin all being more costly per mile. Red Funnel's route from Southampton to Cowes was 28th. In terms of peak-period return passenger fares on 67 routes, Lymington to Yarmouth was 8th, Portsmouth to Fishbourne was 21st and Southampton to Cowes was 42nd. The Isle of Wight routes did not compare quite so favourably at off-peak times; nevertheless, with the possible exception of the Lymington to Yarmouth route, the claim that the Solent is the most expensive stretch of water in the world was not proven. The analysis did not take account of promotional fares that existed on many of the assessed routes, including those on the Solent.

The auditors also assessed how fares had increased over the previous six seasons, but not the long-term change of fares in relation to the inflationary indices. Had they looked into this they would have found that the standard fares had been going up after a period of general decline. This would not have been particularly straightforward to quantify because the fare structure has changed many times over the years. As far as the Fishbourne service is concerned, when the route opened in 1926 there were three fare bands depending on car length. The number of bands rose to seven during the 'sixties and early 'seventies, falling back to two at the time of the audit. Supplements for longer cars were introduced before 1960. Day return passenger fares on the Fishbourne route were introduced in 1931 and abolished in 1953 (they were reinstated in 2000). Separate summer and winter tariffs for vehicles came in during 1977. When the cheaper winter tariffs were first introduced day returns were offered as two-day returns, later increasing to three-day returns, before reverting back to one-day returns once again. In 1984 special 'Bargain Breaks' were introduced, offering reduced rates for various short excursions. Changes to the tariff structure have

continued since the audit. For 1992 only, a peak summer tariff was introduced. From the following year until 1996 the standard summer tariff ran on until the end of the year or beyond. In 1997 the peak summer tariff over the school holiday period was brought back and, from 1998, Easter, May holiday weekends and peak summer Saturdays received an additional supplement. Books of vehicle tickets offering modest discounts had been available since 1933, but in 1994 'Multilink' tickets were introduced offering much larger discounts for Island residents who travel frequently. There is also the special Island resident rate, offering a minimum 37% off the standard mainland fares. Employee discount schemes with a number of Isle of Wight companies also exist. There were many other alterations to the tariffs, far too many to discuss here. It was very complex. The changes in the fares structure is so manifest that there is always going to be an argument for why the tariffs are not unfair. Nevertheless, the handy timetable and fares leaflets (not available in 2004) provide a lasting record of fares over the years. By relating them to the inflationary indices we can find whether or not the often-heard claim that fares today are cheaper (in real terms) than they used to be is really true. In some cases it is true, in most it is not – and the variation is sometimes enormous.

Standard vehicular fares reached their nadir in the late 'seventies and early 'eighties, depending on the type, since when (with the exception of special excursions) they have been generally rising. By the time of the 1990 audit some tariffs remained very reasonable. A car and four people, travelling in the winter of 1990, and taking advantage of the 'all-in day excursion', paid only 41% of the equivalent fare (in real terms) as in 1926, the year the route opened. The driver of a 5.5 metre long car paid 63% (41% for Island residents) of the 1926 fare for an ordinary vehicle return ticket in winter. In summer the fare rose to 74% (55%). The equivalent fare for a 4 metre car was 67% (46%) in winter and 84% (63%) in summer. It was, in fact, foot passengers that came off badly. Passenger fares have rarely been as cheap as they were in the early days and they have been on the increase since the mid 'fifties. By 1990 the passenger return fare was 216% of the effective price in 1926.

After the audit, in 1992, fares for motorcycles and motorcycle combinations were consolidated into a single tariff, seeing winter solo fares double. In 1994 the shorter car category (the one used for the MMC's comparative assessment) was abolished, increasing the winter fare to 107% and the summer fare to 117% of the effective 1926 level. 'Multilink' vehicle tickets for Island residents were initially sold in books of five, ten, 25 and 50. Today they come in books of eight, 12, 25 & 50 and they are without peak period penalties. In 2003, for a car plus driver, they offered between a 32% and 43% saving on the Isle of Wight discounted period return fare (or between a 67% and 72% saving on the peak summer Saturday mainland fare). An Island resident using one of eight 'Multilink' car and driver tickets today would pay the

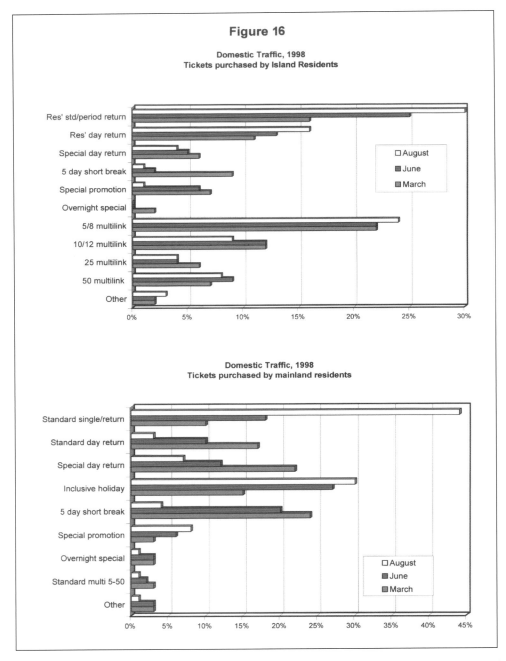

Figure 16

Domestic Traffic, 1998
Tickets purchased by Island Residents

Domestic Traffic, 1998
Tickets purchased by mainland residents

equivalent of 38% of the standard return fare payable in 1926, prior to the introduction of multiple tickets. A ticket from a book of 50 would cost as little as 32%. 'Multilink' tickets are also available for motorcycles and foot passengers, the latter being for Island and mainland residents. Despite the discount, 'Multilink' passenger tariffs are somewhat higher than the effective standard passenger fare in 1926. By 2003, only

'Multilink' car ticket users and those taking advantage of special discounts paid less than in the early days of the route. All standard tariffs, except winter tariffs for cars in excess of 15ft in length and Island resident car tickets, were more expensive. A mainland motorcyclist travelling on a peak summer Saturday seemed to come off worst of all; the fare having gone up by four times the rate of inflation since 1926!

The above comparisons are based on the previous year's September figures of the 'All Items' Retail Price Index for the post-1947 period and the Cost of Living Index pre-1947.

In 2004 the fare structure changed somewhat, with most vehicular tariffs listed as 'from'. Generally speaking, fares were cheapest for travel mid-week or late in the day, with shorter stays away and when booked in advance. There was further discount for booking online. Although, by-and-large, standard fares were not listed and inflation busting increases became hard to determine, some good deals could be had. For example, a day return for a car plus four passengers travelling before the end of March could be up to 33% cheaper than a year earlier and a mainland motorcyclist travelling out on a peak summer Saturday could pay up to 21% less. The message now seems to be to pick your time of travel carefully – if you can. The costliest way to travel, with a vehicle, is just turn up at the booking office and pay for a trip there and then.

The figures for standard fares may not be very encouraging but in fact only a small proportion of ticket sales are now standard. A survey of domestic ticket sales, carried out in the months of March, June and August 1998 showed that most tickets purchased by Islanders were discounted beyond the already discounted residents' rates in one way or another, as Figure 16 shows. In the month of March, 84% of sales were either discounted tickets or day returns, falling to 70% in August. Almost half of tickets sold were 'Multilinks'! Of mainland residents, 90% bought either discounted tickets or day returns in March, falling to 56% in the main tourist month of August.

Additionally, Wightlink point out that the customer enjoys ever improving facilities and now has a much better service frequency to choose from. This is true and it should be remembered that the service started off with nothing more than small and open towboats and nothing like a decent passenger lounge appeared until 1969. Between 1995 and 1999 over £3 million was spent on on-board and terminal refurbishment throughout the three services. Over the same period there was a 26.5% increase in the number of services operated on the Fishbourne route and similar large increases elsewhere. Wightlink claim that the frequency of crossings is the key to increasing the tourist business to the Isle of Wight. People know that it is easy to get to, and if they miss their ferry there will be another one along in half an hour. Wightlink also point out that their wide portfolio of fares offers the greatest discounts for those customers who can be flexible with their travel arrangements. Unfortunately, unlike many foreign holiday destinations, Britain is still largely encumbered with the 'weekend changeover'. In mainland areas this is of little consequence, but on an offshore island it places an enormous burden on the ferry companies during summer weekends. Wightlink say that higher weekend fares are not to make a fast buck but to encourage people to travel at other times in order to spread the load; the wide range of

off-peak discounts also being part of this ploy. It also emphasises that comparisons with fares on the Scottish island services often ignore the fact that they are subsidised. The company further point out that comparisons made with cross-channel fares are sometimes unfair because standard Wightlink fares are often compared with cross-channel promotional fares. P&O's advertised standard return fare for a car and a family of four from Portsmouth to Le Havre was in excess of £500 at peak periods in 2003 – not at all cheap! Furthermore, on the long cross-channel trips the operators have the benefit of the considerable revenue derived from on board restaurant and shop sales – and until 1999 they also made a mint from duty-free sales and the traffic they generated. Nevertheless the P&O services from Portsmouth run at a loss while the French government subsidises the Brittany Ferries services.

Commercial tariffs are a completely different kettle of fish. The commercial sector frequently claims that ferry fares are crippling their businesses and discouraging others from relocating on the Isle of Wight. Commercial vehicle tariffs are a much greyer area than domestic fares, but whilst many smaller businesses must be adversely affected by the additional transportation costs, the two ferry Companies are competitive in this area. Regular users negotiate their own rates (up to 75% discount for some of the larger carriers) and in some cases domestic costs subsidise them. Transportation costs to the Isle of Wight are probably lower than to remote areas of the mainland and Northern Ireland. It is possible that ferry tariffs have no influence on the cost of many goods, although they maybe used as an excuse for higher prices. The following points provide food for thought:

a   Mainstream supermarket prices vary from area to area. This would appear to be dependent on each area's social makeup. Although prices on the Isle of Wight are not the cheapest, they are lower than in many mainland areas, including many large towns and cities along the south coast.

b   A sharp-eyed Island resident many years ago noticed that Isle of Wight tomatoes were cheaper in Portsmouth than on the Island, and cheaper still in London.

c   Petrol prices were much higher on the Island until Tesco started shipping fuel across in road tankers on the car ferries, an inefficient and costly method of transportation compared with the usual bulk shipment via Kingston Wharf at East Cowes.

d   For businesses that relocate on the Isle of Wight there may be ferry costs to pay, but another frequent claim about the Isle of Wight is that wage levels are generally lower than on the mainland.

e   The price of cars is higher in Britain than in mainland Europe. Britain is an island, but is there ever the suggestion that cross-channel ferry fares are to blame?

As far as the domestic traveller is concerned there can be

no doubt that the level of fares creates a huge burden, but it seems not an excessive burden. It should be borne in mind that the ferry companies have increased capacity (and fares) but can still fill their ships up. Regardless of ferry fares, motoring is an expensive business (£102.59 per week, according to an RAC report in March 2004) and it is an expense that people seem prepared to pay. Nonetheless, the payment of ferry fares is an inescapable part of Island life for anybody who wants (or needs) to get on or off. Additionally, Island residents form a captive market; however they do have the benefit of the most substantial discounts and people are usually on the lookout for a bargain, as Figure 16 shows.

Since the majority of people do not benefit from the highest discounts – the less expensive 'Multilink' tickets will be purchased by a minority of frequent travellers – then it is inevitable that there will be complaints about high fares, principally vehicular fares, which cost the most money. It could be argued that there is more justification in complaining about passenger tariffs since they have increased the most and, after all, people cannot travel anywhere without their own bodies. Furthermore, standard passenger fares are the only tariffs that are not discounted for Islanders. Unfortunately there seems little hope of passenger fares in general coming down significantly. If passenger fares were to fall it must happen across the board in order to create a level playing field. Over the years, the public has been gradually abandoning the passenger ferries, instead choosing to travel by car. In 1990, the Portsmouth to Ryde passenger service made a profit of only 1p per passenger trip. It is unlikely to have improved today because passenger numbers are lower than they were then, whilst the fleet size has doubled. It is equally unlikely that a reduction in fares would be rewarded by a huge increase in foot passenger traffic, simply because for most it is not convenient to travel that way any more. Substantial reductions in passenger tariffs would probably see the passenger services flounder and that would do no good at all. It can be surmised from the above that the public's tendency to travel by car has probably been the principal factor in pushing up passenger fares.

Unfortunately for users, many tariffs have been increasing by more than the inflation rate each year, making the services progressively more expensive. Even the 'Multilink' fares are not such good value as they used to be. Whether or not these increases are justified or fair is a moot point. So why are fares so high? One reason is that the Isle of Wight is the only major island within the EU that does not benefit from subsidised ferry transport. Also, it cannot have helped that the MMC gave Wightlink a clean bill of health in 1990 and it is perhaps unfortunate that the audit was carried out at a time when its main competitor appeared to have lost its way. Like it or not, Wightlink and Red Funnel are private companies and a good deal of their revenues are used for repaying debt. At the time of the audit the predecessors to Wightlink were part of Sea Containers, which, in 1984, had purchased the entire Sealink Empire for £66 million. In June 1995 CINVen bought the Isle of Wight services for £107.5 million. Taking inflation into account this is approximately the same amount as Sea Containers paid for the whole of Sealink! In 2001 Wightlink management completed their buyout of CINVen for a total £156 million. Loans are used to fund takeovers, but the fact that the financial institutions are prepared to dole out such whopping sums speaks volumes.

The principal reason that fares are so high must be because, like property prices, they are driven by market forces. But unlike high property prices, high fares are never regarded as good news. Ferry fares keep rising because the demand for tickets keeps rising. If people used the ferries even slightly less then fares would probably fall, as happened during the 2001 foot and mouth crisis when there were some very cheap special offers. It seems unlikely that the public would boycott the ferries as a form of protest, however. People may be united in their condemnation of high fares but as an action force they are powerless individuals.

The ferry companies are really only acting as one might expect a commercial enterprise to act in a free-market economy: they are maximising profits whilst keeping expenditure as low as possible. Nevertheless, they still operate uneconomic services. Clearly, the high standard of service is having more of an effect at encouraging use of the car ferries than the level of fares is at discouraging it. No doubt many people are deterred from visiting the Isle of Wight because the fares are so high and many others say they will not visit again for the same reason. But summer-time loading is still very high and obviously many people still do wish to take their holidays on the Island. Tourists are filling up the ferries like never before, but with cars rather than passengers. At summer weekends foot passengers used to pass through Ryde in their thousands and queue along most of the length of the pier before squeezing on to one of the fleet of six passenger ferries. The old passenger ships could accommodate between 1000 and 1300 passengers but a 'Saint class' ferry with a full load of cars is unlikely to have more than four or five hundred passengers on board. Should the volume of people that flocked through the terminals during the 'fifties visit the Island today, but do so by car, then much of the Isle of Wight's road system would surely grind to a halt.

Chapter 7: Mishaps

Prior to 1983 the type of mishap most likely to befall the Fishbourne ferry was a slipway grounding. All of the ships prior to the 'Saint class' vessels have been stranded at one time or another. Fortunately groundings did not occur frequently, perhaps about once a year on average, but when they did happen they came without a moment's notice and could cause utter chaos, particularly during busy periods. The terminal became totally unusable until the ship was re-floated. The other ships in operation sometimes operated diagonal services to Yarmouth or Lymington. Skippers had to be on their guard during falling tides and had to constantly adjust the position of their ships. Groundings were most likely to occur midway between high and low water, when the tide was in full ebb. They were also far more likely to occur at Fishbourne than at Portsmouth, where the level falls more slowly.

Typically a grounding would be preceded by complete normality; it was only when thrust was applied and the ship didn't move that all hell broke loose. Immediate Tannoy announcements would ask urgently for all drivers to return to their vehicles. Within a couple of minutes the slipway would be a scene of utter chaos. Cars would be strewn everywhere in no order whatsoever, abuse could be hurled, but it was usually to no avail. There was nothing that could be done other than direct vehicles to the company's other terminal and then just wait, typically for five or six hours, for the tide to come in again. In the meantime the terminal would fall silent.

A particularly chaotic grounding occurred on 6 August 1960 when *Wootton* became stranded at Fishbourne. The incident was notable because it occurred on a peak summer Saturday during the period when, even on a trouble-free day, the pioneer ferries were barely able to cope with the traffic. Although *Wootton* was attempting to leave 10 minutes earlier than her scheduled departure time of 3.15 pm she was already aground. Cars were disembarked to lighten her but to no avail. In the meantime *Fishbourne* had arrived and had to drop anchor offshore after she failed to pull her sister free. Meanwhile long queues of traffic built up on both sides of the Solent. In order to free *Wootton* at the earliest possible moment during the rising tide enough cars were loaded on to the ship to weigh down the stern and lift the bow. A launch sent over from Portsmouth was then able to pull the vessel clear. The ship was freed soon after 7.00 pm and then the three ferries operated a shuttle service until 2.35 am, when the last of the stranded cars left Fishbourne. There was praise for the staff on both sides, who remained calm and polite during the chaos.

In May 1965 the non-resident ferry *Lymington* became stranded on the Fishbourne slipway for a period of seven hours. In March 1972, just after BST had begun, the second *Fishbourne* became stuck on the Fishbourne slipway, again for seven hours. Stranded motorists suggested that the clock change was to blame and that somebody forgot that tides do not change to suit altered clocks. The manager described this as "an interesting theory". The following year there was a repeat performance. On Sunday 17 March 1973, the day the clocks went on, *Fishbourne* once again became stranded at Fishbourne. She grounded at 2.45 pm and was not re-floated for 7¼ hours. It was again suggested that the clock change was responsible and the company response was almost the same – "That is an interesting hypothesis." Other known groundings that occurred towards the end of Phase Two are listed below:

13 February 1970
Camber Queen grounded for eight hours at approximately 8.00 pm. *Fishbourne* operated one late evening sailing from Portsmouth to Yarmouth.

11 January 1978
Camber Queen ran aground at Fishbourne. An Admiralty tug failed to pull her clear.

19 February 1978
Caedmon grounded on Fishbourne slipway.

9 May 1979
Cuthred ran aground on the Fishbourne slipway at 2.00 pm. Sailings were diverted to Yarmouth until the vessel was re-floated at 7.20 pm.

18 April 1980
Cuthred stranded on Broad Street slipway at 5.00 am. An emergency service between Fishbourne and Lymington operated until the vessel was re-floated.

5 September 1981
Caedmon grounded at Fishbourne at 8.00 am for 3½ hours.

13 January 1982
Caedmon grounded at Fishbourne slipway.

It was not only car ferries that became stranded on the slipways; in the summer of 1965 an army landing craft, which had been using the Fishbourne slipway between services became caught by the tide (see photgraph on page 96). *Camber Queen* arrived and attempted to haul the stricken craft off. Passengers on board looked on with interest, but those

Accidental slipway groundings were less frequent at Portsmouth where the tide falls more slowly than at Fishbourne. An exception was on 18 April 1980 when Cuthred *was caught by the falling tide at 5am and is seen here well and truly aground. The Voith-Schneider propeller is clearly visible.*

Ray Butcher Collection

Cuthred *trapped on the slipway at Fishbourne on 3 October 1982. Watched by two children, the engineer is crouched under the belting concerned that the Voith-Schneider unit is touching the ground.*

lined up with the rope – stretched tight by full thrust – were in a perilous position. As was usual with such incidents the rescue attempt failed and *Camber Queen* and *Fishbourne* had to operate a long service to Yarmouth for the next few hours. In an attempt to compensate passengers for the inconvenience, running commentaries were provided during the long 'cruise'. On passing Cowes, passengers 'in the know' were amused to hear the Trinity House tender *Patricia* described as the Royal Yacht!

Once linkspans came into use groundings became a thing of the past. That is not to say that the ships could not become trapped at the terminals however. On 14 September 1985, a coach parked at the bow of the 9.00 am ferry from Portsmouth would not start when the ferry berthed at Fishbourne. Its immobilisation was completed by the fact that the brakes were automatically locked on. Although the ship was not strictly speaking 'trapped', no vehicles could get on or off and the ferry remained berthed while attempts were made to free the coach. It was a busy day and as attempts to move the coach failed long queues built up and the two other ferries arrived and waited off Wootton Beacon. Eventually *Cuthred* came in and used the old slipway. This would have been a risky operation had there not been a rising tide at the time because *Cuthred* had shortened ramps, for linkspan use, and had to berth very close to the slipway. With the coach well and truly stuck, the stricken vessel set sail and let her sister use the linkspan before going back to the berth herself. After an hour or two the coach was started, amongst much cheering, and the service returned to some sort of normality.

A similar incident occurred on 7 December 1994 when a lorry became immobilised on the linkspan at Fishbourne when disembarking from the 5.00 am sailing from Portsmouth. It was almost two hours before the vehicle could be moved, all following vehicles on the ship being trapped. The out of service *St. Helen* was brought into traffic to minimise further delays.

Of course many other mishaps have occurred other than ships becoming grounded at the terminals. These have been related to the weather conditions, mechanical failure, some have been the result of human error, and a few have been malicious.

Of the first generation of ships *Hilsea* was the one that always seemed to be in the wars. On 16 January 1945 she sustained damage estimated at £1,500 when she came into contact with a government dockyard craft shortly after departing from the Broad Street terminal. The SR took action to reclaim this amount from the government. Seven months later, on 31 July, *Hilsea* struck a submerged object in the Swashway channel, thought to be the wreckage of the mined paddle steamer *Portsdown*. *Hilsea* was holed and was beached at Southsea where all passengers (and some horses) got ashore safely. Repairs costing another £1,500 were carried out in Southampton but the vessel did not return to service until the end of August.

On 23 April 1947 *Hilsea* was involved in an embarrassing

The bow propeller unit on Cuthred *exposed during the grounding of 3 October 1982. These units were, in effect, this ship's Achilles Heel. Those fitted on the same sized* Caedmon *were greater in diameter and had broad, parallel blades.*

and spectacular accident in Portsmouth Harbour. At the end of her day's duty the skipper decided that the gale force conditions would make it too dangerous to berth the vessel at the Harbour pontoon and he took refuge in the Camber Docks instead. The ship was moved towards the site of the present Gunwharf terminal but the forward prow hinge became hooked over a concrete pile at the corner of the dry-dock entrance. As the tide went out the top corner of the prow remained firmly entangled with the pile and the stern sank deeper into the water and eventually into the mud. As the tide rose again the stern remained firmly embedded in the mud, probably due to a combination of suction and the bow's firm attachment to the quay. Water flooded into the stern winch compartment causing damage estimated at £400. The ship was pumped out by the Portsmouth Fire Brigade on the following morning and *Hilsea* was re-floated.

The same ship was involved in a similar incident at Fishbourne. *Hilsea* collided with the outer mooring dolphin and once again the prow hinge became hooked up. Yet again the stern began to sink into the water as the tide receded but on this occasion the ship had a compliment of vehicles and passengers on board. A line was thrown ashore and the ship was winched off, resulting in an almighty splash! The date of this incident went unrecorded.

Hilsea was involved in a potentially lethal incident while berthing at Fishbourne one day. A length of steel angle became detached from the ship's side when the belting brushed against the jetty on the port side. One end of the angle became embedded in the timber jetty support and, almost

Hilsea *hooked up on the corner of the Camber dry-dock (where today's linkspan is situated) after stormy conditions on 23 April 1947. The stern winch compartment flooded and was pumped out by the fire brigade before repairs costing £400 were carried out. This is a very clear view showing the layout of the after part of the bridge of one the two sisters (*Wootton *was the same). Portsmouth Cathedral tower is prominent on the right.*

Wright and Logan

unbelievably, the other end went through a fair-lead in the bulwark, through the gents toilet door and then coiled up like a spring when it collided with the rear bulkhead of the toilet. Had somebody been relieving himself at the time the consequences do not bear thinking about.

At another unrecorded date the first *Fishbourne* was struck amidships by another vessel during foggy conditions. Although *Fishbourne* was holed above the waterline and was left with a V-shaped slot in her side, she was able to continue on her passage.

The early ferries were so small that vehicles that boarded with too much gusto could easily push them out to sea. There was an incident at Fishbourne when a low-loader with a crane on board pushed one of the ferries across the creek, snapping the mooring lines and leaving itself semi-submerged at the bottom of the slipway.

There was one mishap during the first phase that was of a minor nature, but the scar is still there to this day. The dolphins in the Fishbourne channel were frequently knocked out of position by the ferries but when the outer mooring dolphin was knocked sideways it was decided to straighten it up again. A tug was sent over to pull it vertical, but when the thrust was released the dolphin swung back to its initial angle. The tug then pulled the dolphin well beyond the vertical but this didn't work either so it was simply left. For several decades after the original slipway was abandoned the dolphin lay at this decided angle. Today, it is incorporated into a pier at the Royal Victoria Yacht Club. The tops of the piles were cut off level to support the new decking but underneath the dolphin still has a pronounced tilt.

In more recent times, probably the most serious accident to occur was a double fatality at Fishbourne on the night of 20 November 1986. Two women were drowned after they ignored all instructions and proceeded down the linkspan just as *St. Helen* was departing. Two sailings were cancelled while the car was recovered from 20 feet of water. The women had been returning to the mainland following a visit to their husbands in Parkhurst Prison. Ironically, a barrier consisting of two counter-weighted booms had just been delivered and was awaiting fitment at the linkspan approach.

Thursday 27 December 1979 was not a good day in the history of the Fishbourne car ferry, with one serious and another potentially serious incident being recorded. A gale was already blowing up during the afternoon. *Cuthred* had been withdrawn from traffic and replaced by the out of service *Fishbourne*, a ship that was more capable of staying the course in bad weather. Later in the day *Caedmon* was on passage to Fishbourne when the bow prow ramp was torn away and fell to the seabed. It remains there to this day; nobody is quite sure where because it was not missed until the vessel berthed at the Island terminal. The Master of

Hilsea seemed to be the first generation ferry most likely to get into trouble. On this occasion she had collided with the outer mooring dolphin at Fishbourne and as the tide receded she was left hanging at a precarious angle. A rope was thrown ashore and one of the capstans was used to winch her off, but the evident fall of the tide indicates that an hour or so elapsed before she eventually splashed down.

Ray Butcher collection

Caedmon, not a regular skipper, radioed to the following *Fishbourne* that they had lost their prow. The skipper of *Fishbourne* replied "That's no problem, there's a block and tackle in a hut at the terminal". It was then explained that there was no prow to winch up! The sea had been right through the ship and several cars were damaged. One, which had a sleeping baby inside, could easily have been swept away but luckily the sea knocked it askew and it became jammed in the prow entrance. It is testimony to the stability of these ships that all this had been going on and nobody knew. The vessel was sent to Southampton for temporary repairs, which simply involved plating over the open end. While a new ramp was being manufactured *Caedmon* continued in service for several weeks as a single-ended vessel. Faulty ramp locking pins were to blame. A fault had been reported but it had not yet been acted on. Needless to say, this incident caused great concern to Sealink, and as a result of it improved ramp locking systems were installed on all ships, with warning lights in the wheelhouses. The incident passed without too much publicity, but had it occurred after the Zebrugge accident then the media would undoubtedly have made a five course meal out of it. Since the latter accident marine safety regulations have been considerably tightened up and such an incident should not be possible today.

That same stormy night there was very nearly a second incident. Soon after *Caedmon* lost her prow the skipper on *Camber Queen* aborted a departure from Portsmouth because he was unable to get out of the harbour. By this time *Caedmon* was back at Portsmouth, having sailed light from Fishbourne and *Fishbourne* was making her way back from the Island but on the approach to the harbour entrance she got into serious difficulty and was being swept ever closer to Southsea beach. A request was radioed for *Caedmon* to come out and form a shield but this was turned down. In the meantime, on board *Fishbourne* an engine room alarm went off and her engineer, who was on the bridge, quickly disappeared below. Although the engineer claimed not to have done anything, the skipper suddenly found there was enough power to get the ship away from the beach, narrowly averting a serious disaster.

On another occasion and in almost the same location, *Fishbourne* was less fortunate. In thick fog she struck an iron post, rupturing her hull. She was disentangled from the obstruction and then continued to the Broad Street terminal and she arrived there in the nick of time. The engine room was awash and the water was up to a level where the electrics were about to be taken out. The fire brigade was called to pump her out and temporary repairs were effected while she was grounded on the slipway.

There have been several other fog-related incidents. The ferries used not to operate in foggy conditions if the skippers considered the conditions too dangerous. Pressure to maintain the service, and ever improving radar systems, eventually led to most services operating during fog, but radar is not infallible. On 4 August 1981 the Queen's Harbour Master closed the harbour after *Cuthred* and the submarine *Odin* passed within 80 feet of each other at the harbour mouth during thick fog. Navy personnel described the manoeuvre as 'dangerous'. As related elsewhere, *St. Catherine* ran aground just outside Portsmouth Harbour during foggy conditions on 31 March 1997.

One foggy night either *Fishbourne* or *Camber Queen* sailed straight past the terminal at Fishbourne and ran into the shingle bank near the Ranelagh Works. On seeing bright torchlights through the fog the crew assumed that the shore staff were trying to guide the ship into the berth. Unfortunately they had seen torches held by two policemen who were searching for an escaped prisoner!

One night the skipper on *Cuthred* heard a splash when he was berthing the ship at the Broad Street terminal. On looking over the bridge wing he saw a man in the water between the quay and the ship. He was flailing about holding two bags above the water. The emergency stop buttons were quickly pressed before the man was pulled from the sea. He had fallen in when stepping from the quay through the side access doors at the moment when the gap opened up after the skipper released thrust. The man was holding the bags above the water in a vain attempt to keep the contents dry. It turned out that the victim was an ex-con who had been trying to sneak a free trip across the Solent and his name was Mr Christmas!

Two great storms have occurred during the 'Saint class' era. The first, on 16/17 October 1987 (the storm that everybody remembers), occurred overnight and caused little disruption, but the great storm of 25 January 1990 (the one that everybody forgot) raged through the day and caused the worst disruption to services in the modern era. *St. Catherine*, on the 9.00 am service from Fishbourne took refuge at the Odds and Evens pontoons, but after 4 1/2 hours she was holed above the waterline by a pontoon at HMS *Vernon* while attempting to berth at Portsmouth Gunwharf. The 320 passengers on board eventually had a 5 1/2 hour wait before the vessel was able to dock at the Gunwharf lay-by berth. *St. Cecilia* remained stranded at Fishbourne all day. During the same storm the former Fishbourne ferry *Caedmon* was at sea for six hours. She could not get back up the Lymington River and she was unable to berth at Yarmouth because *Cenred* was stranded there. Eventually her passengers were put ashore in Portsmouth having been denied access at East Cowes where *Norris Castle* was stranded. Meanwhile *St. Helen* was stranded at Dover! She had to put into the Granville Dock there on her way back from her annual survey at Tilbury and remained there for almost four weeks during a sustained stormy period. *St. Catherine* was taken out of service for emergency repairs after the 25 January incident, leaving *St. Cecilia* to operate the service alone, but she was back in service at 4.00 pm on 27 January. Three days later a container broke loose on the same ship due to heavy seas.

St. Catherine was again involved in a foul weather related incident on 12 September 1993. High seas resulted in the injury of a passenger off Gilkicker Point. Most of the cafeteria's crockery and glasses were smashed with some other damage incurred.

In more benign conditions, *St. Helen* became completely disabled off Southsea on 6 September 2000 due to an electrical failure. Two of the three diesel alternator sets in a 'Saint class' ship are required in service at any one time; on the occasion of the incident one unit was off service undergoing a water pump replacement when a piston ceased in a second. Automatic circuit breakers should then have isolated non-essential services, but they failed to function, overloading the third unit, which was soon shut down by its own alarms. Without electrical power to the ship's systems everything defaulted to 'off' and the main engines were automatically shut down. With *St. Helen* drifting lifeless, Bembridge Lifeboat and the coastguard search and rescue helicopter were mobilised as a precaution, because of the vessel's proximity to Southsea beach in a brisk onshore wind. However, the vessel was able to anchor safely and await technical support from on shore. The ship was soon brought back to life when servicing of the first engine was completed and the third had cooled down. This incident was the final nail in the coffin of these unreliable auxiliary engines, which were replaced 18 months later.

There have been a variety of other minor incidents and many of the more recent ones are listed below:

28 May 1974
Services were delayed when a milk tanker fell from the ramp of *Cuthred* at Fishbourne.

29 September 1976
Caedmon brushed against Vernon Wharf at Portsmouth and was withdrawn from service for a few days whilst repairs were carried out.

16 June 1977
Fire was discovered in a lower lounge of *Caedmon* when the vessel arrived at Fishbourne. The ship's crew and the Fire Brigade contained the fire. Arson was suspected as the cause.

25 June 1978
Cuthred sustained a small electrical fire in the fan room at approximately 3.00 am. The vessel was berthed at Broad Street at the time but she was able to take up her sailing.

28 September 1979
Arson was suspected as the cause of a fire on the lower deck of *Cuthred*. The Fire Brigade attended when the vessel docked at Broad Street and damage was confined to a life jacket compartment in one of the lower lounges.

9 June 1984
Cuthred suffered fouling of one of her propellers by a rope during a day when services were already disrupted due to fog.

29 October 1987
St. Helen sustained damage to her stern ramp and some port side plating when she came into heavy contact with the Gunwharf linkspan. She spent two days at Southampton undergoing repairs

13 March 1988
St. Catherine also sustained slight damage after colliding with the Gunwharf linkspan.

11 June 1989
A 'missile' was fired at *St. Helen* breaking a window in the saloon. The vessel was just leaving the Gunwharf on her last trip of the day. Repairs were carried out overnight.

Dover Castle forms the backdrop for this view of St. Helen, *which took shelter from the great storm of 25 January 1990 during her return voyage from refit at Tilbury. She remained in the calm waters of Dover Harbour's Granville Dock for almost four weeks during a sustained stormy period.*

Eddie Clapson

149

14 July 1989
A car caught fire on the linkspan at Portsmouth.

5 July 1990
St. Catherine had a close encounter with a naval vessel whilst approaching Portsmouth Harbour.

28 May 1997
A lorry carrying a cargo of sheep caught fire on board *St. Cecilia*. The fire was quickly extinguished and roast lamb was not served on board.

28 February 1998
St. Cecilia was involved in a mishap whilst departing from Gunwharf on the 10.00 am sailing. Power in the forward engine was lost and a strong northwesterly wind caused her to collide with the fishing boat *Verwachting*, which had two persons on board. *St. Cecilia* was assisted back to her berth where it was established that there were no injuries and damage to both vessels was superficial. The ship was taken out of service as a precaution.

19 September 1998
St. Faith suffered a broken window due to either a stone or an air gun pellet being fired from the shore while the vessel was approaching Portsmouth.

18 March 1999
The driver of an articulated lorry returning to the mainland rather surprisingly failed to notice the Fishbourne terminal entrance and proceeded past two no through road and 6'6" width restriction signs and along the single-track road beyond. The tractor unit reached the far side of the circular road around the green before the driver realised his mistake and found himself trapped. A recovery vehicle took over three hours to pull the truck from its predicament. The owners were billed almost £1,000 for remedial work, which including re-instatement of concrete posts pressed deep into the compacted soil.

21 March 1999
St. Cecilia suffered prow damage as a result of heavy contact with the Gunwharf linkspan. Although able to continue running a late service she was subsequently taken out of traffic for repairs.

4 November 1999
A mentally disturbed man jumped to his death from the top deck of *St. Helen* during a passage from Fishbourne.

10 January 2002
A car was left unclaimed aboard *St. Cecilia* when she arrived at Portsmouth during the evening. The body of the driver was later recovered from the sea off Ryde Pier.

12 March 2002
St. Cecilia was towed into Portsmouth Harbour after a triple engine failure.

12 May 2002
Due to a faulty system, a mezzanine deck on *St. Faith* was buckled when it was raised with the locking pins engaged. The deck was removed and straightened out, not being replaced until over four weeks after the incident occurred.

12 August 2002
St. Faith was forced to drop anchor off Ryde for 90 minutes to allow an overheated engine to cool down.

13 October 2002
Drinks display cabinets and gas cylinders were sent crashing to the floor when *St. Clare* rolled in rough seas. The ship was withdrawn for several days while repairs and modifications were carried out.

27 October 2002
St. Faith was blown into the sail training ship *Prince William* in Portsmouth harbour during gale force conditions. This was of relative insignificance, however, as at approximately the same time the side of the frigate HMS *St. Albans* was demolished by the cross-channel ferry *Pride of Portsmouth*.

7 July 2003
Eleven members of Fishbourne shore staff required medical treatment after hydrochloric acid spilled from a lorry awaiting embarkation. Although the ferries continued to run, outgoing traffic was diverted to Yarmouth for three hours until the acid was washed away.

4 August 2003
Wootton Beacon, the outermost dolphin marking the Fishbourne channel, disappeared beneath the waves after being struck by *St. Catherine* on a fine summer's day. Apparently, this was not the first time that this ship had demolished a post at Fishbourne. It was suggested that the marker should be renamed St Catherine's Beacon after the Pepper Pot obelisk on St Catherine's Down!

October 2003
The bidirectional member of the present fleet, *St. Clare*, very nearly berthed at Fishbourne the wrong way round; not a problem in itself, but the vehicles on board were facing backwards. The ship had proceeded out of Portsmouth Harbour in the reverse direction after waiting for a cross-channel ferry to pass and it would appear that the skipper had not noticed that the ship was back to front until within yards of the destination. The ship shuddered to a halt, reversed down the channel, turned round and came back in again!

October 2003
A couple of weeks after two passengers dived for cover when one of *St. Helen*'s mezzanine decks was almost lowered on to them, a mezzanine deck on *St. Clare* was lowered on to a lorry.

Chapter 8: The future

Ferry companies are not keen to divulge their future plans because they do not want their competitors to know what they have up their sleeves. This chapter, therefore, is largely conjecture and personal opinion.

The future of the Fishbourne car ferry, and indeed that of the other car ferry routes to the Isle of Wight, essentially depends on three factors:

1 Growth or decline of road transport,
2 Competition,
3 The construction of a fixed link.

It is unlikely that people are going to make less use of their cars unless they are forced to. Cars have given people a level of mobility hitherto unknown and this is not likely to be given up voluntarily. The motorcar is now regarded by many as an indispensable part of everyday life. It is the Government's aim to reduce people's dependency on private transport but so far large rises in petrol taxation and vehicle excise duty have been accompanied by a continued increase in the volume of traffic. As long as people will drive 20 miles in the middle of the night to buy a packet of cigarettes from a 24-hour store – and some people do – then there seems little hope that voluntary means of reducing traffic are going to work. It is probably going to require legal restrictions before there is any effect, and the enforcement of such measures is not going to make the government that imposes them too popular come the following general election. Society has been geared around the car. Out of town supermarkets stock more and more everyday goods, soon, perhaps, cars themselves. Present government policy is not to build any more out of town shopping centres, but many already exist and there they are likely to stay. Of course, there is only one way to supply goods to most retail outlets nowadays and that is by road. As road use increases, so does use of the ferries. If the ferry operators are not to play into the hands of their competitors, they are certain to respond to increased demand for road vehicle space on their ships. Unfortunately this will often initiate hostility from sections of the community that created that demand.

At the moment Wightlink has only one serious competitor as far as vehicular traffic is concerned. Red Funnel has invested heavily in modernising its fleet and is increasing its market share of vehicular traffic. Its ships are luxurious and fast, and Southampton is a more convenient port for traffic heading to and from the north, especially since the Newbury bypass was opened. Red Funnel has the obvious disadvantage that it operates a longer route. It would become a more serious competitor if it shortened it, which could happen. The company stated many years ago that it eventually intended to open a car ferry terminal at Fawley, near the mouth of Southampton Water. Red Funnel could then double its service frequency with the same fleet and with no increase in costs. Alternatively they could reduce the passage time on the existing route by introducing high-speed vehicular carrying craft, but it is unlikely that that would be a viable option. Such vessels are expensive in first cost and running costs as well as being less reliable. The extra revenue gained from additional crossings would probably be lost through additional expenditure. In October 2002 Red Funnel announced that their three ships were to be increased in capacity from 140 to 200 cars and that a fourth ship was to be added. Such measures are bound to make Wightlink sit up and take notice because it will give its competitor the capability to substantially increase its market share.

There remains the possibility that another competitor could enter the scene, but if one did so where would it operate? Sheltered, deep water sites on the Isle of Wight are somewhat limited. There are really only three suitable locations – Yarmouth, Wootton Creek and the Medina Estuary. Yarmouth is already tied up by Wightlink (as is Lymington) and so is the eastern shore of Wootton Creek. The western shore is a possibility but not a promising one, being over a mile from the main Ryde to Newport road and linked to it by unadopted roads. The Medina estuary is the most natural port on the Isle of Wight. Red Funnel is already there but there is plenty of scope for the construction of an additional terminal in either East or West Cowes. The drawback with Cowes is that it is rather remote from the existing mainland ports. Of course a new operator could open its mainland terminal closer to the mouth of Southampton Water, just as the existing company has proposed to do, and this is a scenario that Red Funnel must be mindful of. Again, Fawley would probably be the most favoured site, though a terminal there would be of no benefit to foot passengers. It is also sited rather remotely from the motorway network, although a fast and modern road links it. Hamble and Warsash, on the opposite side of Southampton Water, are much closer to both the motorway and Southampton but they are slightly more remote from Cowes. One would imagine that fierce and vociferous opposition campaigns would accompany any attempts to construct a ferry terminal in either of these locations, even though there is already an oil terminal at Hamble. It remains to be seen whether or not a third operator will eventually enter the fray.

Both Stena and Sally have previously attempted to break into the cross-Solent market but any plans appear to have been placed on to the back burner for now. Should a new operator emerge then there is always the likelihood that one company could flounder and the situation would be back to square one.

The third scenario would certainly have the most far-reaching consequences. Proposals for a fixed link have been put forward from time to time since as early as 1871 and whenever one is tabled it sparks a fierce debate. The benefits and drawbacks of a fixed link would be dependent on its type and its siting. Any link would harm the ferry companies in one way or another, unless they built it and charged tolls on it themselves. A railway would probably be the least environmentally harmful link but most people who are in favour of a bridge or tunnel would prefer to see a road link. A road would give them the freedom to come and go as they please and they would not have to pay the extortionate ferry fares; at least, that is the perception. Certainly nobody would be tied to timetables any more, but the siting of a link could not suit everyone. It may not be particularly cheap either. A feasibility study carried out in the late 'nineties suggested that the return fare for a private car through a proposed tunnel would have been about £30, not substantially less than the day return ferry fare for a car and four passengers. It could be conjectured that commercial vehicles tariffs would be significantly higher than this. At the moment, domestic costs subsidise some commercial traffic so a tunnel would not necessarily reduce transportation costs for goods.

Although a fixed road link would make it easier for motorists to get on and off the Island, traffic congestion would almost certainly increase as a consequence. It appears that both urban and rural roads on the Isle of Wight are already far busier than in mainland areas with a similar disposition of the population. Why would this be? Do people on the Island spend more time driving around in their cars than their mainland compatriots? Perhaps; bus fares are expensive, and the Island has a high density of cars per head of population. It is more likely that congestion seems worse because of the nature of the road system itself. On the mainland, traffic naturally migrates to motorways, dual-carriageways and trunk routes, but the closest that the Island comes to any of these is a mile of dual carriageway in the heart of Newport. If gridlock is to be avoided after a fixed link is built then it will be necessary to invest heavily in the transport infrastructure, but this goes totally against present government policy. Major improvements in the road system would adversely affect the character of an Island that has already been blighted by the demands of the ubiquitous motor car.

It is even possible that a fixed link could harm the one industry that the Isle of Wight Council is totally committed to, viz tourism. Wightlink say research has shown that a trip across the Solent is one of the selling points of a holiday / short break on the Island. There may be something in this.

Why do people choose the Isle of Wight for their holidays? It cannot be for peace and solitude or to experience a more relaxed approach to life; they could go to rural areas in many parts of the mainland for that. Could it be for the outstanding natural beauty of the Island? Possibly, but the mainland can offer the same. The beaches? Again, the Isle of Wight is not the exclusive domain of fine beaches. The nightlife perhaps? That seems hardly likely. It could be because there are many excellent and well-publicised attractions to be found, together with a combination of the above features, but I doubt that these are the principal reasons why people visit the Island. Many people probably choose the Isle of Wight simply because of the one factor that sets it apart from the mainland, the fact that it is an island. Install a bridge and it will be no more an island than Portsmouth, Hayling Island or Angelsey.

It seems that the majority of Isle of Wight residents do not want a fixed link and, having found what the cost of using one would be, neither does a good deal of the commercial sector. Fixed link schemes have been proposed several times over the past twenty years or so but nothing has come of any of them so it is reasonable to assume that one will not be built in the foreseeable future.

The Fishbourne ferry's future seems assured but how will it develop in the future? This is far from easy to forecast. Who would have predicted the introduction of a fifth ferry when the fleet capacity already appeared to have reached its natural limit? What the fifth ship does indicate is that Wightlink is most committed to this route, although the remaining routes cannot be ignored. Perhaps future investment would be best served on the Portsmouth to Ryde passenger service? This operates two purpose-built, but elderly catamarans that, historically, have been unreliable, but have seemed much better recently. It also operates two newer, second-hand units that use more fuel, are less easy to handle and were not tailor made for the route they now serve. They are not noted for their reliability either. Although Wightlink says it is happy with the economics of the route, a fleet of three new purpose-built vessels (one acting as a back up) would surely enhance this service. In fact, had Wightlink ordered new catamarans in 2000 rather than purchasing the first second hand ferries since the PS *Heather Bell* in 1870, they could have saved an Isle of Wight shipyard from oblivion and become heroes of the community they serve. And then there is the Lymington to Yarmouth service where the three 'C class' vessels are the oldest ferries on the Solent. Restrictions on the size of vessels navigating the Lymington River means that replacements would have little advantage over the existing fleet. The old ferries are well appointed and still very popular, but they will not last forever. In December 2000, Wightlink's management stated that the Lymington to Yarmouth ships were likely to be the next to be replaced.

Changes will come to the Fishbourne route sooner or later; the question is what changes?

A straightforward improvement would be more equal utilisation of the four Saint class ships, even if that meant investing in on-board shops for the older pair: the newer pair are now used more intensely because they have the better facilities, which generate additional revenue. Equal utilisation would make regular crewing easier to arrange. Regular crewing should lead to a greater sense of pride and competition to have the best ship. The service would thus be enhanced by the individuality of each ship, better reliability and cleanliness. The passenger lounges might currently be kept spic and span, but after crews were reduced in size and not allotted to single ships, some other areas became less polished, such as the engine rooms where the machinery developed a rather unloved in appearance. The vehicle-decks, where passengers form their first impressions, can appear rather unkempt and dirty nowadays and the plastic chains draped across the prows, which cyclists have to negotiate to reach their machines, can be very grubby indeed. The car decks were not painted at all during the 2003 / 2004 surveys and by the following June on some of ships, one in particular, they were looking very shabby indeed.

An obvious and straightforward improvement would be the incorporation of on board shops in the older two Saints. The existence or otherwise of these facilities has been given as the factor that governs the level of usage (in 2002 *St. Cecilia* crossed the Solent almost twice as often as *St. Catherine* and *St. Helen*). If the ships were given equal facilities and more equal utilisation then regular crewing would be easier to arrange. Regular crewing should lead to a greater sense of pride and competition to have the best ship. The service would thus be enhanced by the individuality of each ship, better reliability and cleanliness. The passenger lounges might currently be kept spic and span, but since crews were reduced in size and became less regular, some other areas have become less polished. The promenade decks are sometimes rather shabby and down in the engine rooms the machinery has a rather unloved appearance, although the latter could now change because engineers at least have been allotted to single ships once again. The vehicle decks, where new passengers form their first impressions, can appear rather unkempt and dirty nowadays and the plastic chains draped across the prows, which cyclists have to negotiate to reach their machines, can be very grubby indeed.

However, the principal problem for the operator is peak period congestion, an issue that is now being addressed. At the time of writing (early 2004) listed building consent was being sought to alter the structure of the Grade 2-listed Ryde Pier. This is an early phase of the process to introduce a supplementary car ferry route to Ryde, which would provide a two-hourly service at peak periods – in effect releasing the fifth boat from the main route. It is by no means certain that this scheme will go through; public hostility towards it is

strong and it could be deemed not to be viable.

If it does come to fruition, where could it lead in the future? There would be capacity for a further vessel, with provision of an hourly service to Ryde. When *St. Clare* was under construction there were no plans to build a sister. So, is another ship now on the cards? Rumours have been rife for some time that a new ship named 'St Agnes' is on the stocks and by May 2003 continental lorry drivers were reporting that a ship like *St. Clare* was taking shape at Gdansk. It is doubtful that this is what it seems. Wightlink's new ship may have excellent passenger facilities, but she has been shown to have some operational disadvantages over the rest of the fleet. My guess is that she will either not be repeated or, like *Cuthred* and the first *Fishbourne*, she will be a one-off predecessor to a better design.

The only prediction that can be made with a degree of certainty is that changes will come, and probably sooner rather than later. By the time this work is published it is likely that further changes, or announcements of changes, will already have taken place. After *Hilsea* was built in 1930 the Fishbourne ferry remained virtually unaltered for the next thirty-one years. Such stability is not an option in today's world, change being essential in order to stay ahead of the field. In the bid to gain supremacy companies may find themselves defending unsustainable debts, sometimes through activities not related to the local scene; Sea Containers and ABP have already been forced to shed their cross-Solent activities for such reasons. Wightlink is now an independent operator, unencumbered by external interests, but it is already looking to spread its wings. The Isle of Wight ferries are such a lucrative source of income that it is near certain that the services themselves would survive the passing of an operator. The Fishbourne ferry is in the strongest position of them all and it will almost certainly continue to grow from strength to strength. But it can't last forever.

It is dependent on one other factor – the abundant availability of a finite resource that we are squandering as if there were no tomorrow. We may be awash with it now, but in perhaps in as little as forty years time we won't be. As reserves run low there will surely be an increased risk of global and local conflict: this will not be such a wonderful world. What then – in life after oil? It doesn't bear thinking about, but little concern is expressed at the moment. Perhaps it is regarded as a later generation's problem. Perhaps a solution has already been found but it is being quashed for now by the all-mighty oil companies. Being realistic rather than pessimistic, it is difficult to imagine that any replacement motive power for road vehicles will be as convenient, plentiful and affordable as mineral oil derivatives. Therefore it is probable that personal mobility and services to it, such as the Fishbourne car ferry, will eventually fall into decline.

Figure 17
Hull sections

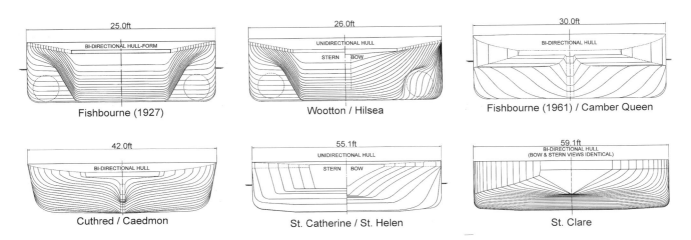

25.0ft
BI-DIRECTIONAL HULL-FORM
Fishbourne (1927)

26.0ft
UNIDIRECTIONAL HULL
STERN | BOW
Wootton / Hilsea

30.0ft
BI-DIRECTIONAL HULL
Fishbourne (1961) / Camber Queen

42.0ft
BI-DIRECTIONAL HULL
Cuthred / Caedmon

55.1ft
UNIDIRECTIONAL HULL
STERN | BOW
St. Catherine / St. Helen

59.1ft
BI-DIRECTIONAL HULL
(BOW & STERN VIEWS IDENTICAL)
St. Clare

Figure 18
Hull sections

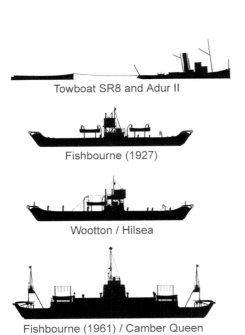

Towboat SR8 and Adur II

Fishbourne (1927)

Wootton / Hilsea

Fishbourne (1961) / Camber Queen

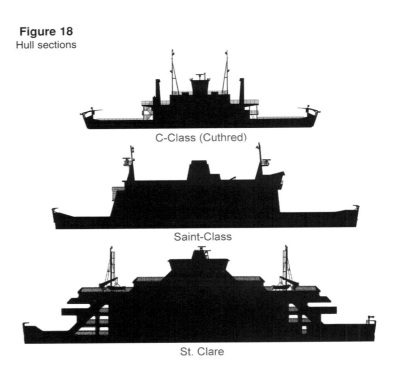

C-Class (Cuthred)

Saint-Class

St. Clare

Fishbourne Ferry Towboat Fleet Data

Name	Description	Built		Builder	Length ft	Beam ft	Draught ft max	Cost £	Withdrawn
Adur II	Steam Tug	1912	(a)	Hepple & Co	75	15¾	7¼	3250	1928 (b)
SR 6	Tow Boat	1870		Hayles	45	16	2	225	c1928
SR 7	Tow Boat	1904		Dibles	48	16	2	250	c1928
SR 8	Tow Boat	1912		Dibles	50	17	2	450	c1930

(a)   Acquired by Joint Committee from REV James in 1919.

(b)   Sold to Shoreham Harbour Trustees in October 1928 for £850. Lost in Bristol Channel, August 1947.

Adur II – steel construction & powered by twin-cylinder steam engine, 40NHP

Towboats 6, 7 and 8 formerly numbered 1, 4 and 5

Fishbourne Ferry Fleet Data

Dimensions

Name	Official number	Signal letters	Launch date	First service	Last service	Broken up	Builder
Fishbourne	149132		21/06/1927	18/07/1927	mid Sept 1961	1967	Denny, Dumbarton
Wootton	149148		06/06/1928	28/06/1928	21/09/1961	1962	Denny, Dumbarton
Hilsea	160936		12/06/1930	21/06/1930	05/10/1961	1970	Denny, Dumbarton
Fishbourne	303149	GXVW	15/03/1961	07/07/1961	05/09/1983	1985 (d)	Philip & Son, Dartmouth
Camber Queen	303157	GXVX	13/04/1961	29/08/1961	02/10/1983	1998	Philip & Son, Dartmouth
Cuthred	337835	GXRX	03/06/1969	28/06/1969	30/01/1987	N/A	Richards, Lowestoft
Caedmon	360676	GTHY	03/05/1973	27/07/1973	01/02/1987 (c)	N/A	Robb Caledon, Dundee
St. Catherine	703495	GCVZ	30/03/1983	03/07/1983	N/A	N/A	Henry Robb, Leith
St. Helen	705464	GDBB	15/09/1983	29/11/1983	N/A	N/A	Henry Robb, Leith
St. Cecilia	712850	MFJT9	04/11/1986	27/03/1987	N/A	N/A	Cochrane, Selby
St. Faith	718794	MMDA5	28/02/1990	16/07/1990	N/A	N/A	Cochrane, Selby
St. Clare	904282	ZNNR5	26/04/2001	20/07/2001	N/A	N/A	Remontowa, Poland

(c)   continues in service between Lymington and Yarmouth.   (d)   lost, Morphu Bay, Cyprus, February 1985.

General

Name	Uni or bi-directional	Yard Price	Car Capacity Total	Car Capacity Main Deck	Car Capacity Mezz. Deck	Passenger Capacity (see note f)	Service Speed knots
Fishbourne	Uni (e)	£13,254	15	15	N/A	99	8
Wootton	Uni	£17,300	16	16	N/A	100	8
Hilsea	Uni	£17,600	17	17	N/A	100	8
Fishbourne	Bi	£174,708	34	34	N/A	165	10
Camber Queen	Bi	£174,575	34	34	N/A	165	10
Cuthred	Bi	£345,000	48 (later 72)	48	24	400	10
Caedmon	Bi	£600,000	52 (later 76)	52	24	756	10
St. Catherine	Uni	£5.0m	142	88	54	771	12
St. Helen	Uni	£5.0m	142	88	54	771	12
St. Cecilia	Uni	£4.76m	142	88	54	771	12
St. Faith	Uni	£6.4m	142	88	54	771	12
St. Clare	Bi	£11.5m	186	81	48 & 57 (g)	878	13

(e)   Initially bi-directional.

(f)   Figures subject to periodic change according to prevailing certification requirements

(g)   Mezz deck, 48; Upper car deck, 57

Weights & Dimensions

Name	GRT gross Tonnage	NRT net Tonnage	DWT Tons t (tonne)	Displ lightship Tons t (tonne)	Displ loaded Tons t (tonne)	Length OA ft	Length WL ft	Beam moulded ft	Beam extreme ft
Fishbourne	136	60	36	163	199	131	110.8	25	25.9
Wootton	149	71	36	176	212	135.5	114	26	27
Hilsea	149	70	36	176	212	135.5	114	26	27
Fishbourne	293	117	81	355	436	166.25	145	30	43
Camber Queen	293	117	81	355	436	166.25	145	30	43
Cuthred	704	357	155t (i)	537t (i)	693t (i)	190.0	180.0	42	51.6
Caedmon	764	404	184t	677t	861t	190.3	180.5	42	51.4
St. Catherine	2036 (h)	856	576t	1418t	1994t	252	246	55.1	70
St. Helen	2983 (h)	908	538t	1455t	1994t	252	246	55.2	70
St. Cecilia	2968	904	594t	1400t	1994t	252	246	55.2	70
St. Faith	3009	914	574t	1420t	1994t	252	246	55.2	70
St. Clare	5359	1607	770t	1939t	2709t	282	277	59.1	69

(h) Criteria for calculating GRT & NRT changed before commissioning of St. Helen.

(i) As built. Similar to Caedmon after fitment of mezz. decks. Displacements for Caedmon are 'as modified'.

Dimensions

Name	Depth ft	Draught ft	Ro-Ro ft	Maximum headroom Above Mezz. Deck. ft	Below Mezz. Deck. ft	Ro-Ro Pre-mod ft	Upper Car Deck ft
Fishbourne	8.0	4.5	11ft 1in	N/A	N/A	N/A	N/A
Wootton	8.5	4.92	12ft 0in	N/A	N/A	N/A	N/A
Hilsea	8.5	5.0	12ft 0in	N/A	N/A	N/A	N/A
Fishbourne	11.0	6.0	15ft 1in	N/A	N/A	N/A	N/A
Camber Queen	11.0	6.0	15ft 1in	N/A	N/A	N/A	N/A
Cuthred	11.25	6.50	13ft 8in	6ft 3in	7ft 0in	14ft 7in	N/A
Caedmon	11.25	6.56	13ft 4in	5ft 11in	7ft 3in	14ft 6in	N/A
St. Catherine	14.86	8.16	13ft 11in	6ft 0in	8ft 4in	N/A	N/A
St. Helen	14.86	8.16	14ft 2in	5ft 11in	8ft 4in	N/A	N/A
St. Cecilia	14.86	8.16	14ft 9in	6ft 3in	8ft 6½in	N/A	N/A
St. Faith	14.86	8.16	15ft 3in	6ft 9in	8ft 6½in	N/A	N/A
St. Clare	15.09	8.56	15ft 7in	7ft 7in	7ft 7in	N/A	7ft 7in

Main engines (1)

Name	No. of Engines	Type (Spec)	Maker	Where Built	Type	Fuel
Fishbourne	2	Gardner 4T7	Norris Henty	Manchester	2-Stroke Crankcase Scavenging	Diesel
Wootton	2	Gardner 4T7	Norris Henty	Manchester	2-Stroke Crankcase Scavenging	Diesel
Hilsea	2	Gardner 4T7	Norris Henty	Manchester	2-Stroke Crankcase Scavenging	Diesel
Fishbourne	2	EGN8	Crossley	Manchester	2-Stroke Scavenge Pump	Diesel
Camber Queen	2	EGN8	Crossley	Manchester	2-Stroke Scavenge Pump	Diesel
Cuthred	2	8RPHCM	Davey Paxman	Colchester	4-Stroke V-form	Diesel
Caedmon	2	ERS6M	Mirlees Blackstone	Stamford	4-Stroke	Diesel
St. Catherine	3	MAN 6ASL25	Harland & Wolff	Belfast	4-Stroke	Heavy oil
St. Helen	3	MAN 6ASL25	Harland & Wolff	Belfast	4-Stroke	Heavy oil
St. Cecilia	3	MAN 6ASL25	MAN B&W	Augsberg	4-Stroke	Heavy oil
St. Faith	3	MAN 6ASL25	MAN B&W	Augsberg	4-Stroke	Heavy oil
St. Clare	4	W5L20C	Wartsila	Helsinki	4-Stroke	Heavy oil

Main engines (2)

Name	No of cylinders per engine	Bore in.	Stroke in.	Engine Output bhp	Total Output to propellors bhp	Speed rpm	Fuel con gal/hr
Fishbourne	4	10.0	12.0	120	240	340	13.5
Wootton	4	10.0	12.0	120	240	340	13.5
Hilsea	4	10.0	12.0	120	240	340	13.5
Fishbourne	8	7.0	9.0	320 (j)	640	650	22
Camber Queen	8	7.0	9.0	320 (j)	640	650	22
Cuthred	8	7.0	7.75	378 (k)	640 (m)	900	?
Caedmon	6	8.75	11.5	400 (n)	800	733	36
St. Catherine	6	9.84	11.81	850 (p)	2550	750	92
St. Helen	6	9.84	11.81	850 (p)	2550	750	92
St. Cecilia	6	9.84	11.81	850 (p)	2550	750	92
St. Faith	6	9.84	11.81	850 (p)	2550	750	92
St. Clare	5	7.87	11.02	965	3860	1000	132

(j) Down-rated from 375 bhp   (k) Each engine also driving generator   (m) Dependant on generator load
(n) Down-rated from 495 bhp?   (p) Down-rated from 900 bhp

Auxiliary engines   **PROPULSION**

Name	Engines/Type	No of engines	Total output kW ë	Voltage	Propellor type
Fishbourne	Single Cylinder Petrol/Paraffin	1	2.5	110 DC	Double Twin Screw
	+ 3 Cylinder Petrol/Paraffin	1	?		
	MaClaren Diesel (replaced 3-cyl engine)	2	30		
Wootton	Gardner 4CC3 Petrol/Paraffin	2	25	110 DC	Double Twin Screw
	Single Cylinder Petrol/Parffin	1	3		
Hilsea	Gardner 2L2 Diesel	2	24	110 DC	Double Twin Screw
Fishbourne	Ruston & Hornsby 4-stroke 6YEZ Diesel	2	120	225 DC	2 x VSP 14E/90
Camber Queen	Ruston & Hornsby 4-stroke 6YEZ Diesel	2	120	225 DC	2 x VSP 14E/90
Cuthred	Ruston 6YEZ Diesel + 2 main engines	1 + Mains	210	225 DC	2 x VSP 14EG/90
Caedmon	English Electric type 6LDTZ Diesel	2	216	415 3-Ph	2 x VSP 16EG/90
St. Catherine	GEC Dorman 6LETZ Diesel (r)	3	468 (s)	415 3-Ph	3 x VSP 21G 11/115
St. Helen	GEC Dorman 6LETZ Diesel (r)	3	468 (s)	415 3-Ph	3 x VSP 21G 11/115
St. Cecilia	Gardner 6YLT Diesel	3	468 (s)	415 3-Ph	3 x VSP 21G 11/115
St. Faith	Gardner 6YLT Diesel	3	468 (s)	415 3-Ph	3 x VSP 21G 11/115
St. Clare	Scania D9 95 MO4S (t)	4 (u)	728	415 3-Ph	4 x VSP 21G 11/115

(r) One unit is reserve only   (s) Normal max. requirement (not all units operational)
(t) Replaced in 2002 by Scania D9 95 MO4S   (u) Driving Stamford HCM 434D2 alternators

NOTE. Official source information for the above tables was frequently at variance. Conflicting data was most common for tonnage, ship dimensions and engine horsepower. Uncertain data have thus been rounded up or down to the nearest whole numbers, or to figures that are believed to be accurate. Maximum ship speeds are often higher than the indicated service speeds.

Glossary

Brake Horse Power (bhp)	The output of a loaded (non-idling) power unit, specifically the power absorbed by a brake that is linked to a power unit under test. 1 bhp = 0.746 kW (kilowatts).
Bulwark	Vertical plating erected at the gunwales to reduce the quantity of water breaking on to the deck.
Companionway	1. A staircase on a ship. 2. Disembarkation ladder.
Deadweight (DWT)	The DWT comprises the cargo, stores, ballast, fresh water, fuel, passengers, crew and their effects.
Draught	The depth of water at which a ship floats. Simply the distance from the ship's bottom to the water-line.
Fair-lead	A hole with a rounded edge, often in a bulwark, to allow the smooth passage of a rope.
GM (Metacentric Height)	A term defining the stability of a ship. The higher the metacentric height the more stable the ship is. specifically it is the distance between the centre of gravity (G) and a point on the centreline of a ship (M) through which passes a vertical line through the centre of buoyancy (the CG of the displaced water) of the rolled ship. For the ship to be stable G must be below M.
Gross Register Tonnage	Not a measure of weight, GRT is a value resulting from the underdeck volume or tonnage of the tween decks and all enclosed spaces above deck. Certain deductions are made for areas that are exempt from measurement. The formulae used for calculating GRT was changed during 1983.
Gunwale	The junction of the deck and the shell plating.
Knot	Unit of speed. The international nautical mile (one second of arc) is 1852m or 6076.1ft. 1knot = 1.151mph.
Lightship Displacement	The weight of the bare ship. Specifically it is the mass of the ship made up of the hull, superstructure, propelling machinery and all fittings provided to make the vessel ready for the sea. Fuel and stores are not included.
Load line	The mark on a ships side indicating the maximum draught to which a ship may be loaded under specified conditions in accordance with the Merchant Shipping Act 1932.
Loaded Displacement	The Lightship Displacement plus the DWT.
Moulded Breadth	Measured at amidship section and is the maximum breadth over the frames.
Net Tonnage	This is given by a formula which is a function of the moulded volume of all cargo spaces of a ship.
Resistance (Drag)	The forces which slow a ship down, comprising: wavemaking, frictional, form drag, eddy making, air resistance and appendage resistance.

Bibliography

Official Documentation

Denny's History Books for pioneer ferries (National Maritime Museum)
Denny's List (National Maritime Museum)
Southern Railway Minutes up to 1946 (Kew)
Timetable/Fares, Handbills 1926 to Present
Traffic Figures 1913 to 1987 (Hand written)
Traffic Figures 1987 to 2001 (Wightlink)

Unofficial Documentation

Books
Clegg, Paul & Styring, John S, *British Railways Shipping and Allied Fleets,* 1969
Rogan,Tony & Ripley, Don, *Designing Ships for Sealink,* 1995
O'Brien, Captain FT, *Early Solent Steamers,* 1973

Compton, Hugh, *Isle of Wight Here We Come,* 1997

Lloyds Register of Shipping, Various

Brown, Alan, *Lymington, The Sound of Success,* 1987

MMC Audit, Cross-Solent Ferries, Her Majesty's Stationery Office, 1991

Lane, Marian, *Piers of the Isle of Wight,* 1996

Allen, PC & MaCleod, AB, *Rails in the Isle of Wight,* 1967

Duckworth & Langmuir, *Railways and Other Steamers,* 1968

Brown, Alan, *Shanklin, Ill Fated Prince,* 1985

Chatterton, E Keble, *The Epic of Dunkirk,* 1940

Robbins, Nick, *The Evolution of the British Ferry,* 1995

Sherwood, Cynthia, *The House on the Point,* (unpublished)

Britton, Andrew, *Once Upon a Line, volumes 1 to 4*, Oxford Publishing Company, 1983–1994

Mills, AD, *The Place Names of the Isle of Wight*

Mackett, John, *The Portsmouth to Ryde Passage,* 1970

Plummer, Russell, *The Ships that Saved an Army,* 1990

Hendy, John, *Wightlink,* 1993

Periodicals

British Ferry Scene

European Ferry Scene

Hampshire Independent, 1861

'Hampshire', November 1985

Hampshire Telegraph and Sussex Chronicle, 1830

Isle of Wight County Press

Isle of Wight Observer, 1861

Isle of Wight Weekly Post

Nammogram (Dutch Oil Company Magazine), 1963

Railway Times, 1862

Ship and Boat International, September 1973

Shipbuilding and Shipping Record

Swashway

The Motor

The Motor Boat

The Motor Ship

The News, Portsmouth

The Southern Evening Echo

Wight Report

Miscellaneous Articles

Morse, Gill, *Car Ferries of the Solent*

Portsmouth to Fishbourne Routes 50th Anniversary

Langford, Terry, *Some Changes in the Ecology of the Solent*

If you enjoyed reading this book, then these Colourpoint publications may also be of interest.

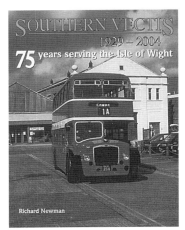

Southern Vectis 1929–2004
75 years serving the Isle of Wight
Richard Newman

1 904242 24 3 £16
192p, pbk,
260 x 210mm,
180 b/w and colour photos.

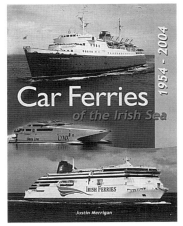

Car Ferries of the Irish Sea 1954-2004
Justin Merrigan

1 904242 25 1 c£16
c160pp, pbk,
232 x 180mm,
c140 b/w and colour photos.

Southern Vectis 1929-2004 is published to celebrate the 75th anniversary of Southern Vectis, the main bus operator on the Isle of Wight. This volume is produced with the offical approval of the company who have opened their archives to the author. It contains a company history, fleet and route lists. This book will be a useful reference for Southern Vectis enthusiasts and modellers alike.

Starting in 1954, the year after the loss of the Princess Victoria, Justin Merrigan traces the development of car ferries on all the routes to Ireland, especially services to Larne, Belfast, Dublin, Dun Laoghaire and Rosslare. The book covers all conventional ferries, as well as catamarans and the latest HSS vessels and is well illustrated with each vessel shown in a variety of liveries and identities.

Passenger Ships of the 20th Century
An Illustrated Encyclopedia
David Latimer

1 898392 70 6 £50 hbk,
400pp 280 x 210 mm,
over 450 photos

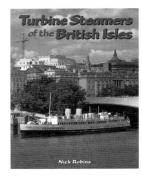

Turbine Steamers of the British Isles
Nick Robins

1 898392 38 2 £11.99
125pp, 232 x 180 mm,
73 b/w photos.

The Decline and Revival of the British Passenger Fleet
Nick Robins

1 898392 69 2 £14.99
160pp, 232 x 180 mm,
134 b/w photos

Death in the North Channel
The loss of the Princess Victoria, January 1953
Stephen Cameron

1 904242 01 4 £13.99
144pp, 260 x 210mm
167 b/w photos.

View the full range of Colourpoint titles at our web site: www.colourpoint.co.uk